IAN MACNEIL OF BARRA

Palgrave Macmillan Socio-Legal Studies

Series Editor

David Cowan, Professor of Law and Policy, University of Bristol, UK

Editorial Board

Dame Hazel Genn, Professor of Socio-Legal Studies, University College London, UK

Fiona Haines, Associate Professor, School of Social and Political Science, University of Melbourne, Australia

Herbert Kritzer, Professor of Law and Public Policy, University of Minnesota, USA

Linda Mulcahy, Professor of Law, London School of Economics and Political Science, UK

Carl Stychin, Dean and Professor, The City Law School, City University London, UK

Mariana Valverde, Professor of Criminology, University of Toronto, Canada

Sally Wheeler, Professor of Law, Queen's University Belfast, UK

Changing Concepts of Contract

Essays in Honour of Ian Macneil

Edited by

David Campbell
Lancaster University, UK

Linda Mulcahy
London School of Economics and Political Science, UK

Sally Wheeler
Queen's University Belfast, UK

Editorial selection and matter © David Campbell, Linda Mulcahy and Sally Wheeler 2013
Foreword, preface and chapters © their individual authors 2013

All rights reserved. No reproduction, copy or transmission of this publication may be made without written permission.

Crown Copyright material is licensed under the Open Government Licence v1.0.

No portion of this publication may be reproduced, copied or transmitted save with written permission or in accordance with the provisions of the Copyright, Designs and Patents Act 1988, or under the terms of any licence permitting limited copying issued by the Copyright Licensing Agency, Saffron House, 6–10 Kirby Street, London EC1N 8TS.

Any person who does any unauthorized act in relation to this publication may be liable to criminal prosecution and civil claims for damages.

The authors have asserted their right to be identified as the authors of this work in accordance with the Copyright, Designs and Patents Act 1988.

First published 2013 by
PALGRAVE MACMILLAN

Palgrave Macmillan in the UK is an imprint of Macmillan Publishers Limited, registered in England, company number 785998, of Houndmills, Basingstoke, Hampshire RG21 6XS.

Palgrave Macmillan in the US is a division of St Martin's Press LLC,
175 Fifth Avenue, New York, NY 10010.

Palgrave Macmillan is the global academic imprint of the above companies and has companies and representatives throughout the world.

Palgrave® and Macmillan® are registered trademarks in the United States, the United Kingdom, Europe and other countries.

ISBN: 978-1-137-26926-3 hardback

This book is printed on paper suitable for recycling and made from fully managed and sustained forest sources. Logging, pulping and manufacturing processes are expected to conform to the environmental regulations of the country of origin.

A catalogue record for this book is available from the British Library.

A catalog record for this book is available from the Library of Congress.

Typeset by Cambrian Typesetters, Camberley, Surrey.

Printed in Great Britain by TJ International, Padstow.

Contents

Acknowledgments		vii
Foreword by Stewart Macaulay		ix
Notes on Contributors		xi
Preface by Rory Macneil of Barra		xv
1	**Introduction** Jay M Feinman	1
2	**'Post-Technique':** *The New Social Contract* **Today** Roger Brownsword	14
3	**What Might Macneil Have Said about Using eBay?** Sally Wheeler	38
4	**The Contract of Employment in 3D** Hugh Collins	65
5	**Neglected Insights into Agreed Remedies** Roger Halson	89
6	**Relational Values in English Contract Law** Hugh Beale	116
7	*Arcos v Ronaasen* **as a Relational Contract** David Campbell	138
8	**In Defence of** *Baird Textiles***: A Sceptical View of Relational Contract Law** Jonathan Morgan	166
9	**Telling Tales about Relational Contracts: How Do Judges Learn about the Lived World of Contracts?** Linda Mulcahy	193
10	**Relational Contract and Social Learning in Hybrid Organization** Peter Vincent-Jones	216
Index		235

Acknowledgments

With the death of Ian Macneil on 16 February 2010 the common law world lost arguably the most important theorist of the law of contract it had known since Lon Fuller. Ian was the principal contributor to the formulation of the relational theory of contract. This book is an attempt by a number of UK scholars who have been influenced by, even if at times they disagree with, the relational theory to honour the achievement of this great theorist. Though it was not possible to arrange for contributions from all the UK scholars who have been so influenced, this collection nevertheless representatively states a powerful challenge to the limits of orthodox contract scholarship in the spirit of Ian's work. It is perhaps fitting that it will appear in the year in which the first English judgment in which the relational theory has played a productive part was handed down: the judgment in the Queen's Bench Division of Leggatt J in *Yam Seng Pte Ltd v International Trade Corporation Ltd* [2013] EWHC 111, [2013] 1 All ER (Comm) 1321, [2013] 1 Lloyd's Rep 526, [2013] BLR 147, (2013) 146 Con LR 39, [2013] All ER (D) 227. A note on this case focusing on Leggatt J's handling of the relational theory will appear in the *Modern Law Review* in 2014.

The chapters in this collection were prepared for presentation at a conference held in March 2012 at the School of Law, University of Leeds, where David Campbell was then Professor of International Business Law. The conference was one of a series of events held to celebrate the opening of the Liberty Building, the School of Law's impressive new home, and was initially suggested by Professor Steve Wheatley, then Head of the Law School, and Professor Joan Loughrey, then Director of the Law School's Centre for Business Law and Practice. The school committed very considerable funds to the support of this conference. The burden of organizing the conference was largely borne by Professor Loughrey, with the very able help of Ms Nicolette Butler, then a doctoral student in the School.

This collection appears in Palgrave Macmillan's series of books on Socio-Legal Studies. We are very grateful to Professor Dave Cowan, General Editor of the series, Mr Rob Gibson, the series' publisher, and Ms Marie Selwood, responsible for production, for their unfailing help.

We should also like to acknowledge our gratitude to the contributors and especially to Mr Rory Macneil, who succeeded his father to become the 47th Chief of the Clan Macneil. Rory has always taken a great interest in the relational theory, to which he has made his own contribution, and gave wholehearted support to the conference.

David Campbell, Linda Mulcahy and Sally Wheeler
10 August 2013

Foreword

At the conference at Northwestern Law School that marked his retirement, I said 'People should not attempt to write about contracts until they have studied Ian Macneil.' While often we exaggerate at such events in order to honour someone, I am still comfortable with what I said. Part of Macneil's contribution is empirical. He insisted that we start with a picture of important business transactions that reflected long-term continuing relationships that involve their own norms and sanctions apart from the commands of the law. Macneil then looked at what a relational approach means for the law that we do and that we ought to have. To say the least, his conclusions were not conventional. Rather, his work was always challenging.

I am pleased that the School of Law at the University of Leeds decided to honour Macneil in the best way possible: gathering an exceptional group of scholars to pay serious attention to his work. Now those of us unable to attend the conference have the chance to read the papers given there.

I hope that in the years to come this book is read widely by those thinking about contract law.

Stewart Macaulay
Malcolm Pitman Sharp Hilldale Professor Emeritus,
University of Wisconsin-Madison, Wisconsin, USA

Notes on Contributors

Hugh Beale is Professor of Law at the University of Warwick in the UK and Visiting Professor at the universities of Oxford and Amsterdam. He was a Law Commissioner for England and Wales from 2000–2007. He was a member of the Commission on European Contract Law 1987–2000, of the Study Group on a European Civil Code and of the team responsible for the Draft Common Frame of Reference. He is a member of the Group of Experts set up by the European Commission to produce the Feasibility Study which preceded the proposed Common European Sales Law. Among his publications, he is an editor (with B Fauvarque-Cosson, J Rutgers, D Tallon and S Vogenauer) of *Casebooks on the Common Law of Europe: Contract Law* (Oxford: Hart Publishing 2010) (2nd edn) and he is the general editor of *Chitty on Contracts* (London: Sweet & Maxwell 2012) (31st edn). He is an Honorary Queen's Counsel and a Fellow of the British Academy.

Roger Brownsword, who is a graduate of the London School of Economics (LSE), has been an academic lawyer for more than 40 years. Currently, he is Professor of Law at King's College London, where he was the founding director of TELOS (a research centre that focuses on technology, ethics, law and society), an honorary professor at the University of Sheffield, and a visiting professor at Singapore Management University. In the area of contract law, his publications include *Understanding Contract Law* (London: Sweet & Maxwell 2007) and *Key Issues in Contract* (London: Butterworths Law 1995) (both with John Adams), *Contract Law: Themes for the Twenty-First Century* (Oxford: Oxford University Press 2006) and most recently the co-edited collection *The Foundations of European Private Law* (Oxford: Hart Publishing 2011).

David Campbell was educated at Cardiff University, UK (BSc (Econ) 1980), the University of Michigan School of Law, USA (LLM 1985), and the University of Edinburgh, UK (PhD 1985). He is a Fellow of the Chartered Institute of Arbitrators. Since 1985, he has taught at a number of British universities and in Australia, Hong Kong, New Zealand, Spain and the USA. He is currently the Professor of Law in the Lancaster University School of Law, UK. He has written on a wide range of legal and social scientific issues in leading UK, Commonwealth and US journals. His books on the relational theory include: *Contract and Economic Organisation: Socio-Legal Initiatives* (with P Vincent-Jones (eds), Aldershot: Dartmouth Publishing 1996); *The Implicit Dimensions of Contract* (with H Collins and J Wightman (eds),

Oxford: Hart Publishing 2003); *Remedies in Contract and Tort* (with D Harris and R Halson, Cambridge: Cambridge University Press 2002); and an edited collection of Macneil's works: *The Relational Theory of Contract: Selected Works of Ian Macneil* (D Campbell (ed.), London: Sweet & Maxwell 2001). His main current research interests are in remedies for non-performance of contractual obligations and in regulatory theory, and particularly in the development of a 'non-Chicagoan' law and economics of these subjects. He is currently working on a book which restates the relational theory of contract, *Contractual Relations*, and (with Matthias Klaes) on a book on Coase's critique of intervention, *Law and Economics and the Concept of Regulation*.

Hugh Collins is the Vinerian Professor of English Law at All Souls College, Oxford. Previously he was Professor of English Law at the LSE, 1991–2013, and a Fellow of Brasenose College, Oxford. He studied law at Oxford and Harvard. He is a Fellow of the British Academy. He has served on the editorial committee of the *Modern Law Review* since 1991, including a period as General Editor, and is co-founder of the *European Review of Contract Law*. Recent book publications include *The European Civil Code: The Way Forward* (Cambridge: Cambridge University Press 2008); *Employment Law* (Oxford: Oxford University Press 2010) (2nd edn); *Networks as Connected Contracts* (by Gunther Teubner) edited with an 'Introduction', pp. 1–72 (Oxford: Hart Publishing 2011); and *Labour Law* (Cambridge: Cambridge University Press, Law in Context Series 2012) (with K D Ewing and Aileen McColgan).

Jay M Feinman is Distinguished Professor of Law at Rutgers School of Law in Camden, New Jersey. He is a well-known expert on contract law, tort law, insurance law and legal education. His many publications include seven books and more than 50 scholarly articles. His scholarly work has been widely cited in the academic literature and by courts, including the United States Supreme Court. Among his professional activities, Feinman is an elected member of the American Law Institute and has served as Chair of the Association of American Law Schools Section on Contracts. He is a member of the New Jersey Bar.

Roger Halson is Professor of Contract and Commercial Law, member of the Centre for Business Law and Practice and former Head of the School of Law at the University of Leeds. He is the author of *Contract Law* (London: Pearson Education 2013) and co-author of D Harris, D Campbell and R Halson, *Remedies in Contract and Tort* (Cambridge: Cambridge University Press 2002) and M Furmston (ed.) (2010) *The Law of Contract* (London: Butterworths LexisNexis) and has published articles on the law of obligations and remedies in many leading academic journals. His work has been cited by appellate courts in England and Wales and overseas.

Rory Macneil of Barra grew up in Ithaca, New York, and now lives in Edinburgh, Scotland, with his wife Sau Ming Kwan and their two teenage sons, Ruari and Seumas. In an early bow in the direction of a scholarly career while at Harvard Law School ('Contract in China: Law Practice and Dispute Resolution' (1986) 38(2) *Stanford Law Review*), he applied relational contract theory to an analysis of Chinese contract cases. He then went on to practise law in San Francisco, Beijing and Hong Kong before founding and running Macneil Pacific, which advised multinationals on investments in China. Macneil Pacific was eventually sold to Sidley & Austin, becoming the basis of Sidley's China and Hong Kong practice, and he joined Sidley as a partner. In 2001 he followed his parents and brother to Edinburgh, partly to be closer to them and the Isle of Barra, and to start another career, as a software entrepreneur. He is now Chief Executive of Research Space, which provides an electronic lab notebook used by researchers in universities to document and share their research data.

Jonathan Morgan is a Fellow of Corpus Christi College, University of Cambridge. His academic interests include contract, tort and public law. His recent books include *Great Debates in Contract Law* (Basingstoke: Palgrave Macmillan 2012) and *Contract Law Minimalism: A Formalist Restatement of Commercial Contract Law* (Cambridge: Cambridge University Press 2013, forthcoming).

Linda Mulcahy is a Law Professor at the LSE having previously held posts at Birkbeck, Oxford, South Bank, the Law Commission and Bristol. Her primary research interests lie in the field of the socio-legal dynamics of disputes and she is a former Chair of the UK Socio-Legal Studies Association. Her empirical work into disputes has been supported by the Economic and Social Research Council, Arts and Humanities Research Council, Nuffield Foundation and Department of Health. She is the author of numerous books and articles including *Contract Law in Perspective* (4th and 5th edns, Routledge: London 2005, 2008) and *Feminist Perspectives on Contract Law* (London: Cavendish 2005). Linda is an editor of *Social and Legal Studies*. Her most recent work focuses on visual jurisprudence and the link between the design of law courts and due process.

Peter Vincent-Jones is Professor of Law at the School of Law, University of Sheffield, UK. His main teaching and research interests are in the areas of contract and public law, regulation and socio-legal theory. He has published extensively on the privatization and contractualization of public services in the UK and Europe and is sole author of the monograph *The New Public Contracting* (Oxford: Oxford University Press 2006). He has been Principal Investigator for research projects funded by the Economic and Social Research Council, the NHS Service and Delivery Organisation, and the European Commission. In 2004 he was Visiting Fellow in the Law Program at the Research School of Social Science, Australian National University.

Sally Wheeler is Professor of Law, Business and Society in the School of Law, Queen's University Belfast. She works on socio-legal accounts of contract law and practice and corporate governance. Within corporate governance, particular areas of interest are corporate social responsibility, corporate boards and board processes and employee participation.

Preface
Rory Macneil of Barra

I thought it would be interesting to look back at my father's life and speculate about possible connections between his scholarly work and his experiences outside academia, including in particular his relationship with the island of Barra in the Hebrides off the west coast of Scotland – the centre of his 'other' life as Chief of the Clan Macneil. I'll start by going back to his childhood.

Two early experiences may have influenced subsequent developments in Dad's outlook and ultimately his scholarly focus. The first was growing up in rural Vermont in the 1930s and 1940s, where the old ways and oral traditions were still alive and many families had local roots going back a hundred years and more. Dad soaked up the history and the sense of community, but as an incomer – the family had moved from New York shortly after Dad's birth in 1929 – was also an outsider. In addition, he was frequently on his own, since his mother, Kathleen, had died when he was five and his father, Robert Lister Macneil of Barra, was often away. As a teenager, he boarded with a large, close-knit neighbouring farming family, which must have further strengthened the sense of being part of yet distinct from a family and the community. I suspect Dad's independence of thought, his fierce self-reliance and his empathy with those who were not part of the 'in crowd' stemmed from these childhood experiences in Vermont.

The second was the two extended visits he made to Barra, with his father and his sisters, in 1938 and 1939, shortly after his father had purchased the southern portion of the island and Kisimul Castle, seat of the Macneils of Barra, which sits on its own islet in Castlebay, 400 metres offshore. Over the next 30-plus years Robert Lister managed the Barra estate, restored Kisimul Castle, and tried to re-institute the traditional role of chief. In Barra too Dad spent time with locals, and heard stories of old times, stories going back not just decades but hundreds of years in a community retaining memories of an earlier way of life which had not completely died out and was preserved through the Gaelic oral tradition. Through the interactions and the stories, he must have developed an understanding of the strength of the community in Barra. Again the sense of being associated with the community yet outside of it must have made a deep impression on a nine and ten-year-old boy.

There is one more stop before turning to the key years of the early 1970s. Between 1965 and 1967 Dad taught law at the University of Dar es Salaam in the newly independent Tanzania. Many people at the university and virtually everyone else had close ties with their villages and in some cases were still living in the village. So Dad developed a first-hand familiarity with yet another set of strong communities. And he began to incorporate this experience into his scholarly work. In 1968 he published *Contracts, Instruments for Social Cooperation, East Africa*, the first book on East African contract law, in which he explicitly grappled with the ways in which contract law deals with contractual relationships embedded in the context of a complex social context, in this case East African tribal societies.

As I mentioned, in 1970 Dad became Chief of the Clan Macneil and inherited the responsibilities for managing a crofting estate, with more than 300 crofts, and Kisimul Castle. A croft, a type of landholding created in the late nineteenth century to give secure tenure to residents of the Highlands and Islands of Scotland, whose ancestors had been removed from or forced off their traditional holdings, came in the twentieth century to be defined as 'a piece of land surrounded by legislation'. Kisimul Castle, an early medieval stronghold which sits on a rock about 400 yards offshore in the middle of a bay at the southern end of Barra, had been restored from ruins by my grandfather in the 1950s and 1960s. Barra is the southernmost of the chain of islands known as the Hebrides which lie to the west of mainland Scotland and to the north and east of Ireland.

Prior to becoming chief, Dad had little to do with the estate or the castle, and was living in Ithaca, busy at Cornell Law School. He could not have been prepared for the commitment required to fulfil his new responsibilities in Barra; over the next several years there was a steep learning curve and he had to make major adjustments in making time for Barra. The pattern developed of spending time in Barra in the summer and during the rest of the year working on Barra matters from Ithaca (and later Chicago), with the estate factor in Barra and the solicitor in Edinburgh.

Although the time spent in Barra was stressful, cramming a year's work into a summer visit, Dad loved being there, re-establishing old acquaintances and making new ones, and playing a productive role in the community. What proved harder than the work and the stress was the resentment from the many people who were ambivalent or even hostile to Dad in his position as landlord. This stemmed not only from the deep-rooted feeling against landlords in the Highlands, but also from the legacy from his father's time in Barra. I suspect the depth of the antagonism came as a shock, but by 1975 Dad was able to articulate it in the context of his father's and his own positions. In the 'Preface' to the republication of his father's account of his restoration of Kisimul Castle, *Castle in the Sea*, he wrote:

> One of the keenest felt disappointments was Robert Lister – his father – 's failure to achieve the ancient position of chiefly primacy on the Island of Barra itself. His desire to be not only chief of the clan, but also of the island was, however, doomed from the start. Not the least of the many reasons for this is that Barra is about as close to a classless society as may be found anywhere in the developed world. When the Macneil family reacquired the Estate of Barra in 1937, the days were long gone when the Laird could command a tug on the forelock, and whatever lingering customs in that direction yet remained happily died out during World War II. (There was, for example, considerable Barra resentment at the near-royal reception accorded the Macneil family upon its return in 1938.) Whatever position the new chiefs wished to enjoy in Barra could come about only from accomplishments and contributions made as members of an equalitarian community.

So Dad's experience in re-engaging with Barra in the early 1970s resulted in intense reflection about communities and relationships, bringing to the surface the earlier contradictions and tensions which had informed his childhood experiences, and following closely on the time spent in Tanzania. It was during exactly these years that he developed a new way of looking at contract law. As you know, this was first manifested in *Cases and Materials on Contracts: Exchange Transactions and Relationships*, a 'casebook' published in 1971 innovative both in its construction and the materials used, and its insistence on understanding contacts and contract law as being embedded in complex human relationships. Then in 1974 – the very year he wrote the preface quoted above – came the publication of *The Many Futures of Contracts*, a full-blown exposition of the theory of 'relational' contract law, setting out a framework for explaining contracts along a spectrum running from simple 'discrete' transactions to complex, long-term relationships.

This is not the place to elaborate on the details of these works – the other authors in this collection are doing that! – but clearly they represent an exploration of issues arising when people engage in making commercial and non-commercial arrangements. One of Dad's core insights was that classical contract law had made the mistake of pretending that contracts were made and carried out in isolation from their social context. His relational theory placed contracts firmly back in the social context which is their lifeblood. What better place could there be than Barra to reinforce this point? And what better vantage point than Dad's – a reflective outsider who was finding himself drawn ever more closely into the heart of the community and its affairs – to serve as a catalyst for seeing that the kinds of relationships he was dealing with in Barra were instances of generalisable principles operating everywhere?

* * *

From 1990, after Mum and Dad moved to Scotland, and Dad took partial and then, in 1995, full retirement from Northwestern University, he devoted even more time to Barra. This resulted in a deepening of his relationships on the island, and, eventually, to a new scholarly interest.

In the early 1990s, the family was able to 'move ashore' from the castle to a house in Castlebay. Canon Angus MacQueen pointed out in his remarks at Dad's funeral service that this step had important symbolic import as well as practical consequences. Being based on the island allowed Dad to interact more easily with everyone in a way that had not been possible given the isolation that accompanied living in the castle.

By the mid-1990s, Dad was turning his attention to two things. The first was securing a long-term future for the castle and the crofting estate. The second was the current and future well-being of the community, as new threats to Barra began appearing with alarming regularity. He approached both matters with characteristic resolution and persistence. After years spent investigating alternatives and crafting and negotiating a detailed, creative and distinctive arrangement, the castle was leased to Historic Scotland in 2000, on the condition that Historic Scotland would have to conserve and manage the castle in a way which preserved its physical fabric and maintained the castle's dual roles as centrepiece of Barra's identity and economy, and symbolic home of Macneils everywhere. And in 2004 he gifted the crofting estate to Scottish Ministers, believing that among the available alternatives the Scottish government was best placed to manage the estate in way which continued to serve the interests of the crofters and the wider Barra community.

Dad's response to the growing threats to Barra's current and future well-being in the forms of omission – e.g. the failure to provide secure transport links – and commission – e.g. the efforts of Scottish Natural Heritage to establish control over both Barra itself and the surrounding seas – was to take a leading role in organizing and galvanizing the community to address these threats, and to represent the community in interactions with civil servants and politicians in Edinburgh. Dad's leadership in these areas also led to working relationships with a whole new group of people in the community. He was thus instrumental not only in various political campaigns but also in the stimulation and training of a new generation of community leaders and activists.

Looking back at Dad's activities in Barra over a 40-year period, it is no exaggeration to say that he reinvented the role of the Highland chief for the twenty-first century. As I mentioned, in 1974 he had written of his own father: 'Whatever position the new chiefs wished to enjoy in Barra could come about only from accomplishments and contributions made as members of an equalitarian community.' How pleased Dad would have been if he could have heard the words spoken 36 years later by Councillor Donald Manford at his funeral service:

> The 46th Chief of MacNeil cared deeply for his people and that respect and affection is returned many-fold. He was a man of dignity, integrity, honesty, moderation and compassion. A wonderful statesman. For this and all the many things that are unable to be said now, when you join your illustrious ancestors; it will not simply be said you were one of the best of them. To us; you are the best of them.

Happily, in his last decade Dad also discovered a new scholarly interest, a fitting culmination of his life's work in that it had Barra at its heart, allowed him to deploy his love of history, was deeply informed by his work on relational contracts, and constituted a campaign in support of an overlooked or misunderstood group, namely Hebridean galley castles, which are in part proxy for the people of the Hebrides. Stimulated by his frustration with the dominant school of historiography, which dates Kisimul Castle to the fifteenth century on the basis of highly selective evidence and Victorian views – Scotocentric as Dad called them – holding that civilisation made its way up from the south with the advent of the Normans, and only belatedly reached the backward heathens of the Hebrides after passing through mainland Scotland, Dad began to explore the origins of what he referred to as Hebridean galley castles, i.e. castles in the Hebrides and the adjacent mainland which were close to the shore and had, he believed, been constructed as adjuncts to the galleys which were the main vehicles of commerce and war in the Hebrides during medieval times.

He got started on this work in preparation for the 2004 Northern Studies Conference, where he had been asked to talk about Kisimul. In preparation he began to look more widely at castles in the Hebrides and elsewhere in the medieval Norse–Celtic seaways. This resulted in a paper, 'Kisimul Castle and the Origins of Hebridean Galley Castles: Preliminary Thoughts'. Much like his early work on relational contracts, the paper is a call to arms. It exposes the flawed assumptions of the dominant school of historiography and the way these lead to unjustified conclusions about late dating of Kisimul and other galley castles. It goes on to call for a proper 'contextual analysis' and sets out issues that need to be investigated in detail and without ideological blinkers before a proper understanding of the history of the galley castles can be written, issues such as comparative mortar analysis of relevant castles, a comprehensive review of early charters, etc.

After 2004 Dad threw himself into detailed study of these issues. His library is piled high with the hundreds of books and articles he was using as reference materials, and he left several papers in draft form. The first fruit of his labours, a series of four maps showing possible galley castles in their contexts of the Hebrides and adjacent mainland, and the wider Norse–Celtic seaways, was completed shortly before his death. The second, an article on how castles are dealt with by the fourteenth-century chronicler John Fordun, was almost complete at the time of his death, and several others were at an earlier stage of preparation. I am working with several Scottish historians on putting together a conference which will take forward the galley castle themes and challenges Dad identified.

In essence, Dad had begun to rewrite the history of the medieval Hebrides from a *Hebridean* perspective. In the twelfth and thirteenth centuries, the Hebrides, including Barra, were at the *centre* of the Norse–Celtic seaways. With their galleys and galley castles, the Hebrideans were producing advanced technology and were part of a thriving, forward-looking set of sea kingdoms. This is hardly the view that comes through from the Scotocentric historiography, which projects back in time the current situation, when the Hebrides are seen to be a backward part of 'the periphery', and, deprived of control over their natural resources like fish and wind and sea power, Hebrideans are caught up in endless battles for survival with bureaucrats in Edinburgh and Brussels.

In his final years, stimulated by this new perspective on the medieval Hebrides, ever creative in his thinking and true to his belief in self-reliance, Dad was developing the concept of a quasi-independent island federation, comprised of the Hebrides, Shetland, Orkney and the Faroe Islands, as a political vehicle that would enable islanders to regain control over their natural resources and free themselves from the shackles of absentee bureaucrats, and in so doing create a framework for sustainable development and a more participative polity that better reflects Hebridean traditions than the stifling state bureaucracy of modern Britain and Europe. This might seem a far-fetched vision today, but who knows how things might develop? As David Campbell said about Dad's contract scholarship after his death, 'even now he remains far, far ahead of his time'.

References

Macneil, I (1968) *Contracts, Instruments for Social Cooperation, East Africa* (South Hackensack NJ: F B Rothman)

Macneil, I (1971) *Cases and Materials on Contracts: Exchange Transactions and Relationships* (Mineola NY: Foundation Press)

Macneil, I (1974) *The Many Futures of Contract* (Los Angeles CA: Gould School of Law, Law Center, University of Southern California)

Macneil, I (2006) 'Kisimul Castle and the Origins of Hebridean Galley Castles: Preliminary Thoughts' in *Barra and Skye: Two Hebridean Perspectives* (Edinburgh: Scottish Society for Northern Studies)

Macneil, Robert Lister (1975) *Castle in the Sea* (New York: Vantage Press)

1
Introduction
Jay M Feinman

The chapters in this volume re-examine the remarkable contributions of Ian Macneil to the study of contracting behaviour and contract law. More important, they do him greater honour by demonstrating the vitality of his relational contract theory in continuing to frame issues for scholars to debate and in providing a vehicle for considering new social and legal phenomena.

Macneil developed relational contact theory as one of a series of efforts to address the inadequacies of neoclassical contract law.[1] Classical contract's most important features for Macneil's subsequent criticism were that it was binary and presentiated, focused narrowly on the isolated, two-party transaction; the law's role was simply to apply formal doctrines of offer and acceptance, consideration, and the like to recognize and enforce the parties' express private ordering. The essence of the criticism of classical law and its reconstruction through succeeding scholarly generations was contextualization, both internal and external to the body of law itself. The internal criticism compared the ostensible doctrines with the results in the cases, finding that the rules did not explain the cases because no formal, general rules ever could. The external criticism, of which relational contract theory would become an important mode, situated the rules in the world of actual contracting practice, a practice characterized by rich social and economic relations, the haphazard ways in which parties bargained and attended to private law, and inequality and disadvantage, all of which undercut the formal notions of calculated private ordering.

Several of the chapters in this volume report and debate the extent to which courts in England and Wales increasingly are focusing on context and therefore developing their own version of neoclassical contract law. Hugh Beale notes that: 'The traditional approach of English law to business-

---

1 A term that he may have coined (Macneil, 1978).

to-business contracts has tended towards abstraction, deliberately ignoring the context in which the agreement was made.' He reports that the tendency toward abstraction may be changing, at least in interpretation cases. Adherence to plain or literal meaning of words is fading in light of a recognition that 'the meaning of words depends on the context in which they are used'; whether or not this development is properly ascribed to inevitable logic, as he would have it, the development is a notable departure from the formality that characterized the classical approach (Beale, p. 135).

Roger Brownsword goes further and asserts that the contextualist development that began in interpretation cases has now spread 'across the whole range of transactional disputes between commercial contractors'. '[T]he contextualist development of the English commercial law of contract that, having been initiated by Lords Steyn and Hoffmann, has now become a wide-ranging form of commercial realism that is sweeping all before it.' Although he suggests that it is fair to 'debate just how radical a departure this is from the classical mode and from orthodox English contract law thinking' the elements of the 'contextualist development' are striking. The first and most fundamental element is that the protection of reasonable expectations in accord with 'commercial common sense' is the goal of contract law. Those reasonable expectations are defined not only by the express terms of the contract but also by implicit understandings of the parties and the commercial context in which they operate. However, agreement, where it is genuine, still reigns; the rules of contract law are only default rules, subject to being varied by the express or implied agreement of the parties, except where public policy clearly dictates otherwise (Brownsword, p. 25, citations omitted).

Both authors attribute the origins of the contextualist approach to cases in the late 1990s (Beale, p. 131; Brownsword, p. 23). In the United States, by contrast, the move toward contextualism had its origins in American legal realism beginning in the 1920s and 1930s and was widely adopted by the courts in the 1960s and 1970s. Brownsword's first element mirrors the title of the first section of Arthur Corbin's important treatise on contract law, the core of which was laid down in the 1920s though not eventually published until mid-century: 'The Main Purpose of Contract Law Is the Realization of Reasonable Expectations Induced by Promises.' (Corbin, 1952, p. 1) The Uniform Commercial Code 2001 (UCC), first promulgated in 1948 and widely enacted in the 1960s, and the Restatement (Second) of Contracts, begun in the 1960s and adopted in final form in 1979, each employ the kind of contextualization reflected in recent cases such as *Rainy Sky v Kookmin Bank* [2011] UKSC 50. As several authors discuss, in that case the court expressed a preference for meanings that reflect relevant background knowledge and surrounding circumstances and, ultimately, 'business common sense'. The UCC, for example, similarly defines agreement as 'the bargain of the parties in fact, as found in their language or by implication from other circumstances including course of dealing or usage of trade or course of performance' (UCC §1–201(b)(3) (2001)).

Oddly enough, at the same time that English courts apparently have moved to contextualism, some US courts have reverted to older approaches that resemble the abstraction of traditional English courts described by Beale. To take only one example, Beale describes the parol evidence rule in English law largely as a relic of the nineteenth century, although subject to resurrection through a merger clause or no-reliance clause. In many jurisdictions in the US, the parol evidence rule in its traditional form remains strong, and the enforceability of a merger clause or a no-reliance clause is extremely important in many transactions. This reversion in contract law has been described as a classical revival (Feinman, 2004), a new conceptualism (Mooney, 1995), or a new formalism ('Symposium: Formalism Revisited', 1999; Scott, 2000), terms which parallel Beale's description of abstraction. In part, this move means less attention is paid to the factual details of a particular case or of the class of cases of which it is representative and to the complexities of real-world contracting as means of better understanding and regulating the parties' contract. It also makes contract law more abstract and rule-based, as the ideal of capable parties transacting in a well-functioning market becomes a primary source of doctrine, and such parties are hypothesized to respond to rules as effectively shaping their behaviour.

It would be a useful exercise in comparative law between jurisdictions with the same common law roots to fully examine these contrasting developments and their sources; although this is not the place for such an undertaking, the comparison is striking. And it is worth noting that in the US the changes in contract law developed in parallel with similarly conservative developments in the other elements of the trinity of private law – tort and property law. All of the doctrinal developments, in turn, were associated with and in part spurred by changes in the political culture. As the UK shared many of those changes – Thatcherism in the UK was analogous to Reaganism in the US – one wonders what a broader analysis of the state of private law would reveal.

In any event, many scholars recognized that neoclassical law corrected some of the errors of classical law but did not go far enough. Neoclassical contract law's attention to commercial context, of which the move away from abstraction in the English courts is an example, is broader than the binary abstraction of classical law, but relational contract theory is broader still. Macneil began with an analysis that was as much sociological as legal, examining the 'primal roots of contract', which led him to broad definitions of 'contract' and 'exchange': '[C]ontract encompasses all human activities in which economic exchange is a significant factor', and 'exchange' includes all interactions in which reciprocity is a dominant element, not just monetizable transactions (Macneil, 1999–2000, p. 877). From this analysis, Macneil identified a set of contract norms stated at a high degree of generality. One thing that the norms do is to suggest the categorization of contracts as discrete or relational or, more accurately, as situated with mixed elements along the discrete-relational spectrum. In examining an individual contract, the norms also can be used to direct attention to elements of the context that are particular to the contract at issue and to the relational context out of which it arises. Accordingly, relational contract theory provides a degree of contextualization that is at the same time more general, more focused and more highly structured than neoclassical law.

As several of the authors note, however, contextualization in relational contract theory, including even the recognition of the discrete–relational distinction, is only a first step, and more is demanded for a complete analysis. Relational contracts do not constitute a distinct class; instead, every contract is relational in the sense that every contractual relation has both discrete and relational elements, and even then the ways in which contracts and contractual behaviour vary are not fully captured by situating a relation along the discrete–relational spectrum.[2] In this respect, Macneil's work is frequently misread by scholars as creating distinct classes of discrete and relational contracts with the entire relational analysis only applicable to the latter category (Feinman, 2000, p. 739).

As Hugh Collins notes: 'The conventional contextual or neo-classical approach refers to the context in order to supplement the contractual agreement or to resolve ambiguities ... Under Macneil's sociological approach, however, one has to start from the outside with the relations between the parties within which context the exchange is made, and then work inwards towards the contract.' (Collins, p. 67) Context is essential but not sufficient. Context must be read through the structure of the ten common contract norms, in which different norms are of different value depending on the nature of the contract. By reference to the social matrix in which the parties' relation is situated, those norms include customs of an industry or other relevant group, rules of a trade association or professional organiza-

---

[2] In his later work Macneil attempted to substitute 'intertwined' as a descriptor for 'relational' when referring to a long-term, extensive contractual relationship, to avoid confusion with the broader use of the term in 'relational contract theory', but the usage never caught on (Macneil, 1999–2000).

tion, and norms generated by any group intersecting with the relation at issue, as well as broader values of the society.

Relational contract theory with its contextualization and more is one of several attempts to respond to the limits of neoclassical contract law. Some approaches also use empirical analysis of actual contracting practices to draw inferences about the appropriate role and content of contract law from that practice; those inferences often suggest that contract law is and should be marginal in the world of commerce. More recent empirical work is of the experimental variety, adopting the techniques of psychological experimentation to attempt to understand contracting behaviour. Other approaches focus on abstraction rather than contextualization; law and economics, at least in its traditional form, and rights theories, such as Charles Fried's *Contract as Promise* (1982), suggest that a systematic approach based on a limited set of fundamental principles and a defined method of applying those principles provides the best means of analysing and determining the content of contract law. And there is the unique contribution of critical legal studies, which draws on empirical and theoretical sources to reveal contract law as problematic, contested and ideological (Feinman, 1990).

Looking at these competitors to relational contract theory, the heyday of critical legal studies has passed (regrettably in my view), empirical work continues to make contributions, law and economics has diversified and occupies a large role in the scholarship, and rights theories surface occasionally. What Linda Mulcahy observes about relational contract theory surely is also true about the others: they always have been more directly influential on the academic discourse than on the courts (and, one might add, are likely to remain so) (Mulcahy, p. 194).

As the chapters here demonstrate, it is likely that relational contact theory remains the richest of the theoretical approaches to contracting and contract law that arose in response to neoclassical contract law. Now some 40 years old, the theory is sufficiently rich and complex to still command development on its own. To take only a few examples from this volume, David Campbell, its foremost contemporary expositor, continues the project of defining and defending it in his chapter, and argues that a relational approach has superior explanatory and normative power than either a market-individualist (classical with a dash of neoclassical) or a welfarist approach to contract law, remarkably illustrating his position by a relational analysis of the much criticized *Arcos Ltd v EA Ronaasen and Son* [1933] AC 470 HL. Collins adds to the refinement of the theory as well. He describes the need for an 'integrated multi-level analysis' that combines focus on the terms of parties' agreements (contractual rationality), a cost/benefit calculus of both short-term and long-term economic interest (economic rationality), and the need for maintaining trust and other elements that support long-term relationships (relational rationality) (Collins, p. 79). Sally Wheeler offers a clarification of Macneil's definition of discrete contract that focuses on large-scale issues of social and economic ordering; given that all contracts have discrete and relational elements, no individual contract is really appropriately labelled 'discrete'. She also refines Macneil's famous illustration of an apparently-but-not-really discrete contract, an isolated transaction for the purchase of gasoline on the New Jersey turnpike, in distinguishing 'between the atomized process of making the contract itself and the informational and network structure that surround it'. (Wheeler, p. 46) But the best demonstration of the true vitality of the theory is shown by its ability to adapt to new issues and situations, including some that Macneil's own work presaged and some that he could not have contemplated.

Jonathan Morgan's chapter and Brownsword's chapter initially demonstrate the extent to which relational theory engages with and to an extent frames scholarly debates long after the theory's formulation. Both discuss the issue of whether and how relational norms might be translated into contract law, an issue that Brownsword states in a now-common form: 'The real question is what the *default* approach of the law should be.' (Morgan, p. 178) The concept of default rules and the debate over how they should be framed has become a central concern of contracts scholarship. The default rules discourse was spurred by classic articles by Ian Ayres (Macneil's colleague at Northwestern University) and Robert Gertner, and Charles Goetz and Robert Scott, who became the principal author of a transformed version of relational contract theory (Ayres and Gertner, 1989; Goetz and Scott, 1981).

Relational contract theory, with its focus on the form of contracting and the contract norms, is useful in shaping the default rules debate. That debate is part of a broader discussion about the possible and desirable links among relational contracting as a social process, relational contract theory as an academic discourse, and contract law as applied in the courts.

A first issue is what Richard Danzig described as 'the capability problem', or the ability of courts to operationalize relational principles in developing rules of law and applying them in individual cases (Danzig, 2004). Mulcahy points out that Macneil and other relationists are aware of the difficulty courts have in defining and implementing relational norms. Part of this difficulty stems from the reluctance of commercial parties to litigate their disputes. Systemic factors cause problems, too. The vanishing civil trial and the decline in the number of appeals concerning contract cases provide fewer occasions for courts to see relational contract cases. Even in those cases, the filtering process of litigation and the tendency of lawyers to favour the framing of arguments stated in traditional legal form and to disfavour novel arguments based on extra-legal norms further diminish the relational grist for the judicial mill.

Even beyond what is possible, Morgan argues that it is undesirable to have more than a limited use of relational theory in law itself. He uses *Baird Textile Holdings Ltd v Marks and Spencer plc* [2001] EWCA Civ 274, [2002] 1 All ER (Comm) 737 to argue that Macneil's account of relational contracting cannot and should not translate into a relational contract law. He recognizes the contribution of relational theory in directing attention to the context in which contracts are made and performed and the frequent relational character of that context, and of the usefulness of Macneil's structure of norms in analysing that context. Yet there are two problems: whether courts can effectively define and enforce the normative structure as rules of law, and whether they should. He cites a wealth of literature that suggests that relational norms flourish even in the absence of legal enforcement, legalizing norms such as trust and co-operation may actually undermine the parties' faith in and reliance on such norms, courts engaging in traditional adjudication are poorly equipped to define and apply the norms, and parties often do not want them to do so in any case.

This type of argument is not new. In an article in 1930, Zechariah Chafee colourfully identified four factors that a court should consider in deciding whether to intervene in an extensive relationship, and three of the four disfavoured intervention. For example, if the court intervenes it may be wading into a 'dismal swamp' where it cannot divine the appropriate norms, and it may cut down the 'living tree' of relationships that flourishes only in the absence of intervention (Chafee, 1930, pp. 1021–9). But, as Brownsword's chapter demonstrates, the argument recently has been reframed and has achieved heightened attention.

Brownsword and Morgan both argue that parties prefer and the law should adopt default rules that are 'strict, formal and rule-based' (Morgan, p. 178) or rules that are 'plain and modest' because such rules 'facilitate[ ] contracting out of the default position' (Morgan, p. 179). In doing so, they rely in large part on empirical research into contracting communities, the form and preferences of contracts between large commercial entities, and non-legal dispute resolution practices. That literature suggests a preference for clear rules and limited judicial intervention, notions that are antithetical to relational contract.

An underlying assumption of this argument is that 'parties that want relational contract law can and should contract for it ... parties are perfectly able to indicate that relational norms are to be used to resolve contractual disputes, if they so desire' (Morgan, p. 181). 'Perfectly able' in theory, but perhaps not so able in practice. And describing how parties 'should' respond to the incentives created by contract law – contracting for relational principles in the face of clear default rules, for example – resembles the heroic assumptions of classical law about the operation of informed parties bargaining on perfect markets. In fact, as much of the empirical literature demonstrates, the assumption that parties will bargain in detail is questionable at all. Roger Halson, for instance, cites the studies demonstrating that parties plan for performance, not breach, a principal subject of the default rules debate. One wonders if parties were more assiduous bargainers under the formalist approach of classical English contract law as compared to parties dealing with the more recent move to contextualism, or as compared to their counterparts in American jurisdictions that moved modestly further in the direction of divining and enforcing relational norms.

There is an even deeper point here that is both theoretical and ideological. Halson notes with respect to liquidated damages clauses a point that might be made more generally about the literature, that 'we are left with a sterile normative defence of freedom of contract, one that is closely tied to its premise that parties know more about their interests than courts do' (Halson, p. 104, citing Posner, 2003, p, 863). The trend in much scholarship, implicitly and often explicitly, has been not just a turn to formalism but a turn toward so-called 'freedom of contract' and against regulation by legislatures or courts. He quotes Eric Posner with respect to the trend that 'the premises of economics push in the direction of freedom of contract' and that direction of travel 'can be resisted only with difficulty' (Posner, 2003, p. 842; Mattei, 1995, p. 432). Halson points out that Macneil's relational theory battles against this trend mightily. 'Yet resist is exactly what Macneil does in *Power of Contract* and this is effected by the careful definition of the concept of power to contract described in detail above.' (Halson, p. 107) That concept incorporates the insight of the legal realists, most notably Robert Hale, that a body of contract law that enforces the acts of a private party is public law, interventionist rather than non-interventionist. In this respect Macneil poses a stark contrast to classical thought and, more importantly, to its modern academic heirs.

With its focus on contracting in context, relational contract theory does not limit itself to judicial enforcement of the contract norms. Mulcahy describes and argues for the expanded use of vehicles of dispute resolution other than courts for the development and application of relational norms. Noting Macneil's early interest in alternative dispute resolution, she describes the expanded use of commercial mediation and argues for increased recognition of it as a locus for relational theory. As in the United States, mediation has become increasingly popular in the UK; parties are often pulled toward less formal, protracted and expensive processes than litigation and, if they need a push, courts under the press of the docket encourage or coerce parties to employ alternative forms of resolution. Two uses of mediation that she notes are particularly relevant in light of relational theory: mediation or at least mediation principles now figure not just as techniques of dispute resolution but also as tools in deal formation; transactional mediation helps parties create relationships rather than just cope with the aftermath of a relationship gone bad. And even in disputes, the purpose is not always to autopsy a dead relationship, but sometimes aims 'to repair an existing relationship rather than just symbolising its end', including the use of creative remedies and forward-looking actions not available to courts.

Beyond the academic debates, several of the chapters demonstrate the strength of relational contract theory in responding to new situations. Peter Vincent-Jones shows the power of relational contract theory in enlightening understanding of hybrid organizations, or the privatized provision of public services. As such entities and programmes become more widely used in the UK and the US, there is a continuing need for improvements in their design, improvements that can be based on empirical research and theorizing about them. Vincent-Jones demonstrates that relational contract theory provides a base of analysis that, combined with social learning theory, sets out the theory and charts a research programme. Once again, Macneil's contract norms provide a useful starting point, particularly with the recognition that the norms in a relationship are both contractual and non-contractual, internal and external. Because the hybrid forms tend to be strongly relational, 'the greater the scope for social learning in negotiating and managing the on-going relationship' (Vincent-Jones, p. 226). Noting the research on the variable use of law in contractual relationships, he lays out a research programme for the study of hybrid organizations that could also feed back into the understanding of more traditional economic contracts.

The most remarkable developments in exchange, broadly understood as Macneil used the term, have come through technological advances of which the internet is the most notable. At the time of the publication of *The New Social Contract* in 1980, for example, Amazon.com and eBay were still a decade and a half from creation. Nevertheless, the concluding theme of that book contrasted 'a dystopian world of La Technique with an imperfect, but more human, world of Post-Technique' (Brownsword, p. 14). As Brownsword notes, this discussion was neither a casual afterthought or a curmudgeonly complaint, and he develops the insight thoughtfully. For example, because communities and networks rise and flourish in cyberspace with little regard for geographic boundaries, from Amazon to commercial trading partners to Second Life, contrasting forms of governance come into play and are debated, including formal, boundary-based law, communal norms, and control through technological devices commonly grouped together as 'code'. He concludes that self-governing communities that organize through and around technology should be nurtured or at least not discouraged by formal law, and that the technologies so important in the constitution and control of those communities should promote conditions in which persons can develop and debate the terms of their moral communities.

Wheeler goes further and suggests that relational contract theory requires further development in the face of the technological revolution and the globalization of exchange. The landscape of informal relations prevailing over formal contracts of production described by Stewart Macaulay and adopted by Macneil has been substantially infringed (Wheeler might say replaced) by production 'cluster[ed] into confined geographical areas that offer a combination of low regulation and low cost labour and access to natural resources', with the resulting products traded in global markets (Wheeler, p. 49). Individual purchases are less commonly transacted face to face and more commonly conducted on eBay, where the seller is unknown to the buyer except by reputation, and the relational component is provided through the structure of the PayPal payment system owned by eBay and trust is reinforced through eBay's dispute resolution process.

What is most striking about these discussions is that the technological conditions could hardly have been anticipated and Brownsword's and Wheeler's own analyses are novel, but the fundamental understandings of the situations and the analyses rests on the pillars of relational contract theory. Here are the recognition that the necessary starting point is exchange broadly defined, that exchange takes place always in relational networks, that norms develop in those networks, that state and norms both have a role to play in regulation, and the most challenging issues are to develop principles of obligation from the norms and practices that should bind the members of the communities. In the new technological and economic situations, and as changes are made, contract law doctrine erected on a model of discrete exchange becomes less and less useful, as Macneil taught.

As several authors point out, however, relational analysis can be particularly useful in warning of the dangers posed by new developments. Wheeler in particular notes that the hybrid organizations described by Vincent-Jones were never intended to realize the norms that are necessary to the development of positive social relationships. She also points out that the employment relation once was the paradigmatic long-term, encompassing relational contract in which the relational norms could flourish, but things have changed:

> Long-term employment with a single provider has been replaced by portfolio careers. Workplace hierarchies are flatter and there is less room for norms that seek to preserve relationships or develop them beyond the limits of the printed conditions of employment. [Therefore] Macneil's relational values are squeezed out of these highly planned arrangements of short and specified duration. (Wheeler, p. 50).

Thus relational contract theory retains vibrancy decades after its creation. The theory is complex enough to require continual refinement. It frames debates even among those who believe its use in courts can and should be limited. And it adapts to and enlightens new social and technological circumstances.

But what of the future? A volume such as this provides appropriate occasion for speculating about the future of relational contact theory. An aphorism variously attributed to Danish physicist Niels Bohr and American baseball player Yogi Berra states that prediction is difficult, especially about the future. Nevertheless, the contributions to this volume as a whole at least raise a few questions worth contemplating about the theory's future.

Theories do not succeed or fail, prosper or wither, solely on their own merits. Thomas Kuhn long ago disabused us of the notion that natural science is simply a truth-seeking, error-correcting process. Even more so as to the study of law, which has no empirical reality against which hypotheses may be tested (or at least where it is easier to obscure the reality in service of a theory). The study of law and economics has prospered in the United States in part because of the substantial financial support it attracted from business and conservative interests who thought its approach and results would be congenial to their political and ideological agendas.

With that situation in mind, one might be concerned about the future of relational contract theory for two reasons. First, the theory has no natural constituency. There is no external group that would obviously benefit from the development and promotion of the theory, as business interests perceived they might have in the early days of law and economics. Nor is there a constituency internal to the legal academy. In the US, at least, philosophical and social science approaches to law, including private law, have become more influential in part because academics with formal training in philosophy and the social sciences have come into the legal academy in larger numbers. Relational contract theory has no cadre of academics likely to be drawn to its cause.

Second, as the authors in this volume illustrate, there is something of a generational challenge. Many of the principal contemporary expositors and analysts of relational contract theory, most of whom are included here, are about a generation younger than Macneil himself and therefore approaching what at least once was normal retirement age. Moreover, many of them were mentored by or colleagues of Macneil (David Campbell and me, for example), an opportunity that is no longer available to scholars. Therefore, the continued success of the theory depends on its use by a younger and more diverse group of scholars.

Despite both these concerns, there is reason for optimism. In a recent study of the most-cited US legal articles of all time, Macneil's 'Contracts: Adjustment of Long-Term Economic Relations under Classical, Neoclassical, and Relational Contract Law' ranked in 90th place (Shapiro, 2012, pp. 1489, 1504). (Relational contract law scholars would be interested in the fact that Stewart Macaulay's 'Non-contractual Relations in Business' ranked at number 15 (Macaulay, 1963) (Shapiro, 2012, pp. 1489, 1504).) That is historical data, but particularly heartening is the fact that the ranking of Macneil's article (and of Macaulay's, too) was buttressed because it was one of the few law review articles to receive many citations in social science journals. The spread of relational contract theory beyond the legal literature is one sign of strength.

That is historical data. Searches of more recent law review articles on the database Westlaw similarly reveal that relational contract and Macneil's version of it are still regularly cited. An admittedly cursory study suggests that the citations fall into two categories.

Some of the articles simply use the category of relational contracts – extensive, long-term relationships – as a distinctive form of contracting. This group of articles is a little dispiriting, or at least not encouraging. Their adoption of the category of relational contracts is by now a mainstream concept, and it is often used only to suggest that traditional contract law contracts that were created for presentiated contracts ought to apply less rigorously and that more contextualization is required. As noted above, and as Campbell among others in this volume makes clear, that is a simplification if not a misunderstanding of the theory.

But many other articles make a much richer use of relational contract theory and, to varying degrees, employ Macneil's broader scope, normative structure and relational method. Included are analyses of relations as diverse as reorganization of companies under the bankruptcy laws, family businesses, employment contracts, construction contracts, and even the relationship between the International Olympic Committee and a city chosen to host the Olympic Games. These articles are more inspiring and present reason for hope for the future of relational contract theory. Scholars and even practitioners writing articles grapple with more of the details of relational contract theory in ways that suggest that it still demands attention and provides insight among contract law scholars and others who grapple with issues involving relational contracting.

References

Ayres, I and I Gertner (1989) 'Filling Gaps in Incomplete Contracts: An Economic Theory of Default Rules' 99 *Yale Law Journal* 87–130

Chafee, Z (1930) 'The Internal Affairs of Associations Not for Profit' 43 *Harvard Law Review* 993

Corbin, A (1952) *Corbin on Contracts* (St Paul MN: West Publishing)

Danzig, R (2004) *The Capability Problem in Contract Law: Further Readings on Well-Known Cases* (Mineola NY: Foundation Press) (2nd edn)

Feinman, J (1990) 'The Significance of Contract Theory' 58 *University of Cincinnati Law Review* 1283–318

Feinman, J (2000) 'Relational Contract Theory in Context' 94 *Northwestern University Law Review* 737–48

Feinman, J (2004) 'Un-making Law: The Classical Revival in the Common Law' 28 *Seattle University Law Review* 1–59

Fried, C (1982) *Contract as Promise* (Cambridge: Harvard University Press)

Goetz, C and R Scott (1981) 'Principles of Relational Contract' 67 *Virginia Law Review* 1089

Macaulay, S (1963) 'Non-Contractual Relations in Business: A Preliminary Study' 28 *American Sociological Review* 55–67

Macneil, I (1978) 'Contracts: Adjustments of Long-term Economic Relations under Classical, Neoclassical, and Relational Contract Law' 72 *Northwestern University Law Review* 854–905

Macneil, I (1980) *The New Social Contract* (New Haven CT: Yale University Press)

Macneil, I (1999–2000) 'Relational Contract Theory: Challenges and Queries' 94 *Northwestern University Law Review* 877–908

Mattei, U (1995) 'The Comparative Law and Economics of Penalty Clauses in Contracts' 43 *American Journal of Comparative Law* 427–44

Mooney, R (1995) 'The New Conceptualism in Contract Law' 74 *Oregon Law Review* 1131

Posner, E (2003) 'Economic Analysis of Contract Law after Three Decades: Success or Failure?' 112 *Yale Law Journal* 829–80

Scott, R (2000) 'The Case for Formalism in Relational Contract' 94 *Northwestern University Law Review* 847–76

Shapiro, F (2012) 'The Most-cited Law Review Articles of All Time' 110 *Michigan Law Review* 1483–520

'Symposium: Formalism Revisited' (1999) 66 *University of Chicago Law Review* 527

2
'Post-Technique': *The New Social Contract* Today
Roger Brownsword

1. Introduction

In the closing pages of *The New Social Contract* (Macneil, 1980), Ian Macneil contrasts a dystopian world of La Technique with an imperfect, but more human, world of Post-Technique. Readers might think that this was something of an afterthought, not closely related to the book's great insights in placing contractual transactions in a context of multifarious relationships and expectations. However, with the development of modern information and communication technologies[1] that not only support new worlds of both consumer and commercial contracting, but also offer opportunities for just the kind of perfect control sought after by La Technique, there are reasons for thinking that the time has come for Post-Technique. That is to say, if we are to retain our essential humanity while enjoying the benefits of new technologies, we do indeed need a new Social Contract that sets limits to the imperialist thinking of Technical Man and the unreflective spread of new technologies – technologies that, in some applications, liberate and empower but, in others, confine and control (Brownsword, 2012a).

Although the technological context in which Macneil was writing was rather different to that of the present century – quite apart from the staggering development and penetration of digital technologies (Harkaway, 2012), there is much greater interest nowadays in the potential of biotech-

---

1 For a helpful overview of the key transformative technological developments, see European Group on Ethics in Science and New Technologies (2012, pp. 15–25). The astonishing pace of recent developments is nicely captured in Harkaway (2012, p. 22): 'The services and companies we think of now as being an integral part of the digital realm are relatively recent. Amazon.com began in 1995, letting people order through its digital shopfront from what was effectively a warehouse system. In the same year, eBay was born, hosting 250,000 auctions in 1996 and 2m in 1997. Google was incorporated in 1998. The first iPod was sold in 2001, and the iTunes Store opened its online doors in 2003. Facebook went live in 2004. YouTube did not exist until 2005.'

nologies, nanotechnologies, neurotechnologies, robotics and the convergence of these technologies[2] – he fully appreciated that the marriage of modern technologies with imperfect humans is not always straightforward. In the area of contracting, the technologies open up new marketplaces to consumers and businesses alike (Schammo, 2008); and there are endless opportunities for self-governing communities to agree upon their own codes of conduct. However, at the same time, the technologies can be designed with a view to channelling conduct in ways that are not always desired (by their users) or desirable (relative to the public interest). In this paper, I suggest that, in Post-Technique, it is imperative that regulators should be sensitive to: (i) the opportunities that technology now presents to aspiring self-governing communities (and, concomitantly, the importance of nurturing and preserving legitimate zones of self-governance); (ii) the need to shield contractors not only against the abusive use of technologies (such as digital rights management technologies) as instruments of control but also the use of old-fashioned contractual power to limit legitimate uses of new technologies;[3] and (iii) the virtue of exercising regulatory restraint in giving problems a technical fix lest this should corrode the context for agents (whether as contractors or as citizens) to express their humanity.

The chapter is in four principal parts. First, in part two, 'The new Social Contract: technology with humanity', I outline Macneil's push-back against Technical Man and his vision of Post-Technique. Secondly, in part three 'Governance in a networked world: Johnson and Post', I set alongside the vision of Post-Technique, David Johnson and David Post's influential analysis of the contrast between Westphalian land-based laws and landless cyberspace, together with their advocacy of a self-regulatory approach to the latter (Johnson and Post, 1996; Post, 2009). Thirdly, in part four, 'Contractual networks as self-governing communities', I turn from the internet to contractual networks. Here, I suggest that the puzzle of how to regulate contractual networks (Amstutz and Teubner, 2009; Teubner, 2011) invites a response that highlights the self-governing nature of such networks – and that treats the relevant self-governing codes as the reference point for determining the reasonable expectations of network contractors. Finally, in part five, 'The threat of La Technique today', I step back to draw out the key features of modern regulatory environments so that we can begin to assess the significance of the changing complexion of the signals

---

2 That said, we should not understate or ignore the persistence and re-application of older technologies (see Edgerton, 2006).
3 For the use (and abuse) of technological protection measures, see Favale (2008); and, for contracts and contract law, see Elkin-Koren (1997).

found in these environments. The fundamental point is that, in Post-Technique, regulators need to be careful about changing the signals from what ought or ought not to be done to what can or cannot be done. If we are to preserve self-governing communities, we need to ensure that contract remains a zone in which there are real options and opportunities for private ordering; and if we are to respect our humanity, we should be extremely careful in licensing the use of any technologies of perfect control.

2. The new Social Contract: technology with humanity

When Macneil introduces his prospectus for a Post-Techniquan society in which the benefits of technological development are captured but without the sacrifice of humanity, it is not entirely obvious how these closing reflections fit into the main (relational) themes of the book. Nevertheless, it is clear that Macneil has been stung into making these remarks by what he perceives to be the rise of Technical Man. Technical Man is a marker for a multitude of undesirable characteristics – notably, for an instrumentally rational and instrumentalizing mindset that prefers to 'destroy spontaneous and unreflective behaviour in favour of deliberate and rational behavior' (Macneil, 1980, p. 108), and that seeks both perfection and power (perfect control) over others. For Technical Man, encounters with imperfect humans are necessarily frustrating; but even if Technical Man cannot yet perfect humans, 'he can try to perfect their institutions' (pp. 109–10). At first blush, we might be tempted by the idea of perfected law, or perfected contract law; however, Macneil sees only dystopian futures for Technical Man (Orwell and Huxley lurk in the footnotes). The centralization, the coordination, the horizontality of La Technique is to be avoided.

The Luddites, just like Samuel Butler's Erewhonians (Butler, 1892), had a way of dealing with La Technique. However, Macneil does not argue that we should destroy all the machines. Rather, Post-Techniquan society strives to achieve a harmonious coupling of technology and humanity. As Macneil sketches this world:

> Post-Technique has not given up desires to maintain high levels of production. Thus its citizens accept the need for large amounts of planning in the realm of production and with it significant quantities of power. But they also are willing to make sacrifices of production to keep it subordinate to greater human needs. Thus Post-Technique is not some greened America in which the manifold goodies of modern technology somehow magically keep pouring out with zero-effect on a spontaneous, opiated world. It is one where the clash between the competing

values is recognized and a balanced reconciliation is sought. Post-Technique is, in short, a humanistic and technological world, which is to say that it is imperfect – an essential characteristic of any good world. (Macneil, 1980, p. 112)

In Post-Technique, 'new designs cause much soul-searching' (p. 113); 'assembly lines are frowned on in favour of team production methods in which the team exercises major decision-making and planning responsibility, often even for the product itself' (p. 113); and it falls to law to preserve decentralization against centralizing tendencies as well as to 'help the decentralized centers [to] keep peace among themselves and [to] cooperate affirmatively' (p. 116). In Post-Technique, the guiding principle is that small is beautiful – just so 'because it reduces power; because it makes ludicrous the idea of "the one best way"; because it has to live with its own imperfections and imperfectibility' (p. 113). In short, small is beautiful 'because small has no need to distort the human spirit into Technical Man' (p. 113).

Notwithstanding Macneil's cautionary remarks about taking the title of his lectures too seriously, the prospectus for Post-Technique does suggest new social contracts, both large and small. The large Social Contract is the one that Macneil envisages in a community that seeks to progress technologically but without loss of its humanity. However, what Macneil could not have foreseen was the way in which modern information and communication technologies would be developed and then would penetrate deep into our daily lives – let alone the articulation of concerns about the new technological instruments of perfect control (Lessig 1999a; Brownsword, 2008). At all events, in our modern networked world, it is clear that, in online environments, there are countless opportunities for netizens to enter into myriad small and spontaneous social contracts;[4] but it is also apparent that, offline, there are opportunities for groups to transact in their own self-regulating way. The body of rules representing the general law of contract does not have to be regarded as the only way. When we unite the larger and the smaller pictures, we see that Post-Technique in our century points to a high-tech community that not only respects fundamental human rights and human dignity but also has a considerable commitment to respect for self-governing communities (including groups that aspire to transactional self-governance).

In the next two parts of the chapter, we can treat the vision of Post-Technique as our hub from which we can explore two important contrac-

---

4 An obvious example is Second Life, which is precisely such a prospectively self-governing community (Post, 2009, pp. 178–86).

tual spokes: first, the development of online platforms for contracting (as well as for a host of potentially self-governing activities); and, secondly, the increasing prevalence of connected contracts in business networks.

3. Governance in a networked world: Johnson and Post

Opening their seminal paper on the regulation of online communications, David Johnson and David Post (1996, p. 1367) wrote:

> Global computer-based communications cut across territorial borders, creating a new realm of human activity and undermining the feasibility—and legitimacy—of laws based on geographic boundaries. While these electronic communications play havoc with geographic boundaries, a new boundary, made up of the screens and passwords that separate the virtual world from the 'real world' of atoms, emerges. This new boundary defines a distinct Cyberspace that needs and can create its own law and legal institutions. Territorially based law-makers and law-enforcers find this new environment deeply threatening.

Generally speaking, legal systems as we have traditionally known them map onto geographical territories with clear boundaries. We know when and where we cross from one legal system to another; within each legal system the authorities enjoy a measure of control and legitimacy. However, in cyberspace, matters are quite different:

> Cyberspace radically undermines the relationship between legally significant (online) phenomena and physical location. The rise of the global computer network is destroying the link between geographical location and: (1) the *power* of local governments to assert control over online behavior; (2) the *effects* of online behavior on individuals or things; (3) the *legitimacy* of a local sovereign's efforts to regulate global phenomena; and (4) the ability of physical location to give *notice* of which sets of rules apply. The Net thus radically subverts the system of rule-making based on borders between physical spaces, at least with respect to the claim that Cyberspace should naturally be governed by territorially defined rules. (Johnson and Post, 1996, p. 1370)

Despite these fundamental differences, traditional regulators respond in ways that assume that business is as usual. Thus:

> The power to control activity in Cyberspace has only the most tenuous connection to physical location. Nonetheless, many

governments' first response to electronic communications crossing their territorial borders is to try to stop or regulate that flow of information. Rather than permitting self-regulation by participants in online transactions, many governments establish trade barriers, attempt to tax border-crossing cargo, and respond especially sympathetically to claims that information coming into the jurisdiction might prove harmful to local residents (Johnson and Post, 1996, p. 1371).

The more that regulators try to claim jurisdiction over an online matter, the more difficult it is for there to be any coherent co-ordination. To try to reduce online transactions to 'a legal analysis based in geographic terms', just like '[e]fforts to determine "where" the events in question occur are decidedly misguided, if not altogether futile' (Johnson and Post, 1996, p. 1378).

According to Johnson and Post, the remedy is to treat cyberspace as a place in its own right. This would overcome jurisdictional competition with regard to defamation, professional qualifications, intellectual property, and so on, as well as facilitating the creation of bespoke online law. Moreover, such a response is not unprecedented: there are distinct echoes, for example, of the Law Merchant, of the *lex mercatoria*, that we associate with the new and rapid boundary-crossing trade of the Middle Ages.

Concluding, Johnson and Post say:

> Global electronic communications have created new spaces in which distinct rule sets will evolve. We can reconcile the new law created in this space with current territorially based legal systems by treating it as a distinct doctrine, applicable to a clearly demarcated sphere, created primarily by legitimate, self-regulatory processes, and entitled to appropriate deference—but also subject to limitations when it oversteps its appropriate sphere. (Johnson and Post, 1996, pp. 1400–1)

Would this entail the end of law? Not at all; to be sure, the relationship between traditional top-down law-makers and subjects will have to change. Nevertheless, 'Law, defined as a thoughtful group conversation about core values, will persist. But it will not, could not, and should not be the same law as that applicable to physical, geographically-defined territories.' (Johnson and Post, 1996, p. 1402)

These themes persist in David Post's much more recent and insightful book, *In Search of Jefferson's Moose* (Post, 2009). Here, Post takes issue with the so-called 'unexceptionalists' who argue that online transactions are nothing special. To be sure, as Eliza Mik (2011) remarks, the online architecture is different – for example, one is rarely 'teleported' into a bricks-and-mortar shop but, in the web world, 'a person browsing recipes can easily [click into] an online book shop' (Mik, 2011, p. 340); even so, unexceptionalists may ask, are the general principles of contract and national laws not still applicable? Against unexceptionalist views, Post argues: (i) that there is too much uncertainty in trying to apply standard conflicts principles to online transactions (parties simply do not have sufficient confidence in knowing where they stand for the full potential of online dealing to be realized); and (ii) that transactors have a right (perhaps even an inalienable right) to make their own law. Yet, Post asks rhetorically, is it not 'crazy' to treat these online communities as self-governing in relation to their online places? Not so, responds Post, because even if we do not know quite how this law-making power might be exercised, we do know that people have the right to make these decisions. He says:

> And I just wish the Unexceptionalists would stop telling us that we don't, that we've somehow given up our right to create new communities and to live under law of our own devising, or that we've finished designing legal institutions and are stuck, forevermore, with the ones we happen to have come up with by 1995.
>
> I wish they'd stop telling people that because they're standing in the way of the hard work and experimentation and innovation that will be required to create fair, well-designed, and effective lawmaking institutions and processes that are appropriate for these places. (Post, 2009, p. 186)

Let me pause to flag up a critically important point. What is at stake is not simply self-governance; there are also important questions about technological management. For, the regulatory environment in these online places is a mixture of local rules *and particular technical features*. So far, we have been focusing on self-governing communities making their own laws; but what about the technological features? Post, drawing attention to the technological infrastructure that facilitates an online consumer purchase, explains the significance of the so-called Referrer field in the HTTP Protocol – this feature supports the business model of Google and many others by enabling website B to identify website A as the place from which a visitor has linked across to website B. Similar points can be made about many technical or design features of the online environment. Here, then, in Post's own words, is the question:

> Who decides? Who decided to put a Referrer field into the HTTP protocol?

> This is what governance questions look like here, in cyberspace. If government is about the process of lawmaking, in a place constructed entirely out of code, where code is law (or at least some kind of law) and where the shape of the code(s) deeply affects the kind of place it is and the kind of things one can and cannot do there, **code-making is governance**. (Post, 2009, pp. 130–1, bold in original)

Having highlighted the significance of technological management, we are in danger of getting ahead of ourselves. The precise significance of the shift from rule to code in the complexion of our regulatory environments will be clarified in the fifth part of this chapter ('The threat of La Technique today'). Our immediate priority is to tie back these remarks to Post-Technique.

It will be recalled that the overarching aspiration in Post-Technique is to enjoy the benefits of new technologies without there being any diminution in humanity and the human spirit. The message that we take from Johnson and Post is precisely that we should celebrate cyberspace technologies but that we should facilitate a self-regulatory approach to the many cyber-places. Whether we are thinking about eBay or Second Life, the model is to allow the trading or gaming communities to develop their own constitutive rules, to enter into their own social contracts. This is not to say that public regulation should be eschewed altogether: when fraudsters operate on eBay, the criminal law is needed; and when the activities of Second Life spill over into the real world, there needs to be a regulatory response. But, the vision is clear: if a group does not like the house rules at Second Life or eBay, then it should set up its own gaming zone or auction site. Small, we should remember, is beautiful.

4. Contractual networks as self-governing communities

We can turn now from online environments to more traditional offline transacting. Here, our focus is not on the classically framed reciprocal exchange between two parties, A and B – where, as Macneil puts it, 'A and B had better be the *only* parties; adding C, D, and other such riffraff is bound to create complicated relations outside the transaction' (Macneil, 1980, p. 61). Rather, our focus is on networks of the kind that are commonly found in commercial practice. The patterns of connection might vary: there are hubs and spokes; chains and strings; clusters and groups, and so on – but the point is that, in all these cases, the transactions are wired for connection; they are networked. What should we make of such contractual connections?

In *Networks as Connected Contracts* (Teubner, 2011), Gunther Teubner discusses 'the appropriate legal regulation of business networks, virtual enterprises, just-in-time systems and franchise chains that are normally concluded in the form of bilateral contracts, but at the same time give effect to multilateral (legal) effects' (p. 73). Characteristically, these business networks 'pursue common projects making use of co-operation between autonomous firms' (p. 92); and, time and again, Teubner returns to the point that an appropriate legal response must reflect the various tensions (or institutionalized contradictions) that drive these networks – for example, the tension between hierarchy (organization) and market (contract), between common purpose and individual interest, between co-operation, and competition and so on.

According to Teubner, there needs to be a new regulatory approach to networks, not so much aimed at directing or channelling the behaviour of the parties but rather at supporting 'stable network expectations by giving them symbolic re-statement in cases where concrete network behaviour contradicts them' (p. 103). Adopting such an approach, it remains to articulate the relevant legal consequences (i) as between the parties to the network and (ii) as between network parties and those non-network parties with whom they contract.

Teubner's discussion of the former (internal network questions) opens with the *Apollo (Optik)* case where a number of German courts were faced with fixing the extent of the franchisor's responsibility to pass on to franchisees the benefit of discounts negotiated by the former with suppliers to the network. The Federal High Court eventually ruled in favour of the clamant franchisees, holding that multilateral connectivity within the franchise may create an obligation to pass on advantages to members of the network. Approving this outcome, Teubner remarks that it is no answer to resolve the dispute in either a one-sided market way (so that the standard contracts rule) or in a one-sided hierarchical (corporate) way: such strategies inappropriately 'force a choice in favour of one of the contradictory business orientations, consigning the other to the obscurity of informality' (2011, p. 183). Hence, when, in response to questions concerning the scope and nature of network loyalty, appeals are made to the overarching network purpose, these must be understood, neither from 'the one-sided perspective of an exchange', nor from the one-sided perspective of corporate totalization, but as encompassing 'the contradiction between the individual and collective elements of networking' (p. 185). In the same way, where there are disputes about the interpretation of standard form contracts that apply to networks, or about the allocation of risk within just-in-time supply networks, or about whether one member of the network may hold another to account (even though there is no direct contractual connection between them), the larger contradictory perspective must be adopted.

With regard to the external liability of the network and its members (and, concomitantly, the internal allocation of responsibility in relation to external liabilities), Teubner says that the reaction of networks 'is one of strategic ambivalence' (2011, p. 239). That is to say, network members can interface with external contractors as disconnected and discrete individual contractors (liable only to their co-contractors) or as mere nodes in the larger network of connected contractors (liability resting with the latter). In German law, there are evidently doctrinal resources to aid external claimants who seek to join defendants from within the network but with whom they have no direct contractual connection; but there remains the problem of apportioning responsibility within the network itself. For this latter purpose, the idea of the overarching network purpose again needs to be relied on. Thus, as Teubner summarizes it, questions of external liability should be regulated by reference to a doctrinal constellation involving 'internal network agreement (agreed third party performance impacts), external client contracts (*culpa in contrahendo* criteria) and overarching association (network purpose)' (p. 261).

Before we take Teubner's analysis any further, we should set it alongside the contextualist development of the English commercial law of contract that, having been initiated by Lords Steyn and Hoffmann,[5] has now become a wide-ranging form of commercial realism that is sweeping all before it in cases such as *Rainy Sky v Kookmin Bank* [2011] UKSC 50[6] and *RTS Flexible Systems Ltd v Molkerei Alois Müller Gmbh and Co (UK Production)* [2010] UKSC 14.[7] I suggest that this development is significant in four ways. First, it makes explicit the idea that the fundamental purpose of the commercial law of contract is to protect the reasonable transactional expectations of business parties (or, stated more pointedly, to resolve disputes in a way that accords with commercial common sense). Secondly, in determining whether a commercial contractor's expectation is reasonable, there

---

5 Seminally, see, *Mannai Investments Co Ltd v Eagle Star Life Assurance Co Ltd* [1997] 3 All ER 352 and *Investors Compensation Scheme Ltd v West Bromwich Building Society* [1998] 1 All ER 98. See, too, *Attorney General of Belize v Belize Telecom Ltd* [2009] UKPC 11, where Lord Hoffmann indicated that contextualism applies not only to questions of interpretation but also to implied terms (that is, to questions of implication).

6 According to Lord Clarke (giving the judgment of the court at [21]): '[C]onstruction is essentially one unitary exercise in which the court must consider the language used and ascertain what a reasonable person, that is a person who has all the background knowledge which would reasonably have been available to the parties in the situation in which they were at the time of the contract, would have understood the parties to have meant. In doing so, the court must have regard to all the relevant surrounding circumstances. If there are two possible constructions, the court is entitled to prefer the construction which is consistent with business common sense and to reject the other.'

7 Where (at [58], [62] and [86]–[87]) Lord Clarke rejects the Court of Appeal's view that there was 'no contract' between the parties as making no commercial sense.

are four recognized reference points: (i) the formal rules of contract law; (ii) the express terms of the agreement (provided that they are compatible with the formal law); (iii) the signals given by a co-contractor (such as the signals of encouragement or acquiescence that base the fair-dealing ideas at the root of equitable estoppel or common law waiver); and (iv) the implicit understanding of contractors who deal in a particular business sector (Brownsword, 2003; Mitchell, 2009). Thirdly, although the distinctively 'contextual' reference points (points (iii) and (iv) above) emerge in disputes involving the interpretation of commercial contracts, it is clear that context is relevant across the whole range of transactional disputes between commercial contractors. Fourthly, following Lord Hoffmann's seminal speech in *Transfield Shipping Inc v Mercator Shipping Inc* [2008] UKHL 48, unless there are clear policy reasons for pitching the formal rules in a particular way (e.g. the rules against penalty clauses or exclusions of liability for negligently caused death or personal injury), the formal rules should be treated as defaults liable to be displaced by the parties (whether by express terms, by conduct, or by implicit understanding as in *Transfield Shipping* itself). We can debate just how radical a departure this is from the classical mode and from orthodox English contract law thinking – but not here. For present purposes, the only question is how this bears on any proposal for the adoption of networks and connected contracts.

Consider, first, how the new contextualism might bear on internal network disputes. On the face of it, a contextual approach applied to the interpretation of standard form terms in just-in-time supply contracts or to a case such as *Apollo (Optik)* would lead quickly to the network setting; and, in many cases, it would probably generate similar outcomes (reflecting heightened expectations of co-operation and proportionate risk allocation). However, the approaches are not identical; they do not have quite the same emphasis and certainly not the same priorities. Whereas, in Teubner's account, networks have a distinctively contradictory nature that should always be reflected in the regulatory response, contextualism sees the network as a self-governing business community. Whereas, for Teubner, the legal challenge is to keep faith with the paradoxical logic of networks, for contextualists, the legal challenge is to keep faith with the parties' understanding of their rights and responsibilities as members of their network. Whereas, for Teubner, it is the logic of the network that grounds stable expectations, for contextualists, expectations are stabilized by a mix of norms, normality and agent interactions. What seems to matter for Teubner is that the law should respect the dynamism and potential benefits of network forms of business organization; what matters for contextualists is that the law should respect functional zones of self-governance. This contrast, notwithstanding, it does not follow that it would be counter-productive or entirely unhelpful for English contract law to specify a set of conditions (as Teubner does)[8] for the realization of a network with its own special rules. However, unless this version of a network and its effects was underwritten by a particular public policy imperative, it would operate merely as a default, as a background reference point for the parties' reasonable expectations. In this background capacity, it would be brought into play only where the parties' foreground expectations lacked the clarity needed to settle the particular dispute.

While contextualists might wish to champion self-governing business communities (for reasons of both agent-autonomy and flexibility in the face of rapidly changing global economic conditions), they need to set limits to self-regulation; business networks cannot be permitted to rule the world. In particular, when networks interface with their clients (whether commercial or consumer contractors), there needs to be a regulatory environment that is sensitive to the larger public interest. As Teubner's discussion of the external liability of networks highlights, there are questions about both the protection of claimants and the internal apportionment of liability. For contextualists, the latter question can be left to the network's own self-governing order; but, once we address the former question, even though we are thinking about contracts we are moving into the realm of public order and the public interest. At this point, each legal system will have its own regulatory purposes and priorities which it will seek to advance in its own way (Brownsword, 2011a; 2013).

To return to Technical Man and Post-Technique, it is in the nature of many business networks that they embed modern technologies (information and communication technologies, radio-frequency identification (RFID) tracking and locating devices, and so on) in their day-to-day operations. With the development of modern technologies, it becomes possible for networks to operate in ever smarter and more efficient ways; and, to a considerable extent, we can see networks being shaped by the technologies that underpin their operations (think, for example, about the contractual networks that will develop around cloud-computing services). It also becomes possible for businesses to exploit their technological advantages in their dealings with customers, leading to calls for regulatory interventions to control overreaching by copyright-holders, infringements of privacy and

---

8 According to Teubner (2011, p. 158), connected contracts will be recognized where, in addition to the standard requirements for a bilateral contract, the following three features are present: (1) mutual references within the bilateral contracts to one another, either within the explicit promises or within implicit contractual practice ('multi-dimensionality'); (2) a substantive relationship with the connected contracts' common project ('network purpose'); and (3) a legally effective and close co-operative relationship between associated members ('economic unity').

so on (Lessig, 2001). If, like the contextualists, we value self-governance but we also value technological improvement, there is a double warning here: both within and without networks, we need to monitor asymmetries of power (particularly when enhanced by technological capability); and, everywhere, we need to keep an eye on the incremental and insidious adoption of technological instruments of governance. In Post-Technique, we should appreciate the technological facilitation of business but we should be wary of technological instruments that empower Technical Man operating as either a private or a public regulator.

5. The threat of La Technique today

New technologies have the capacity to enable self-governance; but they also represent a major challenge, indeed a classical Technical Man threat, to spontaneity, to humanity and to self-governance. In this part of the chapter, in order to understand how the development of new technologies can present such a threat, first, we need to expand on the nature of the regulatory environment and then we can begin to see how technological management impacts on and undermines both prudential and moral humanity (as valued in Post-Technique).

a. Regulation and the regulatory environment

As is well-known, the working idea of regulation is as a sustained, focused and organized attempt to steer conduct (Black, 2005, p. 11). Regulation, so conceived, is operationalized through a cycle of direction, detection and correction. It follows that, in a regulatory environment, there will be various signals that are intended to direct the conduct of regulatees; there will be various means of monitoring conduct to see whether the directions are being followed; and, where deviation is detected, there will be measures for correction. In such environments, regulators signal whether particular acts are permitted (even required) or prohibited, whether they will be viewed positively, negatively, or neutrally, whether they are incentivized or disincentivized, whether they are likely to be praised or criticized, even whether they are possible or impossible and so on (Brownsword and Somsen, 2009; Brownsword and Goodwin, 2012). Whilst some environments are regulated in a top-down law-like fashion (with regulators clearly distinguishable from regulatees), others are more bottom-up, more self-regulatory and more reliant on 'governance' than hard law. Moreover, while some regulatory environments are reasonably stable and well-formed, others are unstable, overlapping, conflictual and so on. So far, so extremely familiar. However, as lawyers, we need to be careful to avoid two framing mistakes.

First, there is *the mistake of legal exclusivity* – which makes the assumption that the only signals in the regulatory environment are formal legal signals. One of the key points about the regulatory environment is that we may find regulators employing a range of mechanisms or modalities that are designed to channel the conduct of their regulatees. Some of these modalities may well be legal. It is not that regulatory environments never feature legal signals; and, in many instances, it will be the legal signals that have the highest profile. Nevertheless, the regulatory repertoire goes well beyond legal signals – including, for example, social norms, the market and architecture (or code) (Lessig, 1999a; 1999b).

This takes us to the second framing mistake, *the mistake of normative exclusivity* – which makes the assumption that the only signals in the regulatory environment are normative (that is, signals that prescribe what ought, or ought not, to be done). Again, laws are normative, as of course are social norms. Market signals might also speak to what ought (or ought not) to be done, not so much as a matter of respect for others but simply what ought (or ought not) to be done relative to one's own interest. For example, where a 'green' tax is added to the price of larger cars or to fuel, we might reason that we ought to drive a smaller car because larger cars are expensive and put a strain on our personal finances. However, if the price of larger cars is increased beyond our means, our reasoning shifts from the normative mode to the non-normative mode of practicability – it is not so much that, as a matter of self-interest, we ought not to buy a large car but that we simply cannot (afford to) do so. When the regulatory modality is that of architecture or code, or the like, we might well find that the signal is one of (non-normative) practicability or possibility. However, as with market signals, there might be elements of both normativity and non-normativity – witness, for example, Mireille Hildebrandt's important distinction between 'regulative' (normative) and 'constitutive' (non-normative) technological features (Hildebrandt, 2008). So, for example, if a car is equipped with sensors that can detect alcohol in the driver, it might be designed to respond normatively (by advising that it is not safe for the driver to proceed – this being an example of 'level 1' technological management) or non-normatively (by immobilizing the car – this being an example of 'level 2' technological management).

With today's Technical Men eager to grasp the new technological opportunities, Post-Techniquans need to be alert to any changes in the registers that regulators employ to engage the practical reason of regulatees. There are three such registers as follows:

1   the moral register: here regulators signal that some act, x, categorically ought or ought not to be done relative to standards of right action (as

in retributive articulations of the criminal law where the emphasis is on the moral nature of the offence); or

2 the prudential register: here regulators signal that some act, x, ought or ought not to be done relative to the prudential interests of regulatees (as in deterrence-driven articulations of the criminal law where the emphasis is on the sanction that will be visited on offenders); or

3 the register of practicability or possibility: here regulators signal that it is not reasonably practicable to do some act, x, or even that x simply cannot be done – in which case, regulatees reason, not that x ought not to be done, but that x cannot be done (either realistically or literally).

Where there is an increasing reliance on regulatory technologies (for example, CCTV, DNA profiling, RFID tracking and monitoring devices, and so on) (Rothstein and Talbott, 2006), there is a real likelihood that the strength and significance of the moral signal will fade.[9] At first, while these technologies operate only in support of (rather than in place of) the criminal law, the dominant signal to regulatees tends to be a prudential one, accentuating that the doing of a particular act is contrary to the interests of regulatees (because, in the event of non-compliance, they will be detected and punished). Similarly, in the context of transactions, the introduction of technologies such as eBay's reputational system tend to accentuate the prudential rather than the moral signals that exhort agents to deal fairly with one another. However, over time, as novel technologies are employed to limit the options that are realistically available to regulatees, the signal becomes that an act is either not practicable (such as trying to board an aircraft for an international flight without going through the security scans) or simply not possible (Koops, 2009). Where the signal is that a particular act is no longer a possible option, regulatee compliance is, so to speak, fully determined. With each step towards such determination of conduct, the grip of Technical Man tightens; with each step the perfection of regulatory control moves closer (Brownsword 2004; 2005; 2008; 2011b; and 2012b).

b. Moral interests and moral community

If the amplification of prudential signals can weaken the basis for moral community, then we might expect the problems to be accentuated where

---

9 For a perceptive analysis, see Larsen (2011, pp. 153–4). Larsen says (emphasis added): 'Another reason speaks against pervasive recording in public space as a strategy for crime prevention. Increasing the threat of punishment does not deprive punishment of its moral message, and highlighting the detection risk of offending does not have to dilute the deontological condemnation expressed in punishment. *Nevertheless, one should not rule out the possibility that an over-reliance on CCTV, with its emphasis on the instrumental appeal to desist from crime in order to avoid paying the cost, might entail a dilution of the moral reasons for desistence.*

the change in the regulatory environment is from normative to non-normative signals. In such strongly managed environments, it is not only the opportunities for employing moral reason that are restricted, there is also a reduction in the space for self-interested (prudential) reason to operate. To draw out some of the implications of this change in the complexion of the regulatory environment, we can start with *self-regulatory* choices and then turn to the *imposition* of technological management.

i) Self-regulation

Let us suppose that we are dealing with an aspirant moral agent. When this person is offered a choice of product design, such as a car, he or she will be thinking about how the technological management secures his or her own safety; but, as an aspirant moral agent, he or she will also be thinking about how the technological features safeguard the legitimate interests of others. So, for example, whilst a purely prudential agent might elect level 1 technology that goes no further than reminding the driver about his or her own safety, a moral agent might elect similar technology that expresses the caution in moral rather than prudential terms, reminding the driver about the safety of other road-users. However, our hypothetical agent, being aware of his or her own shortcomings, might choose level 2 technological management where safe transport is more strongly designed-in (the technology not now being limited to giving an advisory message).

A similar analysis might be applied to contracts. For example, when contractors use electronic agents to negotiate and conclude their deals, a purely prudential agent might elect level 1 technology that simply advises the user about his or her own economic interests. By contrast, moral agents will elect advisory technologies that caution their users against bad faith negotiation; and, for those users who recognize their own weakness of will, level 2 technologies will be adopted (Brownsword, 2011c).

Where level 2 technology is chosen for moral reasons, it is in consideration of the legitimate interests of other road-users (or, in the case of transactions, fellow contractors). Would such self-imposed technological management be problematic?

When moral reason so guides the decision, the agent elects technological non-normative management because this reduces the risk that the legitimate interests of others will be harmed. Although this seems to be in line with the aspirations of moral community, there are three questions that we might raise about the agent's choice. These concern, respectively, the authenticity of the agent's moral performance, the possibility of expressing human dignity and the constraints on dealing with moral emergencies.

First, as the motorist (or contractor) proceeds in a way that the level 2 technological management ensures causes no harm to other road-users (or fellow contractors), one might say that this is not an authentic moral performance; for it is the technology, not the agent, that does all the work. Of course, the concept of 'authenticity' is deeply contested (Levy, 2007, chs 2 and 3). However, even if we concede that the pattern of seemingly 'respectful' driving (or contracting) is no longer an authentic moral performance, we might still argue that moral reason lies at the root of the agent's actions. At the material time, the agent selected level 2 technology and did so for moral reasons. Arguably, this is good enough.

Secondly, when the car is in motion, observing the interests of other road-users, the driver cannot proceed otherwise (assuming no facility for overriding the technological controls). There is no possibility of the driver expressing his or her human dignity by turning away from doing the wrong thing. An agent travelling in a car with level 2 technological management never confronts the choice between doing the right thing and doing wrong – safe driving is the only option. All of this applies *mutatis mutandis* to contractors who employ level 2 technologies. Again, though, the driver (or contractor) is where he or she is only because the earlier design choice was made. If that choice was made freely, then that seems to be the moment at which human dignity is expressed.

Thirdly, en route from east to west, the smart car might encounter an emergency in which, without the technological controls, the driver would have deviated to assist another (as in the stock example of a motorist who exceeds the speed limit in order to get a pregnant woman to hospital) (Yeung, 2011). Similarly, a contractor might be precluded by the technology from adjusting performance in order to respond to an emergency. No doubt, the really smart car (like the really smart electronic agent) will have an override that allows the moral agent to do the right thing in such an emergency. Failing this, when the moral agent elects level 2 technological management, he or she must calculate the potential moral cost of subjecting their conduct to the governance of the technology. Still, from the fact that there is a moral downside to technological management, it does not follow that, all things considered, this is a poor moral choice, let alone signify a loss of moral community.

ii) Imposed regulation

Let us suppose that, after a full and inclusive public debate, the regulatory environment takes on non-normative features; and let us suppose that the rationale for adopting such features is that they are judged to be more effective in protecting relevant moral interests. Let us suppose, moreover, that there is general agreement that the interests to be protected are important and that a technologically managed environment is the right regulatory strategy. Once this non-normative regulatory environment is in place, regulatees lose the opportunity to do wrong by violating the protected interests of others – which, of course, is precisely the point of making this particular regulatory move. However, it also means that regulatees cannot demonstrate in such an environment that they do the right thing for the right reason. How serious a price is this to pay? How serious is it for moral community that agents, in such managed environments, think only about what is practicable or possible rather than what morally is required? Is this a Faustian bargain with proponents of La Technique? Or, is it irrational to insist not only that the right thing be done but that it be done for the right reason?

For present purposes, it is not necessary to do much more than note these philosophically puzzling questions. The answers are not self-evident. However, one of the fundamental points is that there is much more to moral community than the responses of its individual members. In such a community, while it might be fine for an individual to choose to be a passive techno-managed regulatee in some respect, active moral citizenship is also required. If technological management leads to such 'demoralizing' effects, they would need to be carefully monitored; for, they are clearly corrosive of moral community.

iii) In-person moral coding

It is one thing to adopt technological management in consumer products (such as cars or DVDs) or even in places (as we see in the architecture of buildings and roads). Imagine, though, that Technical Man proposes the coding of persons for moral action – for example, that all contractors should be coded to respect the principles of good faith and fair-dealing. In an aspirant moral community, this gives rise to a clutch of questions and concerns, three of which we can highlight.

First, there is the question of whether the coding results from an act of self-regulation. If it is, then what is the difference between this and taking a daily dose of soma, or whatever, that keeps the agent on the moral tracks? Provided that the coding is reversible, then the cases might be comparable and, arguably, it is for each agent to make a choice about whether, all things considered, this kind of fix is the best way to lead a moral life. If, however, the coding is imposed, we might want to distinguish between coding before or at birth (which might be seen in a negative or a positive light) and the enforced coding of mature agents who have perhaps shown themselves to be otherwise incapable of respecting the moral interests of others. We might also want to differentiate between coding that amplifies moral signals (or strengthens moral resolve) and that which simply suppresses harmful or dangerous instincts. Whereas, in the former case, we seem to be designing for the moral life, in the latter it seems to be an exercise in risk management. Clearly, there is much devil in the details of such fixes (Yeung, 2008).

Secondly, there is the question of an agent's moral development. A moral community will be greatly concerned that technologies are not employed in ways that interfere with the development of a capacity for moral reason and an agent's appreciation of morality as a normative code. Here, we need only recall the concerns famously expressed by the President's Council on Bioethics (2003, pp. 105–6) with regard to the administration of methylphenidate (Ritalin) and amphetamine (Adderall) to children whose conduct is outside the range of acceptability. If we rely on biotechnological or neurotechnological interventions to respond to (or manage) our social problems, there is a danger that, as the President's Council puts it, 'we may weaken our sense of responsibility and agency' (p. 106).

Thirdly, there is the question of whether, once a coding intervention is made, is it capable of responding to changes in the community's interpretation of their moral commitments and the way in which fundamental principles should be applied. If the coding simply represses anti-social instincts, or if it strengthens the signal to do the right thing, it might continue to be functional even as the substance of morality changes. However, so long as the moral project is understood as an ongoing one, there will need to be a hard look at in-person measures lest they should inappropriately freeze the substance of the community's moral commitments.

iv) Regulatory guidelines for Post-Technique

What do these sketchy remarks signify for regulators in Post-Technique? The overriding consideration in Post-Technique is that technological management does not interfere with the development of moral reason and the capacity to participate in the life of the community as a moral agent. No doubt, the foreground regulatory environment for children and young persons is that found in the family, at school and in the neighbourhood – and we should not assume that the larger public regulatory environment aligns with these most proximate environments. Nevertheless, regulators need to be sensitive to the possibility that the use of non-normative signals in the background environment might carry over to the foreground.

That said, as Macneil rightly warns, Post-Technique is unlikely to be the best of all possible worlds; there will be tensions and hard choices. For example, consider the case where a techno-regulatory intervention precludes certain kinds of harmful acts, whether those acts are intentional or unintentional – for example, where products (such as surgical instruments) (Yeung and Dixon-Woods, 2010) or complexes of products (such as transport systems) are designed for safety. Primarily, the purpose of such safety measures will be to safeguard users or passengers – for example, by phasing out trains with slam-door carriages (Wolff, 2010), or by making it impossible for trains to pass through signals on red. Given that such measures are designed to make routine activities (such as the journey to work) less risky, it is reasonable to assume that most interested parties judge them to be in their prudential interests; and, if public engagement has indeed shown this to be the case, then all well and good. However, the effect of these measures is not only to replace prudential norms with non-normative design but also to impact on the opportunity to display a moral performance. For example, commuters opening railway train doors might want to show that they do so with due regard for the safety of fellow passengers and persons standing on station platforms. Likewise, train drivers might want to show that they exercise due care by stopping at red signals. Once the train is designed for safety, these displays of due care and concern for others cannot be made in this way. If such displays of moral virtue are valued by Post-Techniquans, do regulators have a short answer to these 'objections'?

One thought is that regulators might be able to say that, where their primary purpose is the safety of passengers, they do not have to answer for any secondary effects – that they are shielded by a doctrine akin to that of double effect. Surely, though, this will not do. Otherwise, this would involve accepting that, because Robert Moses' bridges were built with safety in mind, there is no need for regulators to answer for their secondary (and racially discriminatory) effects (Manders-Huits and van den Hoven, 2009). However, this is contrary to the Post-Techniquan premise that regulators need to be much more sensitive to the impact of relying on architecture, product design and the like as features of the regulatory repertoire.

The other thought is that there is no real loss of moral community when such safety features are introduced because, insofar as the intervention targets acts that are harmful to others, its focus is on unintentional rather than intentionally harmful acts (Rich, 2012). If the technology only prevented non-negligent unintentionally harmful acts, there might be something in this thought. However, technological management also blocks negligent acts as well as intentionally harmful acts. For the sake of argument, let us suppose that it is conceded that regulators do not have to answer for any impingement on unintentional acts (even negligent acts); but the crucial point is that regulators must not interfere with opportunities for intentional wrongdoing. On the face of it, this is a very strange view: what it amounts to is that regulators, whatever other good they may do by using non-normative controls, must not deprive those agents who might intentionally harm others (including, in transactional settings, intentionally harming others by fraud or by breach of contract) of the opportunity to do so if this means that, when such agents do not harm others, they cannot then demonstrate that they are freely doing the right thing. Hence, train drivers must not be prevented from passing through signals when they are on red lest this prevents the driver from showing that he or she does the right thing by stopping on red (and, in the same way, in technologically managed transactional environments, contractors must not be denied the option of opportunistic breach lest this precludes showing that one is doing the right thing by performing the contract). This seems such a strange view that one wonders whether any moral community could reasonably attach such importance to preserving the opportunity to do wrong in order to demonstrate that one does right. Having said that, a moral community might perfectly reasonably attach importance to there being some such opportunities and the question then would be whether train drivers or their passengers, or contracting agents, need this particular opportunity more than they need the design-in features – a question for regulatory debate and deliberation in Post-Technique (Brownsword, 2011b; Yeung, 2011).

Conclusion

Ian Macneil could not possibly have anticipated that the world would become networked at so many levels, that information and communication technologies would develop so rapidly, and that code could become such a powerful regulator. Nevertheless, his discussion of Post-Technique (even without full presentation) is remarkably prescient. Given the changes in both technology and contracting practice since 1980, there is good reason to treat Macneil's discussion as an invitation to rethink our Social Contract – or, at any rate, to review the social licence that we grant to new technologies. For the purposes of such a review, I suggest that two aspects of the licence would be critical.

First, in Post-Technique, it is important that regulators act in ways that nurture or, at any rate, do not undermine self-governing communities, including self-governing contracting communities. For this reason, regulators should respect the private ordering of contractual networks and align contract doctrine so that the reasonable expectations of network contractors are protected. I will not use this platform to rehearse again the reasons why we might doubt the wisdom of trying to impose a pan-European code of contract law (Brownsword, 2011a); suffice it to say that Technical Man would be an enthusiastic advocate of such schemes.

Secondly, at all points in Post-Technique, it is important that technologies do not insinuate themselves into the regulatory environment, whether private or public, in ways that lack transparency or that compromise the fundamental public interest in allowing agents to act on their own judgments of self-interest within the bounds of a moral community. Crucially, there needs to be a vigilant approach towards preserving the conditions for moral community in which agents can express their humanity by debating what they think is the right thing and then acting on their moral judgment. The complexion of the regulatory environment might matter more than we realize and, in Post-Technique, it is absolutely right that before new designs are adopted regulators should engage, as Macneil would say, in much soul-searching.

References

Amstutz, Marc and Gunther Teubner (eds) (2009) *Networks: Legal Issues of Multilateral Contracts* (Oxford: Hart Publishing)

Black, Julia (2005) 'What is Regulatory Innovation?' in Julia Black, Martin Lodge and Mark Thatcher (eds), *Regulatory Innovation* (Cheltenham: Edward Elgar), pp. 1–15

Brownsword, Roger (2003) 'After *Investors*: Interpretation, Expectation and the Implicit Dimension of the "New Contextualism"' in David Campbell, Hugh Collins and John Wightman (eds), *The Implicit Dimensions of Contract* (Oxford, Hart Publishing), pp. 103–41

Brownsword, Roger (2004) 'What the World Needs Now: Techno-Regulation, Human Rights and Human Dignity' in Roger Brownsword (ed.) *Human Rights* (Oxford: Hart Publishing) 203–34

Brownsword, Roger (2005) 'Code, Control, and Choice: Why East is East and West is West' 25 *Legal Studies* 1–21

Brownsword, Roger (2008) *Rights, Regulation and the Technological Revolution* (Oxford: Oxford University Press)

Brownsword, Roger (2011a) 'The Theoretical Foundations of European Private Law: A Time to Stand and Stare' in Roger Brownsword, Hans Micklitz, Leone Niglia and Steven Weatherill (eds), *The Foundations of European Private Law* (Oxford: Hart Publishing), pp. 159–74

Brownsword, Roger (2011b) 'Lost in Translation: Legality, Regulatory Margins, and Technological Management' 26 *Berkeley Technology Law Journal* 1321–65

Brownsword, Roger (2011c) 'Autonomy, Delegation, and Responsibility: Agents in Autonomic Computing Environments' in Mireille Hildebrandt and Antoinette Rouvroy (eds), *Autonomic Computing and Transformations of Human Agency* (London: Routledge), pp. 64–84

Brownsword, Roger (2012a) 'The Shaping of Our On-Line Worlds: Getting the Regulatory Environment Right' 20 *International Journal of Law and Information Technology* 249–72

Brownsword, Roger (2012b) 'Whither the Law and the Law Books: From Prescription to Possibility' 39 *Journal of Law and Society* 296–308

Brownsword, Roger (2013) 'Contracts in a Networked World' in Larry di Matteo (ed.), *Commercial Contract Law: A Transatlantic Perspective* (Cambridge: Cambridge University Press), pp. 116–45

Brownsword, Roger and Morag Goodwin (2012) *Law and the Technologies of the Twenty-First Century* (Cambridge: Cambridge University Press)

Brownsword, Roger and Han Somsen (2009) 'Law, Innovation and Technology: Before We Fast Forward – A Forum for Debate' 1 *Law, Innovation and Technology* 1–73

Butler, Samuel (1892) *Erewhon* (London: Penguin Books) (1935 edn)
Edgerton, David (2006) *The Shock of the Old: Technology and Global History Since 1900* (London: Profile Books)
Elkin-Koren, Niva (1997) 'Copyright Policy and the Limit of Freedom of Contract' 12 *Berkeley Technology Law Journal* 93–113
European Group on Ethics in Science and New Technologies (2012) *Ethics of Information and Communication Technologies* (Opinion No 26) (Brussels: EGE)
Favale, Marcella (2008) 'Fine-Tuning European Copyright Law to Strike a Balance between the Rights of Owners and Users' 33 *European Law Review* 687–708
Harkaway, Nick (2012) *The Blind Giant: Being Human in a Digital World* (London: John Murray)
Hildebrandt, Mireille (2008) 'Legal and Technological Normativity: More (and Less) than Twin Sisters' 12(3) *TECHNE* 169–83
Johnson, David R and David Post (1996) 'Law and Borders – The Rise of Law in Cyberspace' 48 *Stanford Law Review* 1367–402
Koops, Bert-Jaap (2009) 'Technology and the Crime Society: Rethinking Legal Protection' 1 *Law, Innovation and Technology* 93–124
Larsen, Beatrice von Silva-Tarouca (2011) *Setting the Watch: Privacy and the Ethics of CCTV Surveillance* (Oxford: Hart Publishing)
Lessig, Lawrence (1999a) *Code and Other Laws of Cyberspace* (New York: Basic Books)
Lessig, Lawrence (1999b) 'The Law of the Horse: What Cyberlaw Might Teach' 113 *Harvard Law Review* 501–46
Lessig, Lawrence (2001) *The Future of Ideas* (New York: Vintage Books)
Levy, Neil (2007) *Neuroethics* (Cambridge: Cambridge University Press)
Macneil, Ian R (1980) *The New Social Contract* (New Haven CT: Yale University Press)
Manders-Huits, Noëmi and Jeroen van den Hoven (2009) 'The Need for Value-Sensitive Design of Communication Infrastructures' in Paul Sollie and Marcus Düwell (eds), *Evaluating New Technologies* (Heidelberg: Springer Science), pp. 51–60
Mik, Eliza (2011) 'The *Un*importance of being "electronic" or – popular misconceptions about "Internet contracting"' 19 *International Journal of Law and Information Technology* 324–47
Mitchell, Catherine (2009) 'Contracts and Contract Law: Challenging the Distinction Between the "Real" and the "Paper" Deal' 29 *OJLS* 675–704
Post, David G (2009) *In Search of Jefferson's Moose* (Oxford: Oxford University Press)
President's Council on Bioethics (2003) *Beyond Therapy* (Washington DC: Dana Press)
Rich, Michael L (2012): 'The Perfect Non-Crime', *New York Times*, 7 August, A23
Rothstein, Mark A and Meghan K Talbott (2006) 'The Expanding Use of DNA in Law Enforcement: What Role for Privacy?' 34 *Journal of Law, Medicine and Ethics* 153–64
Schammo, Pierre (2008) 'Regulating Transatlantic Stock Exchanges' 57 *ICLQ* 827–62
Teubner, Gunther (2011) *Networks as Connected Contracts*, Hugh Collins (ed. and 'Introduction'), Michelle Everson (trans.) (Oxford: Hart Publishing)
Wolff, Jonathan (2010) 'Five Types of Risky Situation' 2 *Law, Innovation and Technology* 151–63

Yeung, Karen (2008) 'Towards an Understanding of Regulation by Design' in Roger Brownsword and Karen Yeung (eds), *Regulating Technologies* (Oxford: Hart Publishing), pp. 79–108

Yeung, Karen (2011) 'Can We Employ Design-Based Regulation While Avoiding *Brave New World*' 3 *Law, Innovation and Technology* 1–29

Yeung, Karen and Mary Dixon-Woods (2010): 'Design-Based Regulation and Patient Safety: A Regulatory Studies Perspective' 71 *Social Science and Medicine* 540–55

3
What Might Macneil Have Said about Using eBay?
Sally Wheeler

In this chapter I want to look at computer-mediated consumer purchase contracts. These are contracts made in the world of e-commerce using the websites of companies such as Amazon which, so far as consumers are concerned, exist only as electronic presences, and the online presences of conventional 'bricks and mortar' retail establishments. In 2011, the value of retail online sales in the UK was £50.34 billion, representing 12.0 per cent of UK retail trade. In 2008, the equivalent figure was 8.6 per cent of retail sales. In the US, the market share of online sales is 9.0 per cent (Centre for Retail Research, 2011). In Australia and New Zealand, the figure is rather lower at just under 7 per cent, but this is predicted, as in the UK, the US and Europe, to carry on growing (Frost & Sullivan, 2012). The growth of online shopping, previously fuelled by the increase in domestic broadband accessibility, now unsurprisingly mirrors the popularity in ownership of mobile devices that can access the internet; in the UK just over a quarter of adults own a smartphone, and in the US that figure rises to over a third (Ofcom, 2011; Pew Research Centre, 2011).

Continuing online retail sales growth in a period of general contraction for retail sales because of worldwide economic conditions emphasizes the entrenchment of online shopping as a cultural practice. The particular example discussed in this paper comes from a study of contracts made using eBay, which is a marketplace site that acts as an intermediary rather than as a retailer in its own right. As the chapter points out, contracts made using this marketplace differ from contracts made using the online presences of conventional retail establishments or internet sites such as Amazon in that trust has to be established, not in a brand name for goods or in a retail establishment, but in an unknown individual.

Ian Macneil has told us that a discrete contract is a contract made without social relations, but he also suggests that all contracts are relational in that they are embedded in some social relations, however minimal. Even the most discrete contract is, on this latter view, encircled by relations facilitating that exchange (Macneil, 1986, pp. 577; 1987a, p. 32). Those relations are at their most basic formed by four core elements; order, means of enforcement, means of exchange and communication (Macneil, 1999–2000, p. 834). These, Macneil explains, can be evidenced by the simplest of systems; a system which ensures exchange rather than robbery takes place satisfies his conception of social relations even if such a system falls far short of what we might recognize as a legal system or a currency (Macneil, 1974a, p. 724). We might deduce from this that the discrete contract is something that cannot empirically exist and that all contracts are relational, with some just being less relational than others. However, I believe that in much of his work Macneil is using a terminology that does not belong to the language family that is recognized by lawyers, and this results in readings of his position that are not in strict accordance with what he meant. Later in this chapter I try to unpick Macneil's apparently contradictory comments on the relational–discrete distinction. This discussion is important for the accommodation of these computer-mediated contracts within Macneil's framework.

Computer-mediated contracts offer a very different form of social relations from those observed by Macneil, even if all due recognition is given to the appreciation that contract is a field of huge breadth implicit in his observation that the contractual relations of IBM and a McDonald's hamburger franchise are very different (Macneil, 1980, p. 20). In order to place these contracts within a Macneilian framework, it is necessary to see his work, particularly at the micro level of his contract norms, as being rooted in a particular understanding of industrial society and reason forward from that point. Macneil deploys contract, or more broadly exchange, in two ways. At the level of society he uses it to explain the progression from primitive pre-barter economies to advanced monetary-based economies. Within these more advanced societies he ties his conception of the practices involved in individual contract scenarios to a reading of industrial society that is very orientated towards a particular understanding of production and employment relations (Macneil, 1985). The effect of this is that behaviour that Macneil might have characterized as discrete, and as such on the edge of society, now in fact represents behaviour that is much closer to the centre ground of social relations. This chapter builds on Macneil's conceptualization of the discrete norm (Macneil, 1983, pp. 355ff.) in order to contribute to the debate about whether a purely discrete contract is ever possible. My conclusion is that Macneil fails to distinguish between the social processes involved in making a contract and the informational relationships that underpin strategic choices that are made in the contractual interaction. If these two are separated, then a more nuanced and descriptive meaning can be given to the notion of 'discrete' in the world of contract. I explore what this might look like in the third section of the paper.

This analysis sits alongside that of Roger Brownsword in his chapter in that, from a similar starting point, we offer different but complementary ways of thinking about the future of Macneil's model of contract. The abstracting and dehumanizing effect of technology, or the actions of Technical Man that might result from technology, were a concern that Macneil voiced in the closing ten pages of *The New Social Contract* (Macneil, 1980, pp. 108–18). This passage is examined in some detail by Brownsword and I do not intend to go over that ground again. He exposes Macneil's concerns as ones about control and perfection. Technical Man can organize his world so that the 'messy reality' which attends the use of contract (Macaulay et al., 2010, p. 30) need not be part of it. Spontaneity can be designed out of interaction and replaced instead by entirely bureaucratic structures that recognize only demands 'for presentation and discreteness' (Macneil, 1980, p. 110). Macneil's alternative to the world of Technical Man is the life offered in the country he calls Post-Technique. It is to the citizens and legislators of Post-Technique that Brownsword's largely regulatory solution in support of a new Social Contract is addressed. This solution focuses on the control of technology to support self-governance in the pursuit of flexibility and autonomy, but also to regulate it where asymmetries of power emerge. Brownsword's analysis is a sophisticated one that considers prudential, moral and practical regulation.

1. A technological world

Alongside his concerns about the disassociation of Technical Man from social relations we have to set Macneil's observation also from within *The New Social Contract* about the effect of the existence of technology on contract practice. This effect is that contracts require high levels of specification in both service and product production scenarios such that 'even the most specific and measured exchanges [are tied] into on-going relational patterns' (Macneil, 1980, p. 22). The technological world of 2013 is far advanced from anything that Macneil could have thought possible in 1980 but the influence of technology on contracting practice has been that contracts have become less, not more, relational. This is illustrated by the purchase made using eBay; this transaction can result in the most mundane of purchases, but it can also accommodate an impulse buy that stimulates excitement in the least consumption-focused individual. Whatever item I desire to buy – as long as it is not a living animal – the chances are that it will be available through a listing on eBay from a seller somewhere in the world and, if it is not currently listed it, it might be the next time I look or the time after that. In this way eBay becomes a game that can be played every day to quench the desire for consumption activity (Molesworth and Denegri-Knott, 2008). I will not know exactly where in the world my object is located and I will know nothing about the seller other than the other items they are offering for sale. I want to suggest that we see different configurations of power emerging in these transactions compared with conventional consumer shopping scenarios (Rha and Widdows, 2002), and that power is maintained and advanced through artificially constructed devices such as feedback systems, the contents of which are entirely the product of social relations. These are the new communications systems that have replaced any 'dickering over terms' or, perhaps more appropriately to a consumer contract scenario, any face-to-face inquiries about colour choices, delivery times and the possibility of seasonal sale discounts (Licklider and Taylor, 1968).

Advances in technology in general, and in the functionality of the internet in particular after it was opened to commercial applications in the early 1990s (Abbate, 1999; Wu, 2010, pp. 168–75, 262–8), have transformed human life. Broadband technology and telecommunications innovation have resulted in the more precise articulation of what I call vertical relationships between individual *qua* citizen and state and between citizen and corporation. In general terms, we can see that this technology has enhanced the formal and informal democratic process (Coursey and Norris, 2008; Van Laer, 2010) and improved the targeting and delivery of some public services (United Nations, 2008). It is a significant factor in increasing economic development (Czernich et al., 2011), even though we can drill below these generalities into the persistence of the digital divide and the inequalities it creates and exacerbates (Eubanks, 2011, pp. 35–48). It is also the case that the internet has created the opportunity for some relationships which are potentially very unequal, requiring their power imbalances to be addressed by human rights protection and other regulatory controls if these relationships are not to be abusive. Although Brownsword does not give these examples in the course of his account of necessary regulatory structures, he must have in mind the potential for the state to employ surveillance and monitoring technology in relation to an individual's movements, and the acquisition and retention of personal information by corporations through purchase histories and the use of social media utilizing that information to develop the unscrupulous targeting of unsolicited loans often with very high interests rates, age and content inappropriate viewing, gaming possibilities and invasive consumer product marketing. Internet use renders the watching and monitoring of individuals both inevitable and routine (Bennett, 2008).

On a more personal level. the internet has enabled us to live our dreams through using cyber handles and avatars to create literally a Second Life (Denegri-Knott and Molesworth, 2010a), to set up entirely different identities for different purposes, to create communities of interest that are divorced from geographical proximity (Williams, 2006), to construct our own work–life balance through working remotely, and to embrace creativity by moving away from the linearity of thought imposed by traditional structures. However, as with the relationships that I term vertical, the transformative effect of these horizontal developments on the individual is not always positive. The employment opportunities it has created outside of design and invention work are the new satanic mills of call centres and data entry nodes, acknowledged to offer low job satisfaction (Ellis and Taylor, 2006), or the factories located in developing economies that piece together the actual machines that make the use of internet technology possible that have become as notorious as garment sweatshops for their use of child labour and their dangerous working conditions (Bradsher et al., 2012). There is evidence that online communities are created at the expense of maintaining existing relationships that depend on telephone use and direct personal contact (Kraut et al., 1998; Wellman et al., 2002). Unsurprisingly, the literature on technology captures these paradoxes and divides itself between laudation and damnation (Mick and Fournier, 1998).

In horizontal relationships, specifically in the world of contract, technology has rendered the previously reasonably social practice of shopping (Bowlby 1997, pp. 102–4), whether task fulfilment shopping or recreational shopping (Wagner and Rudolf, 2010), a potentially more solitary exercise. Access to credit and an internet connection means one is able to enter into a wide range of transactions without engaging in communication beyond the use of a point, click and buy interface. The sensory stimulation offered by the freedom of the physical space of shopping centres and browsing opportunities is replaced by surfing the virtual world of the web (Cox et al., 2005). The impulse to buy in both cases may come from similar sources, for traditional advertising and window-shopping are represented in the world of the internet by website design and interactive functions (sometimes referred to as the 'stickiness' of a website (Miller, 2000)) and ultimately by the aesthetic power of the screen (Zwick and Dholakia, 2006). The desire to buy, with its concomitant feelings of escape and otherness, may be the same in both contexts, but one involves human contact and the other involves social relations mediated through virtual space (Belk et al., 2003). The purchase made across virtual space is not necessarily more rational, reasoned or needs-orientated than a purchase made in a conventional retail store simply because it can be concluded more quickly. However, the internet does offer the opportunity for the purchase to be more informed and selected from a wider range of possible purchases. Consumers can access a global market, gather information on price and quality variance and potentially connect with other consumers who have made or are considering a similar purchase from the same range of potential sellers. This reverses the informational imbalance that conventionally is said to exist between buyer and seller in favour of the buyer (Pires et al., 2006). Buyers using the eBay platform may draw on this power imbalance when making their purchases, and enhance it through participating in the eBay feedback system.

What binds applications of technology together at the level of the individual is the idea of interactivity – filling in a self-assessment tax return and applying for a loan from a bank are interactive processes. They are about functionality, speed of communication and the relatedness of sequential messages (Rafaeli and Ariel, 2007). These horizontal interactive processes look like relatively discrete social relations in Macneil's terms and involve complex social relations (cf. Walther, 1992) as little as potentially coercive vertical relationships. To discover social relations in internet transactions we have to dig beyond the level of mere interactivity (Downes and McMillan, 2000) limited to a clicked decline or accept to discover a deeper information flow (Rezabakhsh et al., 2006).

Most days when I return from work and certainly at the weekends I peruse eBay, in the compulsive fashion described by fiction writer and icon William Gibson (1999), for any new listings and price changes in the form of bids in the categories that I follow. I am an addicted collector, in a taxonomic sense as opposed to an aesthetic sense (Belk, 1991), of diverse and obscure things that include, as I confess below, Beswick china Beatrix Potter character figures. I use eBay for purchasing everyday household items. But the account of eBay trading in this paper is all about sourcing the 'special' item; hoping intently that the missing piece is there at a price I can afford, choosing the seller, bidding for rather than simply buying the item, and then securing the item through submitting the bid that beats all competitors in the time period the proxy auction allows, all the while hoping that I do not then see a better example of the piece in question on another day. In this way, eBay becomes something of an emotional drama which I play through nearly every day (Denegri-Knott and Molesworth, 2010b). I am not alone in my daily visits to eBay; the calendar year to September 2012 saw 108.3 million active users bid for, list, buy or sell on eBay.

The internet, and eBay in particular, has empowered me and thousands of taxonomic collectors like me to scour the world in pursuit of the objects that I desire. The fastest growing categories of items for sale on eBay have been listings for collectibles such as stamps and medals (Bradley and Porter, 2000). The steps necessary to become a successful collector are truncated and rendered simpler by the internet auction sites like eBay. Planning what to collect (goal formation), hunting for the objects to collect and garnering knowledge of the objects themselves in terms of their scarcity and distinguishing marks is made much easier by the image-rich internet (Ellis and Haywood, 2006). EBay listings contain descriptions and photographs of items. Old auction catalogues, magazines and collectors' guides are available in different eBay listings or from sites such as Amazon. EBay hosts collection pages for those who want a quick overview of particular items. However, all the exhilaration and excitement of the planning phase (Formanek, 1991) is still there as the object to be pursued is decided upon and then courted through bidding. Actual ownership in the form of handling the object and placing it on the shelf-space allotted to it within the collection can be imagined as the clock ticks down to zero on the listing (McCracken, 1988, pp. 110ff.; Olmsted, 1991).

It is possible to become a connoisseur of a particular field, an expert in identifying the item that enhances a collection, much more quickly and with less effort than would have been the case previously (McIntosh and Schmeichel, 2004). The internet accommodates Belk's four types of collector; the passionate collector who collects obsessively as a matter of desire; the hobby collector; the investor collector; and the 'wannabe' collector who collects as a statement of status (Belk, 1998). These types are located within Belk's broader definition of a collector as someone who engages in the 'the process of actively, selectively, and passionately acquiring and possessing things removed from ordinary use and perceived as part of a set of non-identical objects or experiences' (Belk, 1995, p. 479). All of these types share certain self-fulfilling or self-enhancing motivations, even if there is no overarching psychological explanation for what makes people pursue collecting (Pearce, 1992), and these can be accommodated in more general paradigms of behaviour around escape, entertainment and control (Case, 2009).

The significance of eBay in relation to collecting is that collecting behaviour becomes about individuals and their introspection. Despite eBay's hosting of collectors clubs, most of which have very small memberships in comparison with the listings for the items they map onto, the process of internet collecting is a solitary activity. Buyers and sellers can find each other in a virtual market place without needing to meet in a physical space. There is no need to set up organizations to host collectors' fairs or swap sessions. The ICDA (interactive consumer decision aids) technology that eBay uses means that buyer and seller are separated in virtual space. The buyer can make bids and, having set their highest price (not known to the seller or other potential buyers in the same virtual space), eBay will act through a proxy bidding system to place bids on their behalf up to that limit against bids entered by other buyers. There is no face-to-face interaction involved in the way that there is at car boot sales, auction houses or in the traditional shopping scenario, and in the overwhelming majority of sales there is no email contact between buyer and seller until after the sale is concluded, if at all (Resnick and Zeckhauser, 2002). Even then, contact is via an eBay user name and the parties do not know each other's legal identities. There is no role for pre-sale contact because eBay allows only very few variances in contract terms and buyer and seller reputation is created by the parties to previous contracts. Haggling behaviour is not part of the process and the intensity of the purchase experience comes from acquisition not from 'getting a bargain' or negotiating a deal. There is no communication between the actual parties over and above that mediated through the eBay software which also offers access to a similarly mediated payment system operated by its wholly owned company, PayPal, and dispute resolution system if required.

2. Discrete and relational contracts

The eBay transaction described above seems to be concluded with the very minimum of social relations. We might say that it resembles the discrete transaction that Macneil describes thus:

> Discrete contracts are characterized by short duration, limited personal interactions, and precise party measurements of easily measured objects of exchange. They require a minimum of future cooperation between the parties. No sharing of benefits or burdens occurs, nor is altruism expected. The parties are bound precisely and tightly. The parties view themselves as free of entangling strings. (Macneil, 1978, p. 275)

He adds to this description in *The New Social Contract*:

> Everything about the discrete transaction is short – the agreement process, the time between agreement and performance, and the time of the performance itself. The discrete transaction commences sharply by clear, instantaneous agreement and terminates sharply by clear and instantaneous performance; sharp in, sharp out. (1980, p. 11)

And later in the same text he says,

> Discreteness is the separating of a transaction from all else between the participants at the same time and before and after. Its ideal, never achieved in real life, occurs when there is nothing else between the parties, never has been, and never will be. (1980, p. 60)

It is the possibility of isolating this type of contract scenario from its more sophisticated counterpart – the relational contract – that is taken to be the general proposition that can be derived from Macneil's work (Feinman, 2001, pp. 59ff.). The 'gas station on the Jersey turnpike' that is visited by someone who rarely travels the road has become a well-known example of the discrete scenario (Macneil, 1978, p. 857), as has the horse purchase between two strangers (Macneil, 1974b, p. 594). What is less well documented is the career-long struggle that Macneil had to explain that being distinct from the relational contract was by no means all that he meant by the discrete contract. In the footnotes to the gas station example he placed the purchase in a web of social relations based on brand and advertising and in a network of other contracts concerning the provision of credit (1974a, pp. 720–1). He does a similar thing in relation to supermarket purchases; the 'this for that' so characteristic of depersonalized self-service shopping is not a discrete contract but instead one that is embedded in social relationships and a network of other contract transactions: shopper and brand loyalty to product or retailer, credit transactions between shopper and bank, and the customary practices of different supermarket retailers such as 'Taste the Difference' and 'Tesco's Finest' (1987a). There is a distinction between the original examples and the reworked examples that Macneil does not draw in discrete and relational terms and that is the distinction between the atomized process of making the contract itself and the informational and network structure that surrounds it.

As Feinman explains (Feinman, 2001, p. 63), much of Macneil's descriptive vocabulary is confusing and alien to the world in which one might expect it to have the most traction: that of contract lawyers. Terms such as 'presentiation', 'social matrix' and 'solidarity' are not part of the normal terminology of the contract lawyer. This lexicon may perhaps sound more familiar to a scholar rooted in the disciplines of sociology or management. As a taxonomic collector of various objects I share Macneil's admiration for classificatory structures, but the presence of so many schemes and lists do nothing to elucidate his work. This perhaps explains the focus of his work on the social process of contracting to the exclusion of considering the relationships involved in social relations, the former being more susceptible to taxonomic structuring than the latter. To these problems we can add the reworking and refinements of terms that Macneil brought to his model, all of which increase the opaqueness of his work. For example 'relational' is used interchangeably to contrast with 'discrete', but also to refer more generally to contracts embedded in social relations. At one point (Macneil, 1987a; cf. Feinman, 1990) he declared that exchange relations that were the opposite of discrete would be known as 'intertwined'. However, he later lost faith in this proposition (Macneil, 1999–2000). These examples of the way in which Macneil constructed his edifice of contract behaviour go to the heart of the confusion that surrounds Macneil's message about the role he ascribes to discrete contracts in his worldview of contract.

The most common approach to the question of the discrete contract is to situate it at the opposite end of a spectrum to relational contract. Macneil hints at the existence of such a spectrum (Macneil, 1974a, p. 737) and, while it is not something that he develops (1987b, pp. 277ff.), it remains part of his thinking if only as something which has purely mythical force (1999–2000, pp. 894ff.). The most comprehensive and sophisticated discussion of this spectrum occurs in David Campbell's work (Campbell 1996, pp. 41–3; 2001, pp. 28–31; 2013, pp. 178–82) and, as his analysis makes clear, what Macneil means by this idea of a discrete to relational spectrum is not a device for plotting contracts by type from spot to supply chain, or for mapping individual contract scenarios, but a mechanism by which we can examine contract at a macro level.

This is the only way that statements such as:

> Every contract ... involves relations apart from the exchange of goods itself. Thus every contract is necessarily partially a relational contract, that is, one involving relations other than a discrete exchange. (Macneil, 1980, p. 10)

can stand alongside the following:

> Discrete exchange will always be a comparatively rare phenomenon because it performs only the transfer of control function and is only minimally related to physical production of goods and services. (Macneil 1985, p. 488)

and not be seen as contradictions. In the first statement, Macneil is talking about individual contracts and contract scenarios. In the second, his focus is on economic ordering within society at a macro level. He is using the journey from discrete to relational to give a sociological account of how society evolves and then works (Scott, 2013, pp.114–15). His point is that both neoclassical economics and most expositions of contract doctrine that have the 'will' theory as their underlying rationale are incorrectly anchored at the discrete end of the spectrum. They are represented by, or mirrored in, the discrete norm (Macneil, 1983). If an economy was dependent on discrete contracts (a discrete economy, as Macneil describes it (1985, p. 490)) as its primary method of facilitating exchange, productivity would be very low and transaction costs would be very high. Contracts made via the internet using a site such as eBay have very low transaction costs (that is a significant part of their attraction) and so play back into the question of the descriptive force of the term 'discrete'.

Macneil never intended that the label 'discrete' should be appended to particular contract scenarios but rather that these interactions should be seen as more or less relational. This is clear from his use of marriage as an example of a relationship that can be more or less transactional depending presumably on the wishes of the parties involved and the nature of their relationship (Macneil, 1987b). At the level of individual contract scenarios, Macneil's concern is with moving the legal analysis of exchange-based relationships beyond the idea of the simple regulated transaction towards identifying the norms that govern such transactions when they are viewed as continuing relationships between the parties. Macneil's internal contract norms will determine how an exchange works in practice. The suggestion is that some norms will come to the fore when exchanges are more discrete – namely 'implementation of planning' and 'effectuation of consent' – while others, such as role integrity and solidarity, will be more evident in exchanges that are more relational. Factors that are present in the parties' relationship with each other but not included in the contract between them will become part of their obligation to each other. All ten of the norms that Macneil identifies will be present to some degree or another in each exchange. Of these ten norms, five hold special significance for Macneil's scheme. These are *role integrity* and *propriety of means*, which come straight from the list of ten, and three others, which are a combination of the remaining eight. These three are *preservation of the relation* (an expansion of *contractual solidarity* and *flexibility*), *harmonization of relational conflict* (derived from *flexibility* and *harmonization of the social matrix*) and the *supra-contractual norm* (produced from the *harmonization of the social matrix*) (Macneil, 1983; Spediel, 1999–2000). These will be generated in the relationship over time.

Moving on

The difficulty with these as indicators of 'relationality' is that they do not map onto what has become simultaneously both a more atomized, individualized society and a more technologically networked society than the one Macneil described. Macneil's view of contract practice was that it was nestled in a society that was 'Macaulay-esque' in structure. My reference here is to Stewart Macaulay's classic article (Macaulay, 1963) which described contractual practice in machinery-manufacturing plants in Wisconsin in 1962. Macneil's attachment to this world is not surprising. It was the context that first confronted him when he began to set out his contract philosophy. Indeed, one of the first articulations of his support for reliance-based norms reflecting the importance of conduct, trust and reliance between the parties, as opposed to the expectation loss preference of formalist contract law, occurs in the examination of a case concerning car manufacture in Memphis (Macneil, 1962–1963). The empirical work of others that he relied on when developing his normative schema obviously reflected the institutional framework of business practice in this period (Macaulay, 1991; 2000).

The production landscape has changed, however. The buying of widgets from a Wisconsin component manufacturer for a car construction plant in nearby Illinois no longer happens. Machinery manufacturing is unlikely to exist in Wisconsin now and in fact had probably ceased to exist by the early 1990s. A knowledge-based economy with nodal production sites has replaced large-scale manufacturing in developed economies. The dismantling of trade based on nation states and investment barriers has made it easier for industrial production to cluster into confined geographical areas that offer a combination of low-regulation, low-cost labour and easy access to natural resources. The core and the periphery of production are no longer split between developed, industrialized states and non-industrial developing states (Dicken, 2003, pp. 8–32). There are likely to be far fewer 'local' deals enhanced by personal relationships giving rise to concerns about reputation and creating a sort of interdependence and shared code of conduct between the parties. Supply chains are global. The availability of information technology creates more transparency around product price and quality, lessening the need to establish communicative ties and long-term contracts with potential trading partners and as the transaction costs involved in changing and replacing contractual partners have become lower (Sturgeon et al., 2011). Post-sales service and re-order information can be automated through information technology use (Lancioni et al., 2003; Chryssolouris et al., 2004).

There are more contractual relationships rather than less in a world trading economy that is shaped in this way, but they are different from the contract relationships that Macneil saw as typical. Webs of contracts exist around production, but often seek to achieve goals that are not connected to the delivery and price of the end product. For example, garment production and resource extraction often take place in low labour-cost areas and inhospitable climates. Subcontracts, supply chains and logistics firms have replaced vertical integration and, while Macneil did focus a great deal on horizontal arrangements, he did so with vertical integration and domestic-level production, rather than global production, as the backdrop (Macneil, 1975). Subcontracts are the preferred method of relationship not least because the environmental and human-rights risks associated with efficient (low-cost) production can be insulated in the chain to avoid reputational damage to investors' and consumers' views of brand (Harpur, 2008; Hoang and Jones, 2012; cf. Vandenbergh, 2007). Global production is driven by a form of retail consumption in which the brand has triumphed and blurred the boundaries between manufacturers, retailers and the supply chain (Petrovic and Hamilton, 2011). Flexibility of production schedules, delivery dates and contract solidarity have little role to play here. Relationships of trust and interdependence are still important, but they are more likely to be expressed as partnership arrangements and co-production arrangements around brand identity than relationships of contract per se.

The re-engineering and relocation of production and the subsequent financialization of developed economies has created a situation in which service-based employment, with contracts of employment that are fixed-term and temporary in nature, dominate in previously industrialized economic areas as employers try to hedge against the vagaries of product demand and the need for employees with contemporary skills. This is not a universally held view of current employment structures and opportunities (Fevre, 2007) but it is the perception of those who are currently the participants in these sectors of the labour market (Tweedie, 2013). In the context of mapping 'relationality', it is perception that is all-important as contract relationships are embedded in social relations, as those relations are experienced. It is not unusual for several part-time positions to be held at once by those in low-level employment yielding poor job satisfaction (Kalleberg, 2011). Long-term employment with a single provider has been replaced by portfolio careers. Workplace hierarchies are flatter and there is less room for norms that seek to preserve relationships or develop them beyond the limits of the printed conditions of employment (Marsden, 2004). Macneil's relational values are squeezed out of these highly planned arrangements of short and specified duration.

Macneil's norms have been used as the basis for analysis of the public-sector contracting regimes that represent the outworking of the New Public Management approach to governance of the early 1990s. There, contract was used as the vehicle for delivering a range of state-provided services and functions, including the construction and subsequent running of infrastructure facilities, often using private sector actors, to citizens. Macneil's stress on underlying social relations allows us to see these structures as forming relationships almost of a constitutional nature between citizen and state, in which the procedures for monitoring service provision, incentivizing performance and imposing administrative sanctions are laid out (Whitford, 1985; Feinman, 2000). Empirical work of the highest quality has been carried out on these relationships by Peter Vincent-Jones from the 1990s onwards (2000; 2006) who looked at the use of compulsory competitive tendering in local government and evaluated the use of contract by the state to achieve certain policy goals, such as increasing citizen choice or modifying citizen behaviour, in areas as diverse as the conduct of school children in the form of home–school agreements on homework and the delivery of welfare services.

Vincent-Jones's conclusion is that, measured against Macneil's norms, many of these arrangements fall short of delivering their policy objectives. There is insufficient possibility of adjustment that one might expect in an arrangement designed for both parties to achieve wealth maximization, as the arrangements lack the inherent flexibility to adapt to changing circumstances. The norm of reciprocity, which underpins trust, is not present because often the resources on the state side of the contract are insufficient to address the needs of the citizen (Vincent-Jones, 2002). In many of the relationships, but particularly those involving social control contracts, the norm of consent is missing, as there is no opportunity for citizen involvement in design or any public deliberation of policy such that one might expect in a modern democracy (Vincent-Jones, 2006, pp. 311–45). An alternative reading of Vincent-Jones's findings, though unpalatable in social policy terms, is that there was never any intention on behalf of the political and governance entities that use these arrangements that they should reflect the social norms that Macneil identifies as underpinning successful exchange relationships. This would certainly be the critique of them that is offered by Campbell who also questions whether such contracts can ever capture the note of voluntariness that is required in exchange behaviour (Campbell, 2007, pp. 288–92). The absence of this intention does not make these arrangements unsuccessful in terms of the more powerful party to the contract. While there have been periodic tweaks and recalibrations to the model, there has been no wholesale reconsideration of this methodology for service delivery by political entities, nor has there been revolution by citizens or ballot box rejection. What this shows instead is that it has been possible, in the period since Macneil first presented his model of contractual relationships, for these relationships, both in the legal and extra-legal sense of contract, to exist with norms configured rather differently from the way in which they are explained by Macneil. The emerging picture is one that suggests that short-term arrangements of this type are no longer the epitome of the discrete transaction but instead have evolved to exhibit similar relationality, in terms of mutual regard, to that found in more long-term arrangements (Davis, 2007). In order to make these relationships sufficiently stable for public service delivery, both public-sector and private-sector actors have become learning organizations, something that Vincent-Jones suggested would happen, albeit with his caveat that there are insufficient mechanisms for citizens to contribute to that learning (Vincent-Jones, 2007, pp. 272–5). The learning trajectories of organizations are different and are related to evolving political imperatives and local context (Hartmann et al., 2010).

3. Contracting on eBay

Macneil's model of contracting behaviour and his explanations for it have become disrupted. What have traditionally been flexible settings have become less flexible. Short-term exchange relationships have become ones in which there is mutual regard between the parties, while some long-term relationships do not exhibit this. What might have been a signifier for a discrete contract might now describe the relational setting of a more embedded contract. The importance of brand, for example, might point us to look at a series of contracts as a unified process rather than as differently constituted unique relationships with their own constructions of solidarity and flexibility. Macneil's norms can be rearranged to map onto what in some cases are new kinds of relationships and in others are familiar relationships that are differently structured. What is not lost in this rearrangement is the importance of social relations.

In the same way that Macneil sought to 'relationalize' his archetypal discrete contract, the gasoline purchase at the turnpike station, by describing the credit relations that allowed for the gas purchase, the supply of gas to the station, the advertising of the gas brand, and, indeed, the presence of the gas station itself at that particular location on the turnpike, we can 'relationalize' an eBay transaction. A number of charities use eBay to sell off potentially collectable items that have been donated for sale at their shops and collection points. Courses are offered through colleges and independently for those who want to become successful eBay entrepreneurs; several 'how to' guides have been published on eBay selling; and a number of satellite businesses have developed, such as the iSold It drop-off stores, which sell goods on commission for others on eBay. However, whilst placing the gas purchase in a sea of other business relationships is the only way to make it more significant than a brief encounter by the side of a turnpike, this way of describing eBay transactions misses the very much more real and personal social relations that surround each individual transaction in the form of the eBay feedback system.

EBay is not involved in the delivery of goods or the sale of goods as a trading entity. It does not see or inspect items that are being offered for sale or extend its reputation to warranting them or authenticating them in any way. It is an electronic platform charging sellers to list their items and taking a percentage of an item's sale price, in a way similar to a large electronic car boot sale site or a newspaper advertisement column that acts as an intermediary allowing sellers and buyers to match their desires for gain by taking part in either an auction or an immediate sale through online person-to-person trading (Mishra, 2010). However, instead of scanning lists of newspaper advertisements or rummaging through a dusty car boot while being jostled by other potential buyers, object location on eBay is as the result of a tailored search. The seller describes the item offered, often with photographs, posts an end date, a minimum starting bid, and a bid increment. While business listings occur on eBay, the majority of its sales in the collectables market are consumer-to-consumer transactions (Flanagin, 2007).

To be successful as an electronic platform, eBay has to be able to accomplish two things at the level of technical design. It needs to be able to manage a diverse group of buyers and sellers in terms of having recognizable brand identity within which there is sufficient flexibility to accommodate a variety of interests that underlie participation, that is eBay must be able to attract sufficient buyers for sellers to think that listing fees for items they are selling are worth paying. EBay needs to be able to offer reassurance that the risk involved in a one-time exchange and possibly more (although there is evidence that the vast majority of exchanges that take place on eBay are between buyers and sellers that do not deal with each other again) (Resnick and Zeckhauser, 2002) of money for an object that cannot be seen, except in a photograph, or touched is as low as possible. As eBay is an intermediary only, to which no liability attaches, this means that risk must be calculable and manageable by the users. The eBay system requires buyers to pay for their purchases before sellers dispatch them. Consequently, it is upon buyers that the risks of moral hazard (in the form of post-contractual opportunism such as non-dispatch of the item despite receiving payment) and information asymmetry (adverse selection due to unannounced defects) fall (Dewan and Hsu, 2004).

If we return to the earlier example of eBay being employed to source and purchase Beswick Beatrix Potter character figures, at any one time there are approximately 2500 figures on eBay that fall within the descriptive parameters of 'Beswick Beatrix Potter' ranging in starting price bids from £5 to £3999. Some very rare figures may be listed only once in those 2500 listings, other less rare figures may appear 50 times or so, listed by different sellers. The question for a buyer is how to choose a seller that it can trust in a market where there is a choice and in a market where there is only one seller. Engaging in exchange relations on eBay is not about the market reputation of a particular item but much more about a buyer trusting the seller of the product to describe that product accurately and dispatch it after receiving payment.

In the context of Beatrix Potter figures, what matters to the collector is that the figure is not restored but is in its original condition. A perfect figure is worth more than a damaged figure, but a damaged figure is worth considerably more than a restored figure. Damage can often be seen in photographs, but restoration can only be detected by close physical inspection.

Figure 3.1 From the left: Tom Kitten with a Beswick Gold Circle back stamp (produced 1948–1954, BP1a), Cousin Ribby with a Beswick Gold Oval back stamp (produced 1954–1972, BP2), Miss Moppet with a Beswick Brown back stamp (produced 1973–1974, BP3a) and Fierce Bad Rabbit with a Beswick Brown back stamp (produced 1974–1985, BP3b). Note the very small differences between the back stamps of Miss Moppet and Fierce Bad Rabbit in particular.

Also of importance is the stamp that appears on the underside of the figure, 'the back stamp'. This determines the age of the figure as some 13 different variations of back stamp were used in the 50 or so years that these figures were produced (Baynton et al., 1986). Figure 3.1 displays four figures and their different back stamps. It is not the case that older figures are always worth more than newer figures. Some figures were only made with a particular back stamp for a very short period of time and so are valuable for reasons of rarity rather than age. In the absence of a photograph, as a collector I am reliant on the description that the seller gives of the back stamp. An unscrupulous seller can provide false information or feign not to understand the significance of the detail they are being asked to provide and so provide no information or wrong information (Robinson and Halle, 2002).

In some cases, the value of a particular figure depends on very small design details that evolved over the years of production and distinguish one version of the figure from another. Beswick secured copyright permission to design and produce the Beatrix Potter figures in 1948. The modeller, one Arthur Gredington, sometimes changed the shape of a figure

Figure 3.2 Two versions of Benjamin Bunny, both with the same Beswick Brown back stamp (produced 1974–1985, BP3b).

slightly or the colour of particular parts of the figures with the same back stamp. Usually, these changes were as the result of paint availability or because customer feedback suggested that the figures as currently modelled were too fragile for their often rather young owners to handle. For example, there are three versions of the Benjamin Bunny figure, all with the same back stamp, that have vastly different values not least because one of them was only produced for two years (Callow et al., 2008). Figure 3.2 shows two apparently identical Benjamin Bunny figures. However, Figure 3.3 shows that they are rather different if viewed from behind – one has ears that protrude beyond its hat and the other does not. I am reliant on the angle that the seller's photograph is taken from to know for certain whether I am looking at an 'ears out' or an 'ears in' Benjamin Bunny. In other cases I am reliant on the quality of the seller's camera to reproduce accurately the colour of the jacket that the figure is wearing. I have to *trust* the seller if I am to purchase the figure. If I cannot trust them I potentially miss an opportunity.

None of the usual social cues that generate trust and confidence or wariness and mistrust in a face-to-face interaction are present. Nor, given the prevalence of single buyer–seller exchanges can trust in the seller be

Figure 3.3 The same Benjamin Bunny figures viewed from the back. The version with its 'ears out' on the left is worth very much more than the version with its 'ears in' on the right.

established through repeated interactions. Presentation, in Macneil's terms, reigns and so there is no interest from the seller in securing co-operation from the buyer in relation to establishing a relationship that will be both productive and negotiable into the future. As a platform, eBay offers users, and this primarily means buyers, as sellers are free to offer their item for sale again if payment does not materialize, an opportunity to choose their seller using the experiences of others as a trust barometer. It does this through offering a feedback forum. When using this forum, buyers are invited to describe in one word, taken from a pre-selected menu, their view of the quality of experience that the transaction provided: positive, negative or neutral. Sellers can leave only positive feedback for buyers or no feedback at all. This reflects their more immediate power in individual transactions. The buyer can justify their view in 80 characters and then rate, using a starring system, aspects of the transaction such as the accuracy of the item description, the speed of dispatch and the postage costs. As the seller engages in more sales, so a reputation is built up online, and this can be accessed by a potential buyer who can then, using the information in the profile, decide on the likely honesty and trustworthiness of a buyer. Buyers' power then is reflected backwards through transactions.

The feedback system is being used to generate trust through a formalized process in which a buyer, unsure whether to trust a seller not known to them, is encouraged to establish trust in that seller based on the views of other eBay users that are also unknown to them. It is a reputational gossip network where an individual buyer is substituting personal knowledge of a seller or a personal recommendation from someone they know who has dealt with the seller for a much larger volume of recommendations from strangers (Resnick et al., 2000; Van Swol, 2006). In addition to attracting fewer potential buyers, sellers with persistently low feedback scores might find that they are suspended by eBay or restricted in what they can sell by eBay. What emerges from the feedback system is a reputation management methodology whereby both sanction power and signalling power can be exercised by buyers to deal with moral hazard and adverse selection respectively (Dellarocas, 2003).

Reputation created and managed in this way is different to the social relations that surround reputation when single transactions are carried out offline. Online interactions involve leaving negative feedback where the individual who is its object can see it, unlike the conveying of negative reputational information to third parties that occurs offline. An aggrieved buyer may not want this degree of direct exposure to seller even in circumstances where the identity they are presenting is their eBay identity rather than their offline identity. In the absence of the intention to trade with the particular seller in the future, there is no incentive to leave feedback of any sort as the beneficiaries of that feedback will be unknown future traders, although, in fact, it seems that feedback is left in around 60 per cent of transactions (Saeedi et al., 2012).

There is the possibility of feedback being gamed through the use of seller collaboration to increase positive scores or high positive feedback scores being sprung from a vast number of low-price trades to create a misleading picture of reliability when a high-price trade is attempted. It is straightforward for a seller to create an entirely new identity which, while it is not enhanced by positive feedback, has not been sullied by negative feedback either. Notwithstanding these concerns about its absolute accuracy and reliability, the eBay feedback system is clearly considered by the users of eBay to be robust enough to allay their concerns about seller honesty and reliability. Not only is eBay itself an extremely successful business but analysis of transactions also suggests that sellers with higher feedback ratings achieve higher prices for their listings (Ottaway et al., 2003).

Feedback on eBay has the effect of creating social relations between strangers. In this respect it is different from other online presences such as retail stores, where the object is to create trust in the technology itself rather than a person (Shanker et al., 2002). Feedback very quickly provides information from one buyer to millions of potential buyers about a seller they may never encounter, so overcoming the geographical dispersal of buyers. It provides a rich and documented form of support that achieves more granularity than offline reputational discussions are likely to do (Tambyah, 1996). The feedback system is successful in creating relationships of trust because it pulls on the levers of community responsibility and individual participation. It is a tool that empowers individuals to punish or reward a trading partner knowing that others will operate a sanction based on their view, and there is an obligation on individuals to participate by leaving feedback if the system is to appear reliable (Heimer, 2001) to the user community. The idea of relying on feedback has a particular appeal in a current climate in which trust appears to be placed more strongly in 'people just like ourselves' than in other groups such as political or business leaders (Edelman Trust Barometer, 2012; Tett, 2013). The feedback system allows individuals to decide whom they will trust while wrapping their decisions into the fold of community values that they, as buyers, are encouraged to adopt. EBay supports and encourages the idea that buyers are an online community (Mathwick, 2002) with shared values. In its statement of 'community values', eBay asserts, 'people are basically good' and extorts users to 'treat others the way that you want to be treated'.

Conclusion

In this chapter I have set out the case for the continuing utility of Macneil's relational contract theory despite the changing context of contracting behaviour in a world that is very different from the one described by Macneil. Advances in technology and changing economic patterns that impact on how contracts are made and experienced require us to reconsider Macneil's conceptual categories of *relational* and *discrete*. In the contemporary context we must make a more relational assessment of situations that would appear on first sight to be much closer to a discrete situation. The social processes and informational relationships that underpin strategic choices made within the contractual matrix require a more developed analysis in the light of technological developments than Macneil supplied. As interactional structures between actors change and develop as a result of the possibilities opened up by computer-mediated sites of exchange, so Macneil's relational spectrum needs to adapt. Social relations as conceived by Macneil no longer hold sway over transactions in the way that the journey from discrete transactions to relational contracts he maps envisaged that they would. EBay trading contracts rely on community-constructed feedback to counter information asymmetry. As online shopping and trading increases in popularity we may come to see social relations constructed to radiate beyond the contracting partners as the paradigm example of twenty-first-century contract relations, in the same way that machinery supply in Wisconsin was the paradigm contract of the second half of the twentieth century for those of us, who, following Macneil, have rejected the doctrinal model of the purely discrete exchange. Macneil's model of contractual relations remains the only complete counter-explanation to the doctrinal model. However, this does not mean that it can continue to occupy this position without adaption of its norms to reflect the changing nature of society. Indeed, Macneil's constant tinkering with the definitions and explanations for his model of contract demonstrates that it has this flexibility.

References

Abbate, J (1999) *Inventing the Internet* (Cambridge MA: MIT Press)

Baynton, V, H May and J Morton (1986) *The Beswick Collectors Handbook* (London: Kevin Francis Publications)

Belk, R (1991) 'The Ineluctable Mysteries of Possessions' 6 *Journal of Social Behavior and Personality* 17–55

Belk, R (1995) 'Collecting as Luxury Consumption: Effects on Individuals and Households' 16 *Journal of Economic Psychology* 477–90

Belk, R (1998) 'The Double Nature of Collecting: Materialism and Anti-Materialism' 11 *Etnofoor* 7–20

Belk, R, G Ger and S Askegaard (2003) 'The Fire of Desire: A Multisited Inquiry into Consumer Passion' 30 *Journal of Consumer Research* 326–51

Bennett, C (2008) *The Privacy Advocates* (Cambridge MA: MIT Press)

Bowlby, R (1997) 'Supermarket Futures' in P Falk and C Campbell (eds), *The Shopping Experience* (London: Sage Publications), p. 92

Bradley, S and K Porter (2000) 'eBay, Inc. Case Study' 14 *Journal of Interactive Marketing* 73–97

Bradsher, K, C Duhigg and C Ouyang (2012) 'Signs of Changes Taking Hold in Electronics Factories in China', *New York Times,* 26 December www.nytimes.com/2012/12/27/business/signs-of-changes-taking-hold-in-electronics-factories-in-china.html?ref=business

Callow, D, J Callow and F Corley (2008) *Beswick Collectables: A Charlton Standard Catalogue* (Toronto: Charlton Press) (10th revised edn)

Campbell, D (1996) 'The Relational Constitution of the Discrete Contract' in D Campbell and P Vincent-Jones (eds), *Contract and Economic Organisation* (Aldershot: Dartmouth), pp. 40–66

Campbell, D (2001) 'Ian Macneil and the Relational Theory of Contract' in D Campbell (ed.), *The Relational Theory of Contract: Selected Works of Ian Macneil* (London: Sweet & Maxwell), pp. 3–58

Campbell, D (2007) 'Relational Contract and the Nature of Private Ordering: A Comment on Vincent-Jones' 14 *Indiana Journal of Global Legal Studies* 279

Campbell, D (2013) 'What Do We Mean by the Non-Use of Contract?' in J Braucher, J Kidwell and W Whitford (eds), *Revisiting the Contracts Scholarship of Stewart Macaulay* (Oxford: Hart Publishing), pp. 159–90

Case, D (2009) 'Serial Collecting as Leisure, and Coin Collecting in Particular' 57 *Library Trends* 729–52

Centre for Retail Research (2011) www.retailresearch.org/onlineretailing.php

Chryssolouris, G, S Makris, V Xanthakis and D Mourtzis (2004) 'Towards the Internet-based Supply Chain Management for the Ship Repair Industry' 17 *International Journal of Computer Integrated Manufacturing* 45–57

Coursey, D and D Norris (2008) 'Models of E-Government: Are They Correct? An Empirical Assessment' 68 *Public Administration Review* 523–36

Cox, A, D Cox and R Anderson (2005) 'Reassessing the Pleasures of Store Shopping' 58 *Journal of Business Research* 250–9

Czernich, N, O Falck, T Kretschmer and L Woessmann (2011) 'Broadband Infrastructure and Economic Growth' 121 *The Economic Journal* 505–32

Davis, P (2007) 'The Effectiveness of Relational Contracting in a Temporary Public Organization: Intensive Collaboration between an English Local Authority and Private Contractors' 85 *Public Administration* 383–404

Dellarocas, C (2003) 'The Digitization of Word-of-Mouth: Promise and Challenges of Online Reputation' 49 *Management Science* 1407–24

Denegri-Knott, J and M Molesworth (2010a) 'Concepts and Practices of Digital Virtual Consumption' 13 *Consumption Markets and Culture* 109–32

Denegri-Knott, J and M Molesworth (2010b) '"Love it, Buy it, Sell it": Consumer Demand and the Social Drama of eBay' 10 *Journal of Consumer Culture* 56–79

Dewan, S and V Hsu (2004) 'Adverse Selection in Electronic Markets: Evidence from Online Stamp Auctions' LII *Journal of Industrial Economics* 497–516

Dicken, P (2003) *Global Shift: Reshaping the Global Economic Map in the 21st Century* (London: Sage Publications)

Downes, E J and S J McMillan (2000) 'Defining Interactivity: A Qualitative Identification of Key Dimensions' 2 *New Media and Society* 157–79

Edelman Trust Barometer (2012) www.trust.edelman.com

Ellis, R and A Haywood (2006) 'Virtual_radiophile (163.): eBay and the Changing Collecting Practices of the UK Vintage Radio Community' in K Hillis and M Petit with N Epley (eds), *Everyday eBay: Culture Collecting and Desire* (Abingdon: Routledge), pp. 45–63

Ellis, V and P Taylor (2006) '"You Don't Know What You've Got Till It's Gone": Re-contextualising the Origins, Development and Impact of the Call Centre' 21 *New Technology, Work and Employment* 107–22

Eubanks, V (2011) *Digital Dead End* (Cambridge MA: MIT Press)

Feinman, J (1990) 'The Significance of Contract Theory' 58 *University of Cincinnati Law Review* 1283–318

Feinman, J (2000) 'Relational Contract Theory in Context' 94 *Northwestern University Law Review* 737–48

Feinman, J (2001) 'The Reception of Ian Macneil's Work on Contract in the USA' in D Campbell (ed.), *The Relational Theory of Contract: Selected Works of Ian Macneil* (London: Sweet & Maxwell), pp. 59–66

Fevre, R (2007) 'Employment Insecurity and Social Theory: The Power of Nightmares' 21 *Work, Employment and Society* 517–35

Flanagin, A (2007) 'Commercial Markets as Communication Markets: Uncertainty Reduction through Mediated Information Exchange in Online Auctions' 9 *New Media and Society* 401–23

Formanek, R (1991) 'Why They Collect: Collectors Reveal their Motivations' 6 *Journal of Social Behavior and Personality* 275–86

Frost & Sullivan and PCW (2012) www.pwc.com.au/industry/retail-consumer/assets/Digital-Media-Research-Jul12.pdf

Gibson, W (1999) 'My Obsession: I thought I was Immune to the Net and I Got Bitten by eBay' www.wired.com/wired/archive/7.01/ebay.html

Harpur, P (2008) 'Clothing Manufacturing Supply Chains, Contractual Layers and Hold Harmless Clauses: How OHS Duties Can Be Imposed over Retailers' 21 *Australian Journal of Labour Law* 316–39

Hartmann, A, A Davies and L Frederiksen (2010) 'Learning to Deliver Service-Enhanced Public Infrastructure: Balancing Contractual and Relational Capabilities' 28 *Construction Management and Economics* 1165–75

Heimer, C (2001) 'Solving the Problem of Trust' in K Cook (ed.) *Trust in Society* (New York: Russell Sage Foundation), pp. 40–88

Hoang, D and B Jones (2012) 'Why do Corporate Codes of Conduct Fail? Women Workers and Clothing Supply Chains in Vietnam' 12 *Global Social Policy* 67–85

Kalleberg, A (2011) *Good Jobs, Bad Jobs: The Rise of Polarized and Precarious Employment Systems in the United States, 1970s to 2000s* (New York: Russell Sage Foundation)

Kraut, R, M Patterson, V Lundmark, S Kiesler, T Mukopadhyay and W Scherlis (1998) 'Internet Paradox: A Social Technology that Reduces Social Involvement and Psychological Well-Being?' 53 *American Psychologist* 1017–31

Lancioni, R, H Schau and M Smith (2003) 'Internet Impacts on Supply Chain Management' 32 *Industrial Marketing Management* 73–5

Licklider, J C R and R Taylor (1968) 'The Computer as a Communication Device' *Science and Technology* 20–41

Macaulay, S (1963) 'Non-Contractual Relations in Business: A Preliminary Study' 28 *American Sociological Review* 55–67

Macaulay, S (1991) 'Long-term Continuing Relations: The American Experience Regulating Dealerships and Franchises' in C Joerges (ed.), *Franchising and the Law: Theoretical and Comparative Approaches in Europe and the United States* (Baden-Baden: Nomos VeriagsgeseUschaft), pp. 179–237

Macaulay, S (2000) 'Relational Contracts Floating on a Sea of Custom? Thoughts About the Ideas of Ian Macneil and Lisa Bernstein' 94 *Northwestern University Law Review* 775–804

Macaulay, S, J Braucher, J Kidwell and J Whitford (2010) *Contracts: Law in Action* (London: LexisNexis) (3rd edn)

Macneil, I (1962–1963) 'An Exercise in Contract Damages: City of Memphis v Ford Motor Company' 4 *Boston College Industrial and Commercial Law Review* 331–42

Macneil, I (1974a) 'The Many Futures of Contracts' 47 *Southern California Law Review* 691–816

Macneil, I (1974b) 'Restatement (Second) of Contracts and Presentiation' 60 *Virginia Law Review* 589–610

Macneil, I (1975) 'A Primer of Contract Planning' 48 *Southern California Law Review* 627–704

Macneil, I (1978) 'Contracts Adjustments of Long-term Economic Relations under Classical, Neoclassical, and Relational Contract Law' 72 *Northwestern University Law Review* 854–905

Macneil, I (1980) *The New Social Contract: An Enquiry into Modern Contractual Relations* (New Haven CT: Yale University Press)

Macneil, I (1983) 'Values in Contract: Internal and External' 78 *Northwestern University Law Review* 340–418

Macneil, I (1985) 'Relational Contract: What We Do and Do Not Know' *Wisconsin Law Rev* 483–525

Macneil, I (1986) 'Exchange Revisited: Individual Utility and Social Solidarity' 96 *Ethics* 567–93

Macneil, I (1987a) 'Barriers to the Idea of Relational Contracts' in F Nicklisch (ed.), *Der komplexe Langzeitvertrag: Strukturen und international Schiedsgerichtsbarkeit/The Complex Long-term Contract: Structures and International Arbitration* (Heidelberg: CF Muller), pp. 31–46

Macneil, I (1987b) 'Relational Contract Theory as Sociology: A Reply to Professors Lindenberg and de Vos' 143 *Journal of Institutional and Theoretical Economics* 272–90

Macneil, I (1999–2000) 'Relational Contract Theory: Challenges and Queries' 94 *Northwestern University Law Review* 877–908

Marsden, D (2004) 'The "Network Economy" and Models of the Employment Contract' 42 *British Journal of Industrial Relations* 659–84

Mathwick, C (2002) 'Understanding the Online Consumer: A Typology of Online Relational Norms and Behavior' 16 *Journal of Interactive Marketing* 40–55

McCracken, G (1988) *Culture and Consumption* (Bloomington IN: Indiana University Press)

McIntosh, W and B Schmeichel (2004) 'Collectors and Collecting: A Social Psychological Perspective' 26 *Leisure Sciences* 85–97

Mick, D and S Fournier (1998) 'Paradoxes of Technology: Consumer Cognizance, Emotions and Coping Strategies' 25 *Journal of Consumer Research* 123–48

Miller, D (2000) 'The Fame of Trinis: Websites as Aesthetic Traps' 5 *Journal of Material Culture* 5–24

Mishra, M (2010) 'Why is eBay the Most Successful Online Auction' 10 *Global Journal of Business and Management Research* 62–5

Molesworth, M and J Denegri-Knott (2008) 'The Playfulness of eBay and the Implications for Business as a Game-Maker' 28 *Journal of Macromarketing* 369–80

Ofcom (2011) *Communications Market Report* http://stakeholders.ofcom.org.uk/binaries/research/cmr/cmr11/UK_CMR_2011_FINAL.pdf

Olmsted, A (1991) 'Collecting: Leisure, Investment, or Obsession?' *Journal of Social Behavior and Personality* 287–306

Ottaway, T, C Bruneau and G Evans (2003) 'The Impact of Auction Item Image and Buyer/Seller Feedback Rating on Electronic Auctions' 43 *Journal of Computer Information Systems* 56–60

Pearce, S (1992) *Museums, Objects, and Collections: A Cultural Study* (Washington DC: Smithsonian Press)

Petrovic, M and G Hamilton (2011) 'Retailers as Market Makers' in G Hamilton, M Petrovic and B Senauer (eds), *The Market Makers: How Retailers are Shaping the Global Economy* (Oxford: Oxford University Press), pp. 31–49

Pew Research Centre (2011) *Smart Phone Adoption and Usage* http://pewinternet.org/Reports/2011/Smartphones.aspx

Pires, G, J Stanton and P Rita (2006) 'The Internet, Consumer Empowerment and Marketing Strategies' 40 *European Journal of Marketing* 936–49

Rafaeli, S and Y Ariel (2007) 'Assessing Interactivity in Computer-Mediated Research' in A Joinson, K McKenna, T Postmes and U-D Reips (eds), *The Oxford Handbook of Internet Psychology* (Oxford: Oxford University Press), pp. 71–88

Resnick, P and R Zeckhauser (2002) 'Trust among Strangers in Internet Transactions: Empirical Analysis of eBay's Reputation System' in M Baye (ed.), *The Economics of the Internet and E-commerce* (Oxford: Elsevier Science), pp. 127–57

Resnick, P, R Zeckhauser, E Friedman and K Kuwabara (2000) 'Reputation Systems' *Communications of the ACM* 45–8

Rezabakhsh, B, D Bornemann, U Hansen and U Schrader (2006) 'Consumer Power: A Comparison of the Old Economy and the Internet Economy' 29 *Journal of Consumer Policy* 3–36

Rha, J and R Widdows (2002) 'The Internet and the Consumer: Countervailing Power Revisited' 20 *Prometheus* 107–18

Robinson, L and D Halle (2002) 'Digitization, the Internet, and the Arts: eBay, Napster, SAG, and e-Books' 25 *Qualitative Sociology* 359–83

Saeedi, M, Z Shen and N Sundaresan (2012) 'From Lemon Markets to Managed Markets: An Analysis of Reputation System Evolution' www.econ.umn.edu/saeedi/wwwrep.pdf

Scott, R (2013) 'The Promise and Peril of Relational Contract Theory' in J Braucher, J Kidwell and W Whitford (eds), *Revisiting the Contracts Scholarship of Stewart Macaulay* (Oxford: Hart Publishing), pp. 105–39

Shankar, V, G Urban and F Sultan (2002) 'Online Trust: A Stakeholder Perspective, Concepts, Implications, and Future Directions' 11 *Journal of Strategic Information Systems* 325–44

Speidel, R (1999–2000) 'The Characteristics and Challenges of Relational Contracts' 94 *Northwestern University Law Review* 823–46

Sturgeon, T, J Humphrey and G Gereffi (2011) 'Making the Global Supply Base' in G Hamilton, M Petrovic and B Senauer (eds), *The Market Makers: How Retailers are Shaping the Global Economy* (Oxford: Oxford University Press), pp. 231–54

Tambyah, S (1996) 'Life on the Net: The Reconstruction of Self and Community' 23 *Advances in Consumer Research* 172–7

Tett, G (2013) 'Davos Take Note: We Don't Trust You', *Financial Times*, 25 January

Tweedie, D (2013) 'Making Sense of Insecurity: A Defence of Richard Sennett's Sociology of Work' 27 *Work Employment and Society* 94–104

United Nations (2008) *From E-Government to Connected Governance* E-Government Survey (New York: United Nations)

Van Laer, J (2010) 'Activists "Online" and "Offline": The Internet as an Information Channel for Protest Demonstrations' 15 *Mobilization* 405–19

van Swol, L (2006) 'Return of the Town Square' in K Hillis and M Petit with N Epley (eds), *Everyday eBay: Culture Collecting and Desire* (Abingdon: Routledge), pp. 137–50

Vandenbergh, M (2007) 'The New Wal-Mart Effect: The Role of Private Contracting in Global Governance' 54 *UCLA Law Review* 913–70

Vincent-Jones, P (2000) 'Contractual Governance: Institutional and Organizational Analysis' 20 *Oxford Journal of Legal Studies* 317–51

Vincent-Jones, P (2002) 'Values and Purpose in Government: Central-local Relations in Regulatory Perspective' 29 *JLS* 27–55

Vincent-Jones, P (2006) *The New Public Contracting* (Oxford: Oxford University Press)

Vincent-Jones, P (2007) 'The New Public Contracting: Public Versus Private Ordering' 14 *Indian Journal of Global Legal Studies* 259–78

Wagner, T and T Rudolph (2010) 'Towards a Hierarchical Theory of Shopping Motivation' 17 *Journal of Retailing and Consumer Services* 415–29

Walther, J (1992) 'Interpersonal Effects in Computer-Mediated Interaction: A Relational Perspective' 19 *Communication Research* 52–90

Wellman, B, J Boase and W Chen (2002) 'The Networked Nature of Community: Online and Offline' 1 *IT and Society* 151–65

Whitford, W (1985) 'Ian Macneil's Contribution to Contract Scholarship' *Wisconsin Law Review* 545–60

Williams, D (2006) 'On and Off the 'Net: Scales for Social Capital in an Online Era' 11 *Journal of Computer-Mediated Communication* 593–628

Wu, T (2010) *The Master Switch* (London: Atlantic Books)

Zwick, D and N Dholakia (2006) 'Bringing the Market to Life: Screen Aesthetics and the Epistemic Consumption Object' 6 *Marketing Theory* 41–62

4
The Contract of Employment in 3D
Hugh Collins[1]

The contract of employment has often been described as a relational contract (Bird, 2005; Boyle, 2007; Brodie, 2011). Indeed, the contract of employment possesses many features that are frequently highlighted in descriptions of relational contracts: it is likely to be long term, to require co-operation from both parties, and to depend for its successful performance on flexibility and adaptation to changing circumstances. There have even been occasional judicial references to the relational character of the contract of employment: Lord Steyn, in *Johnson v Unisys Ltd* [2001] ICR 480 said: 'it is no longer right to equate a contract of employment with commercial contracts. One possible way of describing a contract of employment in modern terms is as a relational contract.' (at [16]) Ian Macneil, the originator of the idea of relational contracts (Macneil, 1978), often refers to the contract of employment as an example of a relational contract or, more precisely, at the relational end of the spectrum of exchange relationships between the polarities of discrete and relational contracts. For example, he describes employment as 'an extremely relational contract, no matter how strenuously a party tries to make it discrete' (Macneil, 1985, p. 492).

Notice, however, the ambiguity of that last statement. How can the contract of employment be 'extremely relational' if one party is trying to make it function as a discrete contract? In his magisterial study of the contract of employment in the common law, Mark Freedland also pinpoints an ambiguity or 'structural uncertainty'.

> At the heart of this structural uncertainty lies the dichotomy between exchange transactions and relational contracts. Most of the problems about the content and internal structure of personal employment contracts result from doubt and ambiguity

---

1 I am grateful to Aline van Bever for help with this paper.

as to whether and when those contracts are to be regarded more as exchange transactions than as relational contracts. (Freedland, 2003, p. 88)

Freedland tried initially to resolve that ambiguity by suggesting that the contract of employment possesses a two-level structure. On one level there is an exchange of work for remuneration – a discrete contract; and at a second level there are promises to employ and be employed (or to have an ongoing relationship). In this context, Freedland defines the relational dimension of the contract of employment largely by reference to the long-term, ongoing relationship aspect of employment, sometimes described as mutuality of obligation. Yet then Freedland adds a vital insight:

> The idea of the personal employment contract as an exchange transaction remains crucially distinct from the idea of the personal employment contract as a relational contract. *The two ideas coexist as competing paradigms which exert pressures towards different approaches or solutions to issues of the construction or regulation of personal employment contracts.* Because of this, there remain some problems about the internal structure of personal employment contracts which are not fully resolved simply by invoking the notion of a two-level structure. (Freedland, 2003, p. 92, my italics)

The masterly understatement at the end acknowledges how legal reasoning cannot resolve issues arising from the contract of employment by invoking a theory of a two-level structure, because there is no such settled structure. Instead, there are two 'competing paradigms', which constantly jostle for dominance in the legal analysis. The nucleus of the contract of employment is held together by the attraction of opposites: the proton of the discrete exchange and the neutron of the relational contract.

With its daunting metaphor drawn from nuclear physics, this analysis of the contract of employment in fact seems paradigmatic of all attempts, including those of Macneil (1980; Campbell, 2001), to pin down the relational or implicit dimensions of all types of contracts. Every type of contract has both discrete and relational elements and cannot function without both. *The key question becomes: how are these discrete and relational elements bound together to make the contract function successfully and, in the light of that analysis, how should the law understand its task in resolving disputes about the respective obligations of the parties to the contract?* Structural metaphors prove inadequate to this task for the reason that both Freedland and Macneil acknowledge: like protons and neutrons, the discrete and relational dimensions exist in tension, everywhere at once and not in a settled pattern.

Drawing on earlier work (Collins, 1999), this chapter endeavours to answer the key question described above, not by invoking structures, but rather by describing systems in the sense of logics or discourses, as employed in what is commonly labelled 'systems theory' (Teubner, 1993). The first section explores in greater depth the problems that need to be addressed in any approach to the key question. The second section sets out the proposed analysis of contracts in terms of systems by distinguishing three systems that apply to every contract. The third section applies that three-dimensional analysis to the contract of employment with a view to elucidating and resolving the tension between the competing paradigms.

1. Two puzzles of relational contract theory

Macneil's work on relational contract theory is important primarily for its insights about how to study contract law from a sociological perspective. Macneil sought to examine contracts in the round, in their context. Indeed, the category he investigates is 'exchange' rather than 'contract', which, following Peter Blau and other social theorists (Blau, 1964; Gudel, 1998), he conceives as a broader and more fundamental category of social relations. Macneil insisted that lawyers (or anyone interested in contracts) should try to understand all these surrounding norms and social relations as the starting point for analysing transactions and as an essential guide to legal reasoning. This sociological approach goes further than a typical modern contextual approach to the understanding and interpretation of contracts. The conventional contextual or neoclassical approach refers to the context in order to supplement the contractual agreement or to resolve ambiguities. It works from inside the contract viewed as a written or oral agreement and then proceeds outside to the context that surrounds the contract. Under Macneil's sociological approach, however, one has to start from the outside with the relations between the parties within which context the exchange is made, and then work inwards towards the contract.

Macneil's central claim of significance to lawyers is that the classical law of contract focused on particular aspects of contractual relations, such as the written terms of the agreement, but seemed frequently blind to other relational aspects or implicit dimensions, such as expectations of co-operation and adaptation to changing circumstances, which are often key ingredients of a successfully functioning business transaction, especially in long-term business relations (Macaulay, 1963; Daintith, 1986; Campbell and Harris, 1993). Richard Speidel describes well this sociological or relational approach with respect to the contract of employment:

> In a contract of employment, modern contract law assumes that the bargain between employer and employee is independent of context unless there is proof that the agreement is supplemented by norms and practices from the context or regulated by state or federal legislation. Under relational theory, however, the contract of employment is assumed to be part of and dependent on the overlapping matrix of context relationships unless the independence or self-sufficiency of the deal (the truly 'discrete' contract) is established. The bargain cannot be understood until the relationships are described and understood. (Speidel, 2000, p. 826)

In the contract of employment, for instance, the written terms regarding job description, wages and hours, though providing a framework for the exchange, do not provide any guide or insight into the crucial dynamics of the daily functioning of the contract, which relies on dialogue, co-operation, adaptation and fair treatment. It is sometimes said that the most productive types of contract of employment require performance 'beyond contract' (Fox, 1974). This gap between formal terms and actual expectations is recognized and studied in research in management and industrial relations under different rubrics such as 'organisational commitment behaviour' (Smith et al., 1983) and 'the psychological contract' (Rousseau, 1995; Guest, 2004). Although the different labels betray divergent research agendas, the common theme is that everyone recognizes that, for a productive employment relationship to flourish, it is usually necessary for both parties to develop and respect informal norms or relations that go far beyond the express terms of the contract. That argument about the significance of the relational dimension of contracts sets out a reasonably clear agenda for research and potential critique of the classical law of contract (Eisenberg, 1995; Campbell and Collins, 2003), but at least two puzzles with this approach persist.

Macneil's approach has commonly been understood to propose that there is a spectrum of types of contract ranging from mostly discrete contracts, in which informal norms are mostly irrelevant, to at the opposite extreme relational contracts where informal norms play a crucial role in determining behaviour. The first puzzle arises from the observation that contractual behaviour varies according to context or events, not the type of contract concerned. It is possible to find many instances where contractual behaviour seems to become extremely oriented to the precise promises contained in the contract, with detailed examination of the small print in the formal documents, even though the contract itself has many key elements of a relational dimension by containing long-term diffuse commitments, by being embedded in a long-term business relationship, and by being surrounded by expressions of willingness to co-operate and to act in good faith. For instance, the employment tribunals in the UK handle thousands of cases each year where the issue between employer and employee concerns whether the wages and other fringe benefits have been paid in full, which is the kind of dispute that must be resolved by close inspection of the written terms of the contract plus any relevant statutory entitlements (such as holiday pay) without reference to the relational dimensions of employment at all. Equally, it is possible to observe behaviour connected to what appear to be examples of a discrete contract, such as a single purchase of goods at a fixed price from a shop, where the parties demonstrate flexibility, a willingness to take into account the interests of the other party, and in particular a concern on the part of the shop to maximize customer satisfaction regardless of the precise contractual obligations. The puzzle in these examples is that the spectrum between discrete and relational contracts does not help predict how the parties will behave during the performance of the transaction. The contractual behaviour seems to vary over time in connection with a contract: at one point there may be behaviour that exemplifies relational behaviour, but later on, especially when disputes arise, the behaviour may shift toward meticulous insistence on the precise terms of the transaction. This dynamic quality in contractual behaviour cannot be captured by reference to the type of contract concerned on a spectrum between discrete and relational contracts and their implicit norms. As a description or explanation of contractual behaviour, the spectrum theory of discrete and relational contracts does not account for what norms of behaviour predominate at any particular time and how they change.

A second puzzle that arises in the relational theory of contracts is when to use the sociological perspective as the basis for a critique and adjustment of the law of contract. Indeed, this puzzle applies to any approach to contract law, whether sociological or economic, that attempts to derive guidance for the law from an empirical observation of social behaviour. In a contract of employment, for example, the terms may permit the employer to dismiss the employee for any reason on short notice, but in practice in most employment relationships both employer and employee generally conduct themselves according to an expectation that the contract will continue indefinitely unless there is just cause for a dismissal. The question that arises in such cases is whether the court should simply enforce the express terms of the contract or, in order to make the legal obligations conform to the informal expectations of the parties, whether the court should try to reshape the contractual obligations by devices such as implied terms (Collins, 2003a). At one extreme, the formalist can argue that a court should always simply enforce the written contract, because that is straightforward, predictable and fair since that is what the parties explicitly agreed, and any other judicial practice is impracticable and causes confusion and uncertainty. At the other extreme, the realist or contextualist can insist that a court must always match the legal obligations with the actual expectations of the parties, notwithstanding any contrary terms in the written agreement, because those expectations are the true normative foundation of the transaction and are the vital ingredient in the efficiency of the exchange.

The choice between these extremes is the issue that must always be confronted by what may be called 'sociological jurisprudence'. The broad aim of this approach to legal scholarship is to understand from a social scientific perspective the practices and institutions that the law seeks to regulate, and then to help shape the law so that it both supports the effective functioning of those practices and institutions whilst at the same time preventing the corruption and distortion of those practices and institutions. Within this approach, an important methodological question asks how to turn empirical observation into prescriptive norms: a sociological observation and analysis of behaviour may produce a superior understanding of the relationship of contracting and how the parties behave in the light of the norms that they accept, but how should we turn this factual observation into normative propositions concerning legal obligations? Or, more bluntly, how and when should we derive an 'ought' from an 'is'? Should the court endorse and support the non-legal norms that shape the parties' expectations in a contractual relationship, or should the court insist that, in the absence of a consensual reconciliation of interests, it should enforce the parties' settled legal entitlements as expressed in their explicit contract?

One of the problems of Macneil's discussion of contract law and the sociology of exchange is that it provides scant guidance on the answer to that question. Recall that Macneil describes the context of contracts as involving ten non-legal norms of behaviour such as mutuality (or a fair distribution of benefits and burdens between the parties) and flexibility in performance of the contract (Macneil, 1980). In any particular instance, we may agree with Macneil that some contractual behaviour involves the norm of flexibility without reference to the strict terms of the written contract; the question then arises whether or not the law, if it fails to acknowledge and reinforce that behaviour of flexibility, is doing something wrong. Does a failure of the law to respect the contractual norm of flexibility mean that there is something wrong with the law? No doubt the answer to that question depends on the type of contract involved, the history of the relationship, the economic interests of the parties and many other considerations. In a contract of employment, some degree of flexibility is likely to be common in practice and useful to make the transaction function efficiently, so there may be strong case for the law to endorse a requirement of flexibility. In contrast, if we consider the example of a loan by a bank to a business, there are good arguments for the bank being rigid in demanding repayment according to the terms of the contract rather than granting extra time to pay or being flexible in some other respect. Without that ability to insist on the strict terms of the contract, banks may reduce the number of loans offered to customers or increase interest rates. Yet, even in the example of a business loan, there may be arguments for flexibility such as the historic practice of the bank in accommodating a particular customer and the desirability of avoiding the social costs associated with insolvencies. The problem with Macneil's reference to the ten norms of contractual behaviour is that this comprehensive description does not provide guidance to the law about when rigidity is appropriate and when the norm of flexibility should predominate.

These two puzzles concerning the dynamic qualities of contractual behaviour and the methodology of sociological jurisprudence in connection with contracts seem to be to be closely connected. Evidence that there can be relational norms of co-operation and adjustment operating in discrete transactions and also strict insistence on formal agreements in what appear to be relational transactions such as a contract of employment teaches us surely that it would be a mistake to solve the question of sociological jurisprudence with the simplistic solution of applying a non-contextual formalist approach in legal reasoning to discrete contracts and a contextual approach that encompasses the implicit expectations and norms for contracts on the relational end of the spectrum. This solution is a mistake because the type of contract or its place on the spectrum ranging from discrete contracts to relational contracts cannot tell us accurately about the reasonable expectations of the parties and the implicit norms and understandings that arise between them. But to appreciate that a simple bifurcation of contract types into discrete and relational is not an answer to the puzzle unfortunately does not provide a solution to the problem.

2. Three dimensions of contractual behaviour

In order to approach better the problem of the methodology of sociological jurisprudence, it is suggested that one way to simplify the analysis of contractual behaviour is to distinguish between three frameworks of rational behaviour with respect to contracts. These three frameworks provide reasons for action that make sense within those frameworks, but do not necessarily make any sense within the other two frameworks. In the language of systems theory, the suggestion is that contractual behaviour can best be explained by reference to three largely autonomous systems of logic, reasoning and communication that constitute the context of every contractual relation.

a. Contractual rationality

The first framework that guides contractual behaviour is focused on the agreement itself and the way it creates new rights and obligations between the parties. It focuses on the discrete contract itself and the written or oral agreement and the promises contained in it. This kind of rationality is similar to that employed by the classical legal analysis of contracts because it is guided solely by reference to the contract as a thing, a discrete relationship that has been created between the parties. On this level, parties understand and predict each other's behaviour by reference to the agreement, their planning document and the normal customs of the trade. It includes not only the express promises but also implied promises that can be grounded in the presumed intentions of the parties, the customs of the trade or the market sector and, more broadly, what Hugh Beale and Tony Dugdale called the 'unwritten laws' of the contract (Beale and Dugdale, 1975). These market conventions, such as the expectation of whether there should be payment in advance or on receipt of the goods or services, can be understood within the legal framework of the contract as implied promises or terms of the contract.

This focus on the discrete contract itself as a framework is justified because it plays a vital role in contractual behaviour. It is a mistake not to appreciate that, unlike many other social relationships, such as friendship, that may involve an element of reciprocal exchange, contracts are distinctive because of their voluntary nature, their limited commitments defined by the terms of the agreement, and the confined relationship to the parties to the agreement. Just as all contracts have a relational dimension, as Macneil rightly insisted, it is also true that all contracts have a discrete element. They carve out a distinct relationship, usually finite in duration, specific in obligations, personal to the parties to the agreement, yet almost infinitely malleable in its content (Collins, 1999, p. 16). A contract marks the moment of the creation of something new, a binding obligation that did not exist before. Whilst it is true that contracts differ in the extent of the planning for contingencies and the precision of the reciprocal promises, that fact should not obscure the point that the parties have created, or at least have tried to create, a new bond that is separate from their prior relations. This feature of autonomy is true for both discrete contracts and those that are highly relational. Instead of a spectrum of types of contract, it seems more helpful to use the metaphor of levels or dimensions. Every contract must be examined on at least two levels: there is the discrete contract, a construct that is created by agreement and seeks to define, however vaguely, the reciprocal undertakings of the parties; but there is also another level, in which the discrete contract is embedded, a level in which all the norms that Macneil called common contractual norms operate.

b. Economic rationality

This second type of rationality that governs contractual behaviour involves a cost/benefit calculus of both short-term and long-term economic interest. This economic or material rationality both determines the decision to enter a contract and how the contract is performed. Examples of such behaviour during performance of the contract might include the sacrifice of short-term economic interest for long-term benefits such as the continuance of an established trading network. The supermarket is anxious that the consumer should return every week to purchase groceries in order to keep its market share. The component manufacturer's business plan relies heavily on repeat orders from its range of business customers, especially when they are few in number. In the construction trade, despite the competitive tendering systems in place, it is evident that work is given routinely to a select group of preferred suppliers (Eccles, 1981). In this context, where contracts are made in the course of an indefinite number of repeat transactions, economically rational behaviour is likely to ignore the costs and benefits of any particular transaction and to focus instead on the long-term business relationship. Parties predict each other's behaviour by reference to a similar calculation of economic interest.

Macneil suggests that this situation of long-term economic interest in conflict with short-term utility is a feature of relational contracts (Macneil, 1986, pp. 578–9), but in my view this feature exists in all transactions. In the example of buying goods from a corner shop, the shopkeeper has a long-term interest in repeat purchases and the purchaser may value the convenience of a local shop and have an interest in supporting its business. Indeed, the dissonance between short-term interest and long-term interest is likely to be less pronounced in a long-term contract that is more likely to be classified as relational. Macneil is on firmer ground when he points out that in relational contracts co-operation can increase the size of the pie to be divided between the parties, unlike in more discrete contracts where there is typically a zero sum game. These co-operative sorts of contracts are likely to be long-term, where the complexity of the task is likely to defeat precise planning so there will have to be flexibility and performance governance mechanisms. The contract of employment normally fits into this model of a co-operative contract that increases the wealth of both parties. In the case of contracts of employment, like networks of businesses, it is more accurate to say, following Gunther Teubner, that they thrive on an unresolved tension in the economic logics of co-operation and competition (Teubner, 2011).

c. Relational rationality

This third framework of rational action and communication in the context of contracts concerns the preservation of business relations by means of enhancing trust and reputation for trustworthiness. The choice of contractual partner is likely to be strongly influenced by a belief that the other party is trustworthy, reliable, likely to play it straight with his or her cards on the table. Actions will be understood within this framework as either demonstrations of trustworthiness, or the opposite, a sign of betrayal. Parties predict each other's behaviour by reference to the assumed value that they will place on being trustworthy – within the family this will be high and for distant businesses with no known reputation it will be assumed to be low. This context is nicely revealed in the Beale and Dugdale study (Beale and Dugdale, 1975), where they report that reliance on the small print of a contract will be regarded in the context of a long-term repeat business relationship as bad faith. This framework of relational rationality also affects the handling of disputes, where behaviour may be guided by a concern to preserve the relational qualities, or, if things have gone badly wrong, a desire to punish the act of betrayal by vindictive action.

d. Integrated multilevel analysis

These observations regarding the multidimensional character of normative frameworks that guide contractual behaviour lead to the view that a thorough-going sociological approach towards understanding contracts should employ this triple-level analysis. Parties to contracts conduct themselves simultaneously with an eye to their formal and implied commitments, their long-term economic interest and their concern to appear trustworthy. Each of these three levels constitutes a type of rational or logical behaviour enclosed by a particular framework of reasoning and communication. An individual acts in what seems to be a rational or logical way according to the norms and aims of that particular framework. This rational or self-interested action cannot be reduced to material or economic interest, for that would be to prioritize one framework to the exclusion of the others. The claim is that this multidimensional schema enables us to make sense of contractual behaviour more efficiently and satisfactorily than Macneil's approach. This advantage is achieved in part by its greater simplicity. But its most important insight is that it stresses that all three dimensions of contractual rationality function simultaneously in relation to every contract, and that these rationalities compete and may point in opposite directions. This insight provides a key to unlocking what was called in the introduction the puzzle of the dynamic quality of contractual behaviour and the puzzle of the method of sociological jurisprudence or how to derive a legal 'ought' from a sociological 'is'.

The multilevel schema enables us to map and understand what is happening in examples of contractual behaviour that is dynamic and appears to switch rapidly and unpredictably between what Macneil would describe as relational and discrete contract norms. When behaviour switches in that way, what is happening is that the parties are shifting between the different frameworks. The three levels can and often do point in opposite directions. They answer the question of the party to a contract of 'What should I do?' in different and contradictory ways. A party to the contract may decide to prioritize contractual rationality by insisting on the terms of the contract, or play the long game of economic self-interest in being co-operative and accommodating, or may decide that the conduct of the other party has been so untrustworthy that they will take vindictive action, perhaps cancelling the contract even if they take an unnecessary loss and become themselves in breach of contract.

The multilevel frameworks of rational action also permit us to understand better the task confronting sociological jurisprudence. Remember that the endeavour of sociological jurisprudence is to try to support better the functions of legal institutions such as contracts by matching legal norms in appropriate ways to social norms of behaviour. The problem identified earlier with the agenda of sociological jurisprudence is to determine when the law should recontextualize its legal reasoning about a dispute with a view to matching the legal norms more closely to the informal norms. That problem can now be restated in the following terms. In relation to contracts, the question is: when should the law limit its contextual framework to the level of contractual rationality, which is the characteristic approach of what is called classical contract law, and when should the law acknowledge the presence and significance of the other frameworks of economic rationality and relational rationality (remembering that they are always present in every transaction)?

The answer proposed to that question of recontextualization is that the law should always take account of all three frameworks of the multilevel analysis. The reason for insisting on the inclusion of all three frameworks is a claim that contracts must always function and succeed within the presence of all three frameworks, for, if one is missing, the transaction will not be made, or if made, function unsatisfactorily. What binds the parties to a transaction is a combination of an express agreement or promise, a perception of material benefit both in the short and the long term, and a view that the contractual partner is trustworthy enough to deal with. The triple frameworks of rational action are always in play, though one or other may be prioritized at a particular time by the parties themselves.

In view of that contention about the need for an approach that integrates the triple dimensions of analysis, how should a court decide a contractual dispute? How can a court always take into account all three frameworks that guide contractual behaviour? The task is certainly difficult, but the key is to preserve a harmonious balance between the three frameworks or levels of rational action. In order to promote the successful functioning of contracts, what the law should do is to discourage or prohibit behaviour that is guided by one framework to the exclusion of the others. For instance, behaviour that is exclusively within the framework of contractual rationality, so that there is an insistence on the precise terms of the contract and its small print, should be discouraged where such behaviour runs contrary to considerations of short and long-term economic interest and is also perceived as a betrayal of trust. Discouragement of such behaviour can be achieved technically by many devices, such as interpretation of contracts, implied terms and adjustments to the measure of compensatory damages. For instance, an implied term based upon business necessity or rationality will serve to reinsert economic rationality into the norms governing the dispute. Similarly, an implied term involving a standard of good faith or its equivalent may discourage conduct that, whilst consistent with the express terms of the contract and economic self-interest, represents a betrayal of the contractual relationship owing to its opportunistic or deceitful nature. In the case of *Williams v Roffey Bros and Nicholls (Contractors) Ltd* [1991] 1 QB 1, for instance, by the time the issue resulted in litigation, the main contractor was trying to insist on the terms of the original contract and was claiming that any variation to raise the price had been invalid on the ground of lack of consideration. The Court of Appeal correctly viewed this exclusive reliance on contractual rationality as inappropriate and by finding consideration through 'practical benefit' reinserted long-term economic interest into the evaluation of the dispute. The court also viewed the reneging on the promise of an additional payment as a violation of the relational dimension of the contract, Russell LJ observing, for instance, that: 'It would certainly be unconscionable if this were to be their legal entitlement.'

3. Three-dimensional analysis applied to the contract of employment

> [C]onsider an employee of a small business who has been treated very decently by his employer for thirty years. He quite

naturally comes to expect decent treatment throughout the relation including through retirement. Moreover, he relies on that expectation; and if the expectation is not realized, the employer may very well have derived benefits from the reliance by the employee that, in terms of the relational as it is existed, are unjustified. We can, and do, infer promises in such situations, but they are far from the defined promises of discrete transactions. (Macneil, 1978, p. 898)

This is an example repeated several times by Macneil to illustrate the implications of relational contracts and how the law should respond to their implicit obligations. Although the example may now look out of date in an era when employers have been withdrawing occupational pension schemes, it illustrates well the sociological jurisprudence approach approved by Macneil. By a combination of economic reliance and an expectation of decent treatment, Macneil regards it as appropriate to imply a promise to pay a pension even though there is no explicit contractual commitment. But the question we need to ask is: what is the justification for implying such a substantial promise in this case based upon the flimsy grounds of the employee's expectation of decent treatment and the possibility that the employer had benefited economically from the greater motivation of the employee generated by that expectation? This final section considers the example of the contract of employment in greater depth with a view to demonstrating how the multilevel analysis of contractual rationality described above can elucidate an answer to that question. First, however, it is necessary to explain how the three frameworks of contractual behaviour map onto a typical contract of employment.

a. Three frameworks of contractual behaviour in the context of employment

i) Contractual rationality

With respect to contractual rationality, the principal framework is provided by the terms of the contract of employment. These terms include the implied terms designed to fill in gaps that are based upon the presumed intentions of the parties. In addition, however, the contract of employment is likely to be supplemented by other express rules. In the context of employment, an important market convention or custom concerns whether or not a collective agreement reached between an employer and a representative trade union applies to a particular contract of employment. A contract of employment may be created informally by an oral offer of work but usually these days there is a written contract that sets out the principal terms such as a job description, wages and hours or work. Most employers supplement this agreement with other rules such as staff handbooks or works rules. The rule-book is likely to put flesh on the bare bones of the contract, specifying, for instance, fringe benefits and how adjustments to hours and wages will be made. The rule-book will also include additional material not mentioned in the contract, such as a disciplinary procedure, general responsibilities and explanations of how the organization is supposed to work, lines of management responsibility and how to get things done. If there is a collective agreement, this will provide an additional body of substantive rules and procedures to be followed. Other formal meetings between representatives of the employer and the workforce, such as works councils, may further add to the rules governing the workplace. Beyond these formal documents there will be 'custom and practice', which contains the implied agreements on how jobs should be done and how a particular job role is defined. The employee will discover in the workplace, therefore, a plethora of rules, some explicitly incorporated into the contract of employment as terms, others by implication on the ground of custom and others, though not legally binding in themselves, having indirect legal force because of the implied obligation of employees to obey the lawful instructions of employers (Arthurs, 1985).

ii) Economic rationality

In the context of the contract of employment, long-term material interest usually plays a pivotal role in determining the behaviour of the parties. In most instances, it is in the long-term interest of both employer and employee to continue the relationship because of the mutual gains arising from the division of labour and co-operation. Even in the absence of laws protecting employees from dismissal, the costs to the employer of recruiting and training new staff and the losses caused to employees by periods of unemployment discourage labour turnover. It is usually cheaper for an employer to try to improve the performance of the existing staff by careful monitoring of performance and training. For the employee, it usually makes long-term economic sense to stay in a job because the gradual acquisition of skills and experience from working for a particular employer will lead to higher wages than those available on the open labour market. In the terminology of new institutional economics, this investment in skills in many jobs is a form of sunk investment that binds the employee to a long-term contractual relationship.

Given these benefits that may accrue to either party to employment through long-term co-operation, there is likely to be a tension between the express contractual commitments and the expectations of the parties based on economic rationality. For instance, the contract of employment is likely to include terms that permit its termination following a short period of notice for any reason or no reason at all. In effect, the terms of the contract that describe a temporary arrangement that may be quickly concluded at any time contradict the economic interests of both parties in a long-term arrangement.

From the perspective of the employer, economic rationality requires that employees are motivated to work hard, to be committed to the aims of the business and to use their discretion in the performance of the work to improve its profitability and effectiveness. The employer has many techniques available to encourage 'organizational commitment behaviour'. As well as promises of material rewards through promotion ladders and performance-related pay, the employer can try to improve identification of the employees with the aims of the business through giving employees voice within the organization, by adopting transparent and fair managerial practices and treating each person with dignity and respect, as, for example, by adopting family-friendly personnel practices. Human resources management is mostly about identifying and using techniques to improve organizational commitment behaviour.

iii) Relational rationality

It is also possible to discern beyond any express or implied agreement a broader set of diffuse expectations on the part of employees that will be encouraged and reinforced by employers. These diffuse expectations or beliefs may include such items as the view that if an individual employee works hard and shows real commitment to the business beyond any formal requirements of the contract, this conduct will be recognized and rewarded by the employer somehow – perhaps by a wage rise or promotion, or perhaps in some less material way such as winning the prize for 'manager of the year' or 'law teacher of the year'. In organizational theory, these diffuse expectations of reciprocity have been labelled as 'the psychological contract' (Rousseau, 1989; Marks, 2001; Stone, 2001). This psychological contract refers to a belief on the part of the employer or employee regarding expectations of reciprocal behaviour. From the employee's point of view, such a psychological contract might state something like: 'If I work hard and do my job well, I will be able to keep my job.' This psychological contract is likely to be reinforced by experience and patterns of behaviour in the sense that, over a period of time, indeed it is true that those employees who work hard and do their jobs well keep their jobs, whereas others who fail to match up to these requirements are dismissed or are not promoted. The psychological contract is also likely to be reinforced by general statements from the employer, such as a comment from the manager on hiring to the effect that 'If you work hard, you will have a good job here.' Employers have a considerable interest in reinforcing the psychological contract because it is likely to increase the commitment of the workers to the organization, thereby extracting from the employee what is described as performance 'beyond contract' to the long-term economic benefit of the employer.

It is important to appreciate that the psychological contract in this sense is not a contract in any recognizable legal sense. In organizational theory, the psychological contract is distinguished both from the explicit contract and the implied contract (Roehling, 2004). The explicit contract denotes the terms of the contract and the rules mentioned above. The implied contract concerns matters such as implied terms, including the custom and practice of the workplace. The psychological contract is regarded as a matter of belief, not a reciprocal undertaking. Evidence for its existence is found in a contrast in reactions from employees to some kind of adverse action by the employer: a breach of the explicit or implied contract is regarded as a breach of an undertaking or understanding, whereas breach of the psychological contract is seen as a betrayal of trust (Morrison and Robinson, 1997).

b. Application of the multilevel analysis to employment

We can now reconsider the example given by Macneil concerning the informal expectation of a pension on the retirement of an employee with a view to applying the sociological method. The express and the implied terms of the contract are part of the autonomous contract which the parties have created. The parties can orient themselves to those terms on the level of contractual rationality, as interpreted according to the context of all the workplace rules. In this instance the employer can use contractual rationality to deny the existence of any express or implied terms that support a claim for a pension. On the second level, there is the economic calculus of long-term interest, which derives from investments in the relationship, such as training, and the benefits to be achieved through co-operation, flexibility and adaptation. To achieve those economic benefits, it will often be necessary for both parties to perform in ways not envisaged by the contract at all, by the employee working longer hours, taking on new responsibilities, or the employer reorganizing the system of production. In Macneil's example, it seems likely that the employee has performed with a high level of commitment to the aims of the business. If so, it is in the long-term economic interest of the employer to encourage such behaviour in various ways through rewards such as pay increases and promotions. This economic rationality supports some kind of claim on the part of the employee for recompense, though not necessarily the granting of a pension. On the third level concerning relational behaviour and trust, we encounter what has been called the psychological contract, where the issue is not so much whether the employer has conformed to the contract or acted in an economically rational way, but whether the employer has appeared trustworthy or has betrayed the employee. We would need to consider whether the employer had played fairly or made misleading statements and promises or stood by knowing that the employee was relying on financial support after his retirement. Although these enquiries require further information in order to complete the analysis, this would be the way to determine whether or not a court should permit the employer to insist upon contractual rationality. We can apply this approach to a number of other examples drawn from UK law.

i) Working to rule

On the multilevel theory of contractual behaviour, these three frameworks of contractual behaviour will exist in tension and frequently conflict. For instance, if the employees resolve to work to rule – in other words comply exactly with the contract and rule-book but do no more – this behaviour will almost certainly conflict with the long-term rational economic interests of the employer and perhaps both parties. A work-to-rule involves prioritizing contractual rationality and excluding the other two levels.

English courts struggle with an analysis of the legal position. The employer wants to insist that a work-to-rule is a breach of contract (and therefore a strike to which special rules apply), because no doubt, as intended, the work-to-rule is disruptive to the employer's business. Yet, how can performance in accordance with the terms of the contract amount to a breach of contract? The solution is found in an implied obligation imposed on the employee to perform the contract in good faith. The implied term is described as 'a duty to serve the employer faithfully within the requirements of the contract'.[2] But what amounts to such good faith behaviour if not performance of the contract according to its letter?

The multilevel theory of contractual behaviour suggests that the implied term of good faith has in this context a precise meaning. It requires the employee to behave in the long-term economically rational way that is envisaged in any contract of employment. The employee must not put short-term interest ahead of long-term interest by withdrawing co-operation. Good faith does not necessarily require the employee to be honest or reasonable, but insists that the long-term economic interests of both parties are served best by co-operation and flexibility that go beyond the explicit and implied rules of the contract. The implied term of good faith also

---

2 Buckley LJ, *Secretary of State for Employment v ASLEF (No 2)* [1972] ICR 19 (CA).

connects to the psychological contract. In a case concerning the 'withdrawal of goodwill', the employee was held to be in breach of contract even though to outward appearances she was performing her job as normal.[3] The court found that her position as a manager meant that her employer was entitled to trust her to exercise her discretion in the interests of the employer and not with a view to disrupting the business. The implied obligation may not be as strong as a duty to co-operate, but it does involve a duty not to damage the economic interests of the employer or to betray the employer's trust. Applying the method of sociological jurisprudence, it seems correct for the courts to discourage such behaviour by the introduction of an implied term, because such behaviour renders the contract of employment dysfunctional. In other words, the court appropriately recontextualizes the contract by restoring the economic and relational dimensions to the transaction and enforcing an appropriately tailored legal obligation against the employee.

ii) Bankers' bonuses

A matching example concerns an employer's insistence on the letter of the contract. This concerns terms in contracts that provide for discretionary bonus payments and deferred stock options. In these cases, the employee claims a valuable benefit such as a £1-million bonus. The employer objects that the bonus was expressly stated in the contract to be purely discretionary, within the exclusive control of management. If that view of the contract is correct, the employer can deny the bonus to an employee by, for instance, dismissing her shortly before the bonuses are due to be paid.

The courts have sometimes permitted employees to win such claims on the ground that the discretion was not wholly unconstrained and that it should be used for a rational purpose in the light of the general reason for employers awarding bonuses as part of a remuneration package.[4] By not granting a bonus or some other discretionary reward, the employer may be acting capriciously, arbitrarily, or irrationally in breach of an implied term that governs the exercise of the discretions.[5] The problem with that legal reasoning is that, as well as giving short shrift to the express terms of the contract which emphasize the discretionary nature of the bonus (contractual rationality), the court has to explain why it is irrational for the employer to refuse to award a bonus and save itself £1 million when it has already dismissed the employee.

---

3 *Ticehurst v British Telecommunications* [1992] ICR 383 (CA).
4 *Horkulak v Cantor Fitzgerald International* [2004] EWCA Civ 1287, [2005] ICR 402 (CA).
5 *Mallone v BPB Industries plc* [2002] EWCA Civ 126, [2002] IRLR 452 (CA).

From the perspective of the triple frameworks of contractual behaviour, however, it is evident that the employer's stance is privileging contractual rationality over long-term economic interest and the relational dimension. Long-term economic interest seems to point towards the granting of a bonus when performance has matched expectation, because there is a risk that other employees will quit if they doubt the credibility of the promise to award bonuses for good performance. Furthermore, within the framework of relational behaviour, it seems clear that the denial of a bonus is a significant betrayal of the psychological contract under which city traders believe, with much encouragement from employing banks, that they will receive vast fortunes if they give total commitment to the job. In these cases, the courts use the device of an implied term to reinforce long-term economic interest and the psychological contract. The legal reasoning can be criticized for its pretence that the court is enforcing the autonomous agreement or requiring the employer to behave in a short-term economically rational way, though no doubt these fictions are necessary to fit the decision within established legal doctrine.

iii) Unilateral pay cut

In order to obtain the full picture of the employment relationship, it is necessary to go beyond the law of contract to include statutory rights. These rights provide mandatory entitlements for employees such as protection against unfair dismissal and against discrimination on the ground of various protected characteristics such as sex and race. In the context of the UK law, the statutory protection against unfair dismissal is particularly interesting in throwing light on contractual behaviour in the contract of employment.

Consider, for instance, the case where an employer's business is doing badly during the recession, and the employer decides that the entire workforce should submit to a 10 per cent wage cut. Whilst most workers reluctantly accept the diminution in wages, one employee insists on his contractual entitlement, perhaps not only as a matter of principle but also for fear of not being able to keep up existing financial commitments. The employer dismisses the employee for refusal to accept the pay cut. Is this an unfair dismissal? On a traditional contractual analysis, the employer is committing a repudiatory breach of contract by imposing a wage cut and the employee is entitled to refuse to accept the breach of contract and to insist on the preservation of the original bargain.[6] Under the law of unfair dismissal, however, such a dismissal is almost certainly fair: the employee's

---

6   *Rigby v Ferodo Ltd* [1988] ICR 29 (HL).

refusal to accept the pay cut that has been imposed for a legitimate management purpose is unreasonable behaviour and the employer can reasonably dismiss the employee for that reason.[7]

Here again there is a clash between the autonomous contractual rationality, which upholds the employee's claim for his or her regular wages, and the long-term economic interest of the parties, which is supported by the law of unfair dismissal. Whereas the common law of contract supports the contractual rationality of insisting upon the contractual term governing wages, the law of unfair dismissal recontextualizes the transaction by insisting that the long-term interest of the parties in a successful relationship must govern their rights and obligations. The psychological contract is also relevant in such a case. If the employer had insisted that a particular employee should accept a wage cut, while all his co-workers could keep their existing pay, it seems likely that the dismissal would be found to be unfair on the ground of inequitable treatment. Even under the common law, that victimization of one employee is likely to be regarded as a breach of contract in the form of the implied term of mutual trust and confidence.[8]

iv) Casual workers and umbrella contracts

For casual workers, there is probably a document or letter that describes the job, the pay and makes other arrangements such as training. The amount of work available is indeterminate, however, so the employer states that the worker will be employed 'as required' or words to that effect. The ensuing practice will be that the casual worker will be summoned to work whenever there is a job to be done, which may turn out to be most days. In many of these cases, employers use a pool of trained workers from which they select employees for a particular job. Although it is not a necessary feature of the arrangement, it is also usually understood that employees may refuse to take on a particular job at their choice. The legal question that often arises in connection with casual work is whether the parties entered into a long-term contract of employment (an umbrella contract) or merely established a non-binding framework agreement that would supply the terms applicable to any short-term hiring on a particular occasion. It is said that, in the absence of a promise by the employer to offer work and a promise by the employee to perform work if requested, there is no 'mutuality of obligation' or consideration, so there can be no long-term contract of employment (or any long-term contract at all). As a form of 'requirements contract', it is merely a framework agreement, which fixes

---

7 *Hollister v National Farmers' Union* [1979] ICR 542 (CA); *Richmond Precision Engineering Ltd v Pearce* [1985] IRLR 179 (EAT).
8 *Transco plc v O'Brien* [2002] EWCA Civ 379, [2002] ICR 721 (CA).

the terms of any subsequent engagement, but is not a contract to perform work in return for pay itself.

If a court confines its examination of this issue to the documents that the parties have signed, the circumspect offer of work 'as required' is likely to force the conclusion that there was no long-term contract of employment. If attention is broadened to the economic interests of the parties on the second level, the quality of the long-term commitment becomes more evident. It is clear that the employer needs to be able to draw on a pool of workers and will need to attract trained workers to that pool by regular offers of work. Similarly, the workers themselves are unlikely to have any other source of income, so they will normally accept any work offered. Moreover, they may discover that if they refuse work too frequently they will not be called on again, which places some pressure on them only to refuse work occasionally. For these reasons of long-term economic interest, employees are likely to be working most weeks of the year for a significant number of hours.

Beyond these economic interests, there may be further psychological dimensions to the arrangement. Employees may have an expectation, for instance, that there will be a fair distribution of work among the pool of casual workers. Employers may have an expectation that the workers, even when not performing work, will be loyal to the company by, for instance, not disparaging its product. Employers may have the further expectation that employees will not reject offers of work without a good reason, such as child care commitments or illness.

A particular example of this issue of an umbrella contract of employment was considered by the House of Lords in *Carmichael v National Power plc* [1999] ICR 1226, which concerned guides for groups of tourists around a nuclear power plant. Lord Irvine (speaking for the whole House) treated the issue of the existence of an umbrella contract as a question about the terms of the contractual arrangement and examined the written terms of the agreement, as supplemented by an oral discussion between the parties. He concluded that there was no permanent contract of employment, because both parties had objectively agreed and understood their agreement to include no mutuality of obligation. He observed, however:

> The parties incurred no obligations to provide or accept work but at best assumed moral obligations of loyalty in a context where both recognised that the best interests of each lay in being accommodating to the other.[9]

---

9   [1999] ICR 1229E.

In this statement, there is recognition of the long-term economic interest that in practice bound the parties together, but Lord Irvine insists that this creates merely a moral obligation, not a legal one. The reference to an obligation of loyalty reflects the finding of the tribunal that the guides felt obligated to the manager and could not let him down by not being available to take a tour. Lord Irvine makes no attempt to integrate the three levels of contractual behaviour, but relies solely on the contractual framework.

In contrast, the Court of Appeal in *Carmichael* had found the existence of a long-term umbrella contract. Ward LJ held that the agreement reached included an implied obligation on the company to provide a reasonable share of work for each guide whenever the company had work available and on the guides to take a reasonable amount of work.[10] Chadwick LJ formulated the implied term slightly differently: a promise by the guides to provide the service on being given reasonable notice and a promise by the employer that any work available would be offered first to the trained guides before anyone else.[11] Either version of this implied term could be justified on the ground of business efficacy since it corresponded to the long-term economic interest of both parties and deviation from it would probably provoke termination of the arrangement. Freedland supports this kind of approach as consonant with a relational approach to the contract of employment (Freedland, 2003, p. 104). From a systems theory perspective, the significant difference between these judgments is that the House of Lords prioritizes the contractual rationality of the parties, whereas the Court of Appeal approaches the issue of the existence of an umbrella contract by reference to the long-term economic interests of both parties. There also seems to be an element of a psychological contract or trust dimension in the suggested implied terms, which involve fair treatment through a fair distribution of work and the idea that the guides would not unreasonably refuse work because of a feeling of personal loyalty towards the manager. The Court of Appeal's judgment embraces a three-dimensional analysis, whereas the House of Lords fails to integrate either the economic or psychological relational dimensions of the contract of employment.

Conclusion

A three-dimensional analysis argues that what Freedland detects as a structural uncertainty in the contract of employment is in fact a clash between different rationalities that are applicable to every type of contract. When making and performing contracts, the proton of contractual rationality

---

10 [1998] ICR 1167, 1187.
11 [1998] ICR 1194, 1196

binds with the neutron of economic rationality, with the electron of the relational dimension or psychological contract forming an indistinct boundary to the contractual context. When the law is required to adjudicate contractual disputes, it is a mistake to privilege one of those rationalities in legal reasoning, whether it may be the classical law's emphasis on contractual rationality, the law-and-economics school's emphasis on economic rationality, or the relational-contract-law school's reinsertion of the relational dimension. The best legal analysis always seeks to integrate all three dimensions and resists the prioritization of one over the others. The examples chosen in the field of the contract of employment demonstrate that more often than not the courts intuitively reach for an integrated multidimensional solution. When they fail to do so, as in *Carmichael* in the House of Lords, the multidimensional analysis explains where the court went wrong and how the law may be repaired.

References

Arthurs, H (1985) 'Understanding Labour Law: The Debate over "Industrial Pluralism"' *Current Legal Problems* 83

Beale, H and T Dugdale (1975) 'Contracts between Businessmen: Planning and the Use of Contractual Remedies' 2 *British Journal of Law and Society* 45

Bird, R C (2005) 'Employment as a Relational Contract' 8 *University of Pennsylvania Journal of Labor and Employment Law* 148

Blau, P M (1964) *Exchange and Power in Social Life* (New York: Wiley)

Boyle, M (2007) 'The Relational Principle of Trust and Confidence' 27(4) *Oxford Journal of Legal Studies* 633

Brodie, D (2011) 'How Relational Is the Employment Contract?' 40 *Industrial Law Journal* 232

Campbell, D (ed.) (2001) *The Relational Theory of Contract: Selected Works of Ian Macneil* (London: Sweet & Maxwell)

Campbell, D and H Collins (2003) 'Discovering the Implicit Dimensions of Contracts' in Campbell et al. (2003), pp. 25–50

Campbell, D and D Harris (1993) 'Flexibility in Long-Term Contractual Relationships: The Role of Co-Operation' 20 *Journal of Law and Society* 166

Campbell, D, H Collins and J Wightman (eds) (2003) *Implicit Dimensions of Contract: Discrete, Relational and Network Contracts* (Oxford: Hart Publishing)

Collins, H (1999) *Regulating Contracts* (Oxford: Oxford University Press)

Collins, H (2003a) 'Introduction: The Research Agenda of Implicit Dimensions of Contracts' in Campbell et al. (2003), pp. 1–24

Daintith, T (1986) 'The Design and Performance of Long-term Contracts' in T Daintith and G Teubner (eds,) *Contract and Organisation* (Berlin: Walter de Gruyter), p. 164

Eccles, R (1981) 'The Quasifirm in the Construction Industry' 2 *Journal of Economic Behaviour and Organisation* 335

Eisenberg, M A (1995) 'Relational Contracts' in J Beatson and D Friedmann (eds), *Good Faith and Fault in Contract Law* (Oxford: Clarendon Press)

Fox, A (1974) *Beyond Contract: Work, Power and Trust Relations* (London: Faber)

Freedland, M R (2003) *The Personal Contract of Employment* (Oxford: Oxford University Press)

Gudel, P J (1998) 'Relational Contract Theory and the Concept of Exchange' 46 *Buffalo Law Review* 763

Guest, D E (2004) 'The Psychology of the Employment Relationship: An Analysis Based on the Psychological Contract' 53 *Applied Psychology: An International Review* 541

Macaulay, S (1963) 'Non-Contractual Relations in Business' 28 *American Sociological Review* 45

Macneil, I R (1978) 'Contracts: Adjustment of Longterm Economic Relations Under Classical, Neoclassical and Relational Contract Law' 72 *Northwestern University Law Review* 854–905

Macneil, I R (1980) *The New Social Contract* (New Haven CT and London: Yale University Press)

Macneil, I R (1985) 'Relational Contract: What We Do and Do Not Know' *Wisconsin Law Review* 483–525

Macneil, I R (1986) 'Exchange Revisited: Individual Utility and Social Solidarity' 96 *Ethics* 567–93

Marks, A (2001) 'Developing a Multiple Foci Conceptualization of the Psychological Contract' 23 *Employee Relations* 454

Morrison, E W and S Robinson (1997) 'When Employees Feel Betrayed: A Model of How Psychological Contract Violation Develops' 22 *Academy of Management Review* 226

Roehling, M V (2004) 'Legal Theory: Contemporary Contract Law Perspectives and Insights for Employment Relationship Theory' in J A-M Coyle-Shapiro et al. (eds), *The Employment Relationship: Examining Psychological and Contextual Perspectives* (Oxford: Oxford University Press), p. 65

Rousseau, D M (1989) 'Psychological and Implied Contracts in Organizations' 2 *Employee Responsibility and Rights Journal* 121

Rousseau, D M (1995) *Psychological Contracts in Organizations: Understanding Written and Unwritten Agreements* (Thousand Oaks CA: Sage)

Smith, C A, D W Organ and J P Near (1983) 'Organisational Citizenship Behaviour: Its Nature and Antecedents' 68 *Journal of Applied Psychology* 653

Speidel, R E (2000) 'The Characteristics and Challenges of Relational Contracts' 94(3) *Northwestern University Law Review* 823

Stone, K V W (2001) 'The New Psychological Contract: Implications of the Changing Workplace for Labor and Employment Law' 48 *UCLA Law Review* 519

Teubner, G (1993) *Law as an Autopoietic System* (Oxford: Blackwell Publishing)

Teubner, G (2011) *Networks as Connected Contracts*, H Collins (ed.) (Oxford: Hart Publishing)

5
Neglected Insights into Agreed Remedies
Roger Halson

Introduction

While I was planning the paper upon which this chapter is based, I was also considering another question, whether to buy any wine from the 2009 Bordeaux harvest which had been heralded as the vintage of the century – this despite the fact that Bordeaux seems to celebrate 'the vintage of the century' at least once every ten years. It is said that it is very difficult to judge the quality of a wine early in its life when only cask samples of the wine are available prior to bottling, maturation and review by wine critics, the 'doyen' of whom (according to Jacques Chirac), Robert Parker, is by training a lawyer. Tasting after bottling is slightly more reliable, though I understand that it takes a very expert palate to reach behind the overpowering tannins that linger after recent disgorgement from oak barrels to assess accurately a wine's likely eventual quality.

Perhaps it is the same with law review articles: their standing compared to others can accurately be judged only at some considerable time after their publication. If so, this is perhaps the perfect time to look back upon an article by Ian Macneil, 'The Power of Contract and Agreed Remedies' (hereafter *Power of Contract*), that appeared in the *Cornell Law Quarterly* in 1962. Presumably, the article was completed in 1961, when Ian may have read in the papers that the Bordelais were extolling the virtues of that year's harvest as, yes, the vintage of the century despite its subsequent demotion to '[o]ne of the legendary vintages of the century' (Parker, 2003, p. 98). My use of the wine metaphor is itself intended to be a tribute to Ian Macneil, whose writings are often characterized and enriched by the use of elegant and effective simile and metaphor. My own favourite is that which he used in *Whither Contracts?* to describe the practice of a lawyer dealing with a contractual conflict when all possibilities of a co-operative solution had been exhausted; he described it as 'not unlike ... [that of] a scientist who has had to dry out a jellyfish before his instruments of examination can be used on it' (Macneil, 1969). However, I will now abandon the wine metaphor until the conclusion of this chapter.

The subject matter of *Power of Contract* is the law relating to agreed remedies. In particular, Macneil focuses upon liquidated damages and penalties and he cautions against reasoning from decisions involving the forfeiture of payments and deposits, a caution which I will follow in this chapter. This area of law has over the years confounded many respected writers on contract law, being described as: 'anomalous' (Goetz and Scott, 1977, n. 12; and Coopersmith, 1990, p. 267); 'puzzling' (R Posner, 1979, p. 290; and E Posner, 2003, p. 860); 'controversial' and 'contradictory' (Coopersmith, 1990, p. 267); 'paradoxical' (Hillman, 2000, p. 718); and 'curious' (Edlin and Schwartz, 2003, p. 34). After a few prefatory remarks, my aim in this chapter is to see to what extent *Power of Contract* provides a forgotten key to solving this puzzle.

In a number of ways that will be readily understood by relationalists, empirical studies of contracting behaviour (helpfully reviewed in Wightman, 1996, ch. 4; and Hillman, 1997, ch. 7) reveal that, when parties negotiate a contract, their focus is positive not negative. In classic studies in the US and the UK respectively, Stewart Macaulay (1963) and Hugh Beale and Tony Dugdale (1975) noted that parties discuss, and through their contractual documents plan, usually for performance rather than breach. This is reflected in the standard diet fed to law students, remedies very often feature near the end of traditionally arranged expositions of the subject (Fuller and Perdue, 1936; Macneil, 1969; and Halson, 2005), its late appearance effectively its abandonment by the student, or indeed the lecturer. Notwithstanding the implicit views of contractors and traditional contract scholars, the penalty rules are of huge economic and societal significance. I will illustrate this by reference to recent litigation in the UK concerning the use of so-called 'unauthorized overdrafts' in *Office of Fair Trading v Abbey National plc* [2009] UKSC 6, [2009] 3 WLR 1215 (the *Abbey* case). This point about the importance of the common law penalty jurisdiction is not jurisdiction specific. A recent survey in the US (Klass, 2007, p. 35) reported that '[t]he mandatory rules against penalties ... appear as vibrant today as ever'.

Before examining the *Abbey* case, it is helpful to establish some consistent terminology, something noticeably lacking in many 'non-Macneilian discussions' of this area of law. The so-called penalty jurisdiction incontrovertibly extends beyond terms requiring the payment of a sum of money to include other detriments such as the retransfer of shares at undervalue (*Jobson v Johnson* [1989] 1 All ER 621) or the loss of an opportunity to obtain a refund (*Euro London Appointments Ltd v Classens International Ltd* [2006] 2

Lloyd's Rep). Indeed, recently and controversially, in *Andrews v Australia and New Zealand Banking Group Ltd* [2012] HCA 30, the Australian High Court has, by reference to analogous equitable principles, outflanked the traditional limitation to clauses requiring the performance of an obligation, usually the payment of a sum of money, upon the payor's breach of a contractual obligation owed to the payee, for which *Export Credits Guarantee Department v Universal Oil Products Co* [1983] 1 WLR 399 is usually cited as authority. It is, however, easier to focus upon the paradigm case in order to establish a consistent and neutral terminology. A clause in a contract which provides for a sum of money to be paid upon the payor's breach of that contract will be described by the non-predictive term, 'a stipulated damages clause'. Only when such a clause is unenforceable is it termed a penalty, and only when it is enforceable is it called a liquidated damages clause. In this way we will be able to avoid the semantic trap identified by Macneil: 'the built-in determination of invalidity or validity implied by the words penalty and liquidated damages' (Macneil, 1962, n. 16). Viewed *ex post*, a contractual clause requiring a payment to be made upon the payor's breach of contract will be either an unenforceable penalty or a valid liquidated damages clause.

A contrary view that 'a dichotomy between a genuine pre-estimate of damages and a penalty does not cover all the possibilities' was expressed recently in *Lordsdale Finance plc v Bank of Zambia* [1996] QB 752 by Colman J, and later supported in the Court of Appeal by Arden LJ in *Murray v Leisureplay plc* [2005] EWCA Civ 963 at [15]. However, in *Murray*, Arden LJ's approach was dismissed by Buxton LJ (at [111]), with whom Clarke LJ agreed, who emphasized that it was 'important to note that the two alternatives, a deterrent penalty; or a genuine pre-estimate of loss; are indeed alternatives, with no middle ground between them'. The simpler and more certain Macneil schema, preferred by the majority in *Murray*, and the associated terminology, has been followed by other academic writers (Clarkson et al., 1978, n. 1; and Olazabal, 2004, p. 513).

Some idea of the commercial significance of the *Abbey* litigation can be gleaned from a quick look at the 'all star' cast and compendious judgment. At first instance, Andrew Smith J (*Office of Fair Trading v Abbey National plc* [2008] EWHC 875 (Comm)) was assisted by 11 Queen's Counsel and *all* the 'magic circle' firms of solicitors, before producing a judgment that ran to no less than 450 paragraphs examining the standard contractual terms offered to personal customers by all the leading UK banks: Abbey National plc, Barclays, Clydesdale, HBOS, HSBC, Lloyds TSB, Royal Bank of Scotland, and by Nationwide, a mutual building society. The Clydesdale Bank, which had the smallest share of the market, had over 2.4 million personal customers in the UK! In three separate hearings the judge examined whether the standard terms of eight separate financial institutions were penal. In two cases he concluded that none of the terms considered were in fact penal and in the third that only a small number were.[1] Following the inevitable appeal, the Court of Appeal concluded that, though the different types of charges levied for unauthorized overdrafts were 'akin to default charges which are triggered by a breach of contract' [2009] EWCA Civ 116 at [107], the banks had so structured their contract with their customers that these charges could not be struck down as unenforceable penalties at common law.[2]

The reason why this conclusion of Andrew Smith J (see n. 2 above) was not challenged by the Office of Fair Trading (OFT) in the Court of Appeal was because a contractual provision only falls to be reviewed by that common law jurisdiction if it provided for a payment (or equivalent) to be made as a result of the payor's breach of contract. In all the cases before the judge the overdraft was unauthorized in the sense of not having been approved in advance, but the implied 'request' (usually the simple act of 'spending' money beyond the agreed limits) for such an overdraft that was not pre-approved was *not* itself a breach of contract. This is crucial because, despite Lord Denning's elegant exposure in *Bridge v Campbell Discount Co Ltd* [1962] AC 600 of the 'absurd paradox' that a court 'will grant relief to a man who breaks his contract but will penalise the man who exercise[es] a contractual option' (p. 629), the currently prevailing law is that, if there is no breach of contract by the customer, there is no 'trigger' for the penalty jurisdiction.

The contrary position has been enacted elsewhere[3] and was the basis of a first instance decision in Australia (*Integral Home Loans Pty Ltd v Interstar Wholesale Finance Pty Ltd* [2007] NSWSC 406). The New South Wales Court of Appeal overturned this decision (2008) 257 ALR 292), but invited the High Court of Australia to reconsider this area of law. This was done in *Andrews v Australia*, though the High Court ultimately declined to extend the ambit of the penalty jurisdiction at common law, instead granting relief

---

1 See respectively *Office of Fair Trading v Abbey National plc* [2008] EWHC 875 (Comm) 625 at [449], *Office of Fair Trading v Abbey National plc* [2008] EWHC 2325 (Comm) at [131] (inviting further submissions with regard to some terms) and *Office of Fair Trading v Abbey National plc* [2009] EWHC 36 (Comm) at [33].
2 This conclusion of Andrew Smith J, [295]–[324], was not challenged by the OFT in the Court of Appeal, see at [11].
3 More extensive powers of review have been enacted elsewhere, e.g. South African Conventional Penalties Act 1962 (see Hepple (1961) 78 SALJ 445) and the Law Reform Act 1993, s. 5(1) (New Brunswick, Canada) The agreement in *Bridge* would now be subject to the Consumer Credit Act 1974 as amended. In a working paper (Law Commission, 1975), the Law Commission referred to the paradox noted by Lord Denning and at para. 22 came to the 'provisional view ... that the court should have the power to deal with such clauses in the same way whether or not they come into operation by breach'.

by the application of equitable principles. Thus it can be seen that when the *Abbey* case reached the Supreme Court the only issue before the court was the proper interpretation of the Unfair Terms in Consumer Contract Regulations 1999 SI 1999/2083. However, it was the common law power to review contractual terms as penalties that had dictated the form of a significant part of most people's personal banking contracts.

Despite, or perhaps they would say, because of, the cast of hundreds involved in the *Abbey* litigation, no doubt costing millions, the facts are, at a formal, general level, simple to state. Following an investigation, the OFT sought a declaration under the Unfair Terms in Consumer Contract Regulations against a number of leading banks that the standard terms and charges those banks levied for transactions initiated by customers who at the time had insufficient funds in their account to meet the requested payment (so called 'unauthorized overdraft' charges) were void. The 1999 regulations, made under s. 2(2) of the European Communities Act 1972, were transposed into domestic law under Council Directive 93/13/EEC, which renders any 'unfair' contract term not binding on the consumer (Recital 4). The regulations apply only to terms which have not been 'individually negotiated' (reg. 5(1) and reg. 6(2) provides that, when a term is expressed in 'plain intelligible language', the assessment of the fairness of that term 'shall not relate ... to the definition of the main subject matter of the contract, or ... to the adequacy of the price or remuneration'. 'Adequacy' here means 'appropriateness' (*Director General of Fair Trading v First National Bank plc* [2002] 1 AC 481 at [64]). This restriction was central to the Supreme Court's criticism of the decision of the Court of Appeal. In the Supreme Court, the banks succeeded on the ground that the fees levied in respect of unauthorized borrowing should properly be regarded as part of the consideration paid by customers for the package of banking services they were entitled to receive. This meant that, so long as these, though perhaps not all other,[4] charges were expressed in plain intelligible language, the fairness of the terms under which they were raised was excluded by reg. 6(2) from challenge under the regulations. What is perhaps more interesting from a relational perspective is how the importance of the penalty jurisdiction goes almost unnoticed. This is because sophisticated contractors will frequently structure their contractual undertakings in a way that avoids the power to review a contractual clause as a penalty (Halson, 2010,

---

4 There may be payments that are not regarded as constituting either 'price or remuneration' or those that do may still be challenged as unfair on grounds that do not relate to their quantitative appropriateness for the goods or services supplied. See *Office of Fair Trading v Abbey National plc* [2009] UKSC 6, [2009] 3 WLR 1215 (the *Abbey* case) *per* Lord Phillips PSC at [101], and Baroness Hale of Richmond JSC, at [57]–[61] and [101] respectively.

paras 8.129–34). In other words, skilful drafters may be able to ensure that the penalty jurisdiction is simply not applicable to a particular provision, notwithstanding that the provision operates coercively and in a manner similar to a stipulated damages clause.

This evasion technique is used in other common law jurisdictions and in relation to many other contract types (Perillo, 2009, pp. 530–7). In the oil and gas industry, purchasers often undertake to take delivery of a specified minimum quantity and to pay for this whether or not they accept delivery. The contract will typically also provide compensation in later years through larger delivery quantities for fuel that was paid for but not accepted in earlier years. Such 'take or pay' contracts are routinely upheld in the US (Brooke, 1992). A similar result was reached recently by the Commercial Court in *M & J Polymers Ltd v Imerys Minerals Ltd Polymers* [2008] EWHC 344 (Comm), [2008] 1 Lloyd's Rep 541 at [45], which, for the first time in England and Wales, had to consider the penalty jurisdiction in relation to a take or pay clause. The Commercial Court did not hesitate to uphold the clause ('the evidence was wholly clear') in a contract for the supply of chemicals, but only after the application of the penalty jurisdiction. The court acknowledged that such a clause was 'not the ordinary candidate (at [44]) for the application of the penalty rule, but that it did fall within its ambit. However, the clause was considered (at [46]): '*commercially justifiable*, [the parties had] *comparable bargaining power* and ... *did not have the predominant purpose of deterring a breach of contract ... in terrorem*' (emphasis in original) and so was enforceable.

The final parts of this chapter will seek to evaluate *Power of Contract* from doctrinal and theoretical perspectives before proposing and developing the application of its insights to resolve current difficulties in this area of law. Section 3 will document the formal influence of *Power of Contract* as it is manifested by direct and indirect citation in the academic literature and case law. Section 4 will evaluate its relevance to broader relational contract theory and Section 5 the potential value of the article in resolving difficult issues in the law relating to liquidated damages. In order to do this, it is first necessary to explore in more detail in Section 1 the major themes of Macneil's sophisticated argument in *Power of Contract* and set this in the context of other, mainly subsequent, contributions to understanding the underlying rationale for this jurisdiction (Section 2).

1. Ian Macneil's Power of Contract

In common with many of Ian Macneil's other writings, *Power of Contract* does not submit easily to synthesis (Campbell, 2001, 'Preface', commenting on Macneil, 1974). There is a density to the writing that means that summary seems to inevitably involve loss. This problem is compounded by the fact that the footnotes often contain considerable insights, some of which I have already referred to (again, see Campbell, 2001, 'Preface', for Campbell and Macneil's views on this). Practical constraints force some elimination to be necessary, so a non-exhaustive account of the themes of *Power of Contract* follows.

a. Freedom and power of contract

The concept of freedom of contract is one of a cluster of concepts to which the late Arthur Leff would apply his well-turned description of an 'emotionally satisfying incantation' (Leff, 1967, p. 485, referring to unconscionability). At the risk of prejudging the assessment of the burgeoning subsequent literature considered in the next section, it is clear that 'the premises of economics push in the direction of freedom of contract' and that this direction of travel 'can be resisted only with difficulty' (E Posner, 2003, p. 842; and Mattei, 1995, p. 432). Interestingly, Ugo Mattei also notes the somewhat surprising fact that such arguments are also made in socialist legal systems (when they can now be found!). *Power of Contract* (1962, n. 9) contains a typically thorough mini-essay on remedies for breach of production contracts in communist states. Yet, in the opening paragraphs of *Power of Contract*, Macneil immediately signals his resistance to this momentum. The article begins by recognizing that there are 'two sides of freedom of contract'. The first is freedom from restraint, effectively, an immunity from legal sanctions for making or receiving promises. Other commentators prefer to describe this aspect of freedom of contract as the *freedom to contract* (Barnett, 1992, p. 1181; and Speidel, 1982, p. 194 'the spirit of a people ... may be measured by the opportunity and incentive to exercise "freedom to contract"'). The second is the power of one transactor to secure legal sanctions against another when that other is in breach of its contractual commitments; Macneil believed that this second sense is better described as a 'power to contract'.

The question Macneil poses is effectively whether the non-enforcement of penalties does represent a clash of ideologies, 'or whether instead the law's stance on such clauses is a tacit acknowledgment that the functions of contract can be fulfilled in those cases notwithstanding the law's refusal to countenance those particular remedies' (Macneil, 1962, p. 495). The apparent contradiction between the comforting incantation of freedom of contract and the non-enforcement of penalties is, according to Macneil, a *false opposition*. In his view it would only have force against the backdrop of a system under which 'any promise seriously meant is a contract' (Macneil, 1962, p. 496). Yet the common law's insistence on consideration and other prerequisites to the enforcement of a contract and, perhaps more importantly, its commitment to substitutional remedies such as damages reveals a very different legal landscape. He then seeks to define contract in a way that 'comes closer to the facts of legal life' (Macneil, 1962, p. 496). Macneil disclaims any intention to address the larger themes that dominate his subsequent work and accepts as a 'working hypothesis'[5] (Macneil, 1962, p. 496) the analysis proposed in the celebrated but controversial (Markovits, 2004, p. 1496, is a recent disputant) two-part article by Lon Fuller and William Perdue, 'The Reliance Interest in Contract Damages' (Fuller and Perdue, 1936) that promises are enforced to protect reliance and prevent unjust enrichment, and that the formal protection of expectations is a means whereby hidden or unprovable reliance is protected.

Having adopted this premise, Macneil argues that the penalty doctrine is consistent with the power of contract (Macneil, 1962, p. 500). This argument builds upon an analysis of a contract as comprising two parts: a base promise, 'the substantive parts of the contract, ie all material agreements and terms of condition, other than the agreed remedy' (Macneil, 1962, n. 18), and a stipulated damages clause. Macneil argues that the protection of the identified interests is satisfied by an award of unliquidated damages sufficient to protect the base promise alone; it is not necessary to protect reliance upon a stipulated damages clause that under the present law is considered to be an unenforceable penalty. The law's refusal to protect the promise to pay the stipulated sum does not offend the interest analysis in Macneil's view because the contract demonstrates the promisee's willingness to predicate his own performance upon the base promise and the promisee, at the time of contracting, knows that stipulated damages clauses which offend the penalty rule will be unenforceable (Macneil, 1962, pp. 499–500).

Macneil conceded that this analysis cannot hold when the promisee has a well-founded expectation that he will receive the stipulated sum. Such a scenario is termed one of 'alternative base promises' (Macneil, 1962, p. 500), an analysis which Macneil believes was unknowingly, but nonetheless incorrectly, applied by the English Court of Appeal in *Campbell Discount v Bridge* [1961] 2 WLR 596 – see above for the decision of the House of Lords (Macneil, 1962, n. 19). *Euro London Appointments Ltd v Claessens International Ltd* [2006] EWCA Civ 385, [2006] All ER (D) 79 is a more modern illustration. An employment agency's terms of business provided that: the agency's fee must be paid within seven days of invoice; employers were entitled to a proportionate refund if the engagement of an introduced employee terminated prematurely; but there was no entitlement to a refund

---

5 Interestingly, in 2001, Macneil described Fuller as only effecting a 'half-escape from classical and neo-classical contract'. See Macneil's 'Biographical Statement' in Campbell (ed.) (2001).

if the agency's invoice was not paid within seven days. When employees introduced to the defendant by the claimant terminated their contracts prematurely and the invoice was not settled within a week, the defendant argued[6] that the limitation upon the availability of a refund was a penalty. The Court of Appeal rejected this argument. The penalty jurisdiction applied only to contractual clauses requiring a payment to be made when the payor was in breach of contract. The limitation upon the availability of a refund was simply not such a clause: 'The short answer to the ... point on penalty is that the Agency was suing for its agreed fee. That cannot have been a penalty.' (*per* Lawrence-Collins J, at [44]).

b. The 'intention' test

In the course of his meticulous attempt to discover exactly what test the courts are applying when ascertaining the validity of a stipulated damages provision, Macneil discusses the question 'whether the intention of the parties at the time of contracting determines whether a clause is a penalty or liquidated damages' (Macneil, 1962, n. 21). Again, and typically, this is investigated in an extensive footnote but the quality of analysis is not in the least affected by this placement. Macneil notes the frequent refrain in the US courts that the intention of the parties is determinative, but also notes that, in practice, it rarely is. This is because intention is usually ascertained by reference to the reasonableness of the pre-estimate of loss, and so consideration of intention in addition to the reasonableness enquiry is superfluous in most cases.

A formal distinction between UK and US law is relevant here: US law explicitly refers to the necessity that a stipulated damages clause be a *reasonable* estimate of loss, whereas the test laid down by Lord Dunedin in *Dunlop Pneumatic Tyre Co v New Garage and Motor Co* [1915] AC 79 (the *Dunlop* case) refers to a 'genuine' pre-estimate of loss. The distinction may be one of form rather than substance. In *Phillips v A-G of Hong Kong* (1993) 61 BLR 41, p. 60, Lord Woolf, who agreed that *Dunlop* 'authoritatively set out' the law in this area, later stated that 'the test is objective' (and, at p. 59, 'the issue has to be determined objectively'). In *McAlpine v Tilebox* [2005] EWHC 281 (TCC), [2005] BLR 271 at [48], Jackson J said that the essential enquiry has both objective and subjective elements. He noted that, although many cases in this area repeat the mantra of a 'genuine pre-estimate of loss' formula, in application '[t]he test is primarily an objective one, even

---

6 The argument was based upon a 'wider principle' derived from *obiter dicta* of Dillon and Bingham LJJ in *Interfoto Picture Library Ltd v Stiletto Visual Programmes Ltd* [1988] 1 All ER 348 (clause in delivery note obliging recipient to pay sums for retention of delivered goods not incorporated into contract).

though the court has some regard to the thought processes of the parties at the time of contracting'. Further, in *Murray v Leisureplay plc* [2005] EWCA Civ 963, [2005] IRLR 946 at [69], it was said that 'in the context of Lord Dunedin's speech, the test of genuineness is objective'. It is certainly the case that deposits, as opposed to stipulated damages provisions, are subject to a formal test of reasonableness (*Worker's Trust and Merchant Bank Ltd v Dojap Investments Ltd* [1993] 2 All ER 370).

Although the modern jurisdiction may be traced to earlier decisions, in *Wallis v Smith* (1882) 21 Ch D 243, p. 261, Jessel MR described *Astley v Weldon* (1801) 2 Bos & P 346 as 'the foundation of the ... subject', it is the clear summary of principle expressed as a number of rules by Lord Dunedin in the 'leading authority'(*Lansat Shipping Co v Glencore Grain BV (The Paragon)* [2009] EWHC 551 (Comm) at [17], *per* Blair J) of *Dunlop* that is usually regarded as the definitive statement of the law applicable to stipulated damages clauses in England and Wales. In *Philips Hong Kong Ltd v A-G of Hong Kong* (1993) 61 BLR 41 at p. 56, Lord Woolf said that these rules 'authoratively set out' well-settled proper guidance in distinguishing between liquidated damages and penalties, and Arden LJ referred to 'the continued usefulness of the authoritative guidance given by Lord Dunedin' (*Murray v Leisureplay plc* [2005] EWCA Civ 963 at [44]).

In *Dunlop*, Lord Dunedin (p. 86) said that:

> The essence of a penalty is a payment of money stipulated as *in terrorem* of the offending part; the essence of liquidated damages is a genuine covenanted pre-estimate of damage.

This statement contains two definitions: of a penalty and of a liquidated damages clause. Each derives from a different source, respectively the judgments of Lord Halsbury in *Elphinstone v Monkland Iron & Coal Co* (1886) 11 App Cas 332, p. 348, and Cotton LJ in *Wallis v Smith* (1882) 21 Ch D 243, p. 267. The proffered definition of a penalty does *not* provide a test sufficient to identify one. Taken literally it appears to import a sort of *mens rea* requirement on the part of the person for whose benefit the clause is designed to operate. Yet the cases applying the definition do not turn on whether the beneficiary of the clause *intended* it to operate in a coercive way. Rather the focus is upon the definition of a liquidated damages clause, and a penalty is simply treated as its negative counterpart, i.e. a clause that provides for something *in excess of* a 'genuine ... pre-estimate of loss'.

On this view 'a payment of money stipulated *in terrorem* of the offending party' describes a conclusion of law arrived at by the application of the 'genuine pre-estimate' of loss test, to which it adds nothing. A similar analysis has now been endorsed by the Court of Appeal in three cases (*Cine Bes Filmcilik VE Yapimcilik v United International Pictures (Cine)* [2003] EWCA Civ

1669; *Murray v Leisureplay plc* [2005] EWCA Civ 963 at [106] and [109]; and *Euro London Appointments Ltd v Claessens International Ltd* [2006] EWCA Civ 385 at [30]–[31]). It would seem that for many years English courts have simply ignored the requirement of intent and have only recently articulated the (entirely sensible) consequences of this inaction. Closer attention to *Power of Contract* or to an important but neglected (it is not mentioned in McGregor, 2009, or *Treitel*, Peel, 2010) *obiter dictum* of Lord Radcliffe in *Bridge v Campbell Discount Co Ltd* [1962] AC 600, p. 622, might have expedited this conclusion.

c. The timing of any applicable test

Whether or not a term is a genuine pre-estimate of loss is judged at the time of contracting (*Dunlop*, pp. 86–7). It follows that the 'disproportion principle' (stated by Lord Dunedin in *Dunlop* and *Public Works Comr v Hills* [1906] AC 368), i.e. the test for a penalty that compares the sum stipulated with the 'greatest loss that could conceivably be proved to have followed from the breach', is to be judged by reference to this point in time. The actual loss which is incurred might provide 'valuable evidence' as to what was conceived at the time of contracting to be the consequence of breach (*Philips*, p. 59, *per* Lord Woolf). This clear position under English law also prevailed in the US prior to the enactment of the Uniform Commercial Code (UCC) (Macneil, 1962, p. 533; and Perillo, 2009, p. 532). However, both UCC 2-718 and the Restatement (Second) Contracts, s. 356, now state that the reasonableness of the clause should be judged in the light of *either* anticipated *or* actual loss and so introduce two different times by reference to which the clause may be judged (*Equitable Lumber v IPA Land Development* (1976) 344 NE2D 391; and Perillo, 2009, p. 533).

The litmus test for these competing timings would be a case where the clause was judged to be a reasonable estimate at the time of contracting but where no actual loss in fact ensued. Cases in the US are divided on whether the stipulated sum is recoverable in these circumstances (Perillo, 2009, p. 533). Some of this confusion derives from the requirement asserted in many US cases that a stipulated damages clause will be enforceable only where there exists uncertainty in relation to the assessment of actual losses. English cases have increasingly emphasized this in order to justify substantial recovery, e.g. £2 million paid to Kevin Keegan following his constructive dismissal as a football manager (*Keegan v Newcastle Utd FC* [2010] IRLR 94), but have stopped short of stating that uncertainty of this kind is a prerequisite for the recovery of liquidated damages. In the US, building on the option of a later time of assessment, the argument is put that where it is known that there are no actual losses there is no uncertainty, and so the clause should not be enforced.

The major trend in the cases analysed by Macneil is that correspondence between the sum stipulated and the extent of actual harm was irrelevant because the loss, even at the time of trial, could not be measured with a high degree of confidence. However, where the promisee's loss could be established, Macneil supports the result in most cases where recovery has been restricted to actual loss on the basis that the contractor's power of contract is not necessarily infringed by a court's refusal to enforce a clause where there is no actual loss (Macneil, 1962, pp. 504–9). In so doing Macneil may be said to be in 'good' company as this was the position taken by the only English common lawyer to be canonized, Sir Thomas More! (*Wyllie v Wilkes* (1780) 2 Doug 519; and see Coopersmith, 1990, n. 5) Saintly association aside, such a 'hindsight-based analysis' (Coopersmith, 1990, p. 283) will fail to capture many of the benefits others have associated with such clauses as risk allocation devices. To take a single example, Robert Scott and George Triantis (2004, p. 1490) have argued that stipulated damages clauses should be viewed as contractual with the consequence that 'the inquiry dictated by the penalty rule – [in the US] whether stipulated damages reflect the actual or expected loss to the seller when the buyer walks away from the exchange – is wholly inapt' because in most circumstances the option price (i.e. the sum stipulated) will, like other traded commodities, be 'a function of its value to the buyer and its cost to the seller'.

A brief overview of recent writings seeking to apply economic analysis to the law of penalties is contained in Section 4, but it should be mentioned here that there is some subsequent support (based upon different reasoning of course) for the approach taken by Macneil. Johnston (1990, p. 647, citing Macneil at n. 79), for instance, has argued that the *ex post* monitoring of the relationship between the promisee's actual loss and the sum stipulated as required in the US version of the penalty rule provides a valuable incentive to high value promisees to reveal the value of the contract to them at the same time deterring low-value promisees from imitating high-value ones to get the 'bonus' of an unnecessary stipulated damages cover. How, if at all, Macneil would integrate these arguments into his account of agreed remedies is, of course, a matter of speculation. However, what is clear is that the analysis he developed is faithful to the premises he assumed.

d. Varying and hypothetical breaches

Stipulated damages clauses will frequently provide for recovery of a single sum in respect of a variety of types of breaches, a situation I will call 'varying breaches'. *Wise v United States* 249 US 647 (1918) provides a simple illustration. In this case the US Supreme Court considered and upheld a liquidated damages clause in a contract for construction of two buildings which stipulated a daily rate for delay, irrespective of whether one or both were incomplete. Macneil's typically full analysis describes a tripartite classification of possible legal responses to a stipulated damages clause applicable to varying breaches when other commentators have tended to analyse the situation in terms of a binary, enforce or don't enforce, response (Macneil, 1962, p. 509). Macneil proposes the following categories: (1) clause enforceable; (2) clause enforceable if it would be enforceable as to any of the breaches to which it applies; and (3) it is enforceable if the clause is otherwise enforceable in regard to the breach which has actually occurred.

For the Macneil cognoscenti there are perhaps the stirrings here of a 'rich classificatory apparatus' (Macneil, 1981), the need for which became the subject of a major debate with Oliver Williamson who thought that 'Serious problems of recognition and application are posed by such a rich classificatory apparatus' (1979), but to whom Macneil responded that such '"a rich classificatory apparatus" ... is essential if contractual relations are to be both understood and subjected to successful, realistic, and reasonably consistent analysis' (Macneil, 1981, p. 1025 n. 26; and Leib, 2010, p. 666, discussing the debate and questioning the ability of judges to handle such apparatus). Macneil shows how the strict application of an approach which rendered a clause unenforceable if applicable to breaches of varying importance 'would destroy practically all agreed damages clauses', emphasizing the pervasive nature of the problem as one which 'lurks and is ignored in almost every case involving an agreed damages clause' (Macneil, 1962, pp. 509 and 512). This is because it would be almost impossible to foresee all the ways in which a breach can occur let alone every consequence thereof. The strict approach is associated with the older 'intention-of-the-parties' test which now has less influence than before (Macneil, 1962, p. 510; Halson, 2010, para. 8.122). Macneil criticizes each expression of the 'not enforceable, if providing a single sum for varying breaches rule' as each will infringe the power of contract thesis whenever the breach which actually occurred is one in respect of which legal remedies are not fully adequate to protect the promisee's reliance, restitution and expectation interests (Macneil, 1962, pp. 511–12).

In his classic formulation of the penalty jurisdiction in the *Dunlop* case (p. 87) Lord Dunedin said that where a single sum is payable on the occurrence of 'one or more or all of several events, some ... serious and others but trifling', a presumption (previously this principle had operated as a rule of law: see *Astley v Weldon*) is said to operate that the sum is a penalty. It seems likely that the presumption will be weaker when the loss likely to result from breach will be difficult to assess. In England and Wales, this stems from the separate rule that a sum is not prevented from being liquidated damages simply because 'precise pre-estimation [is] almost an impossibility'. On one view, in the *Dunlop* case, the respondents undertook 27 separate obligations,[7] in respect of each breach of which they undertook to pay £5. Lord Dunedin's presumption was rebutted because the damage caused by each breach would be 'of such an uncertain nature that it cannot be accurately ascertained' (p. 89). Lord Woolf has recently said that, particularly with regard to commercial contracts, the court 'has to be careful not to set too stringent a standard' and should discourage argument based on 'unlikely illustrations' (*Philips*, pp. 58–9). Macneil supports this approach, which he thinks follows *a fortiori* when courts minimize reference to the promisee's actual losses: if a court 'refuses to be fully concerned with the breach which in fact occurred' then there seems 'little justification, for concerning itself with hypothetical breaches' (Macneil, 1962, p. 512).

In the *Dunlop* case, Lord Parker said that it was acceptable to stipulate for the recovery of a sum which represents the average damage which would be incurred in the event of breach (pp. 98–9, though the maths he used is questionable; see Halson, 2010, para. 8.123, n. 8). However, what is not acceptable is to stipulate for the payment of a sum which might be a proper reflection of loss if the obligation were breached in its most serious way, but where it could also be breached in less injurious ways as well (*Ariston SRL v Charly Records* (1990) *Financial Times*, 21 March). Further, if a sum is stipulated which can be regarded as a genuine pre-estimate of the loss that could and in fact did occur, the clause will nonetheless be a penalty if in respect of other contemplated breaches it would be excessive *(Ariston* quoting *Dunlop*, p. 102, *per* Lord Parmoor; and *Pigram v A-G New South Wales* (1975) 132 CLR 216, p. 221, *per* Barwick CJ).

e. 'Underliquidation' clauses

A contractual clause may sometimes provide for the recovery of a sum of money which is calculated to be less than a genuine pre-estimate of loss. Such a clause is a hybrid and shares characteristics with a liquidated damages clause (it does not seek to set recovery in excess of anticipated loss) and a limitation clause (it seeks to limit recovery to less than actual loss). Such clauses may be referred to as 'underliquidation clauses' (Fritz, 1954). They appear to be readily enforced on both sides of the Atlantic (Scott and Triantis, 2004, p. 1435, n. 21; Halson, 2010, para. 8.127; and Walt, 2009, s. 2).

The judicial acceptance of underliquidation clauses might be thought to

---

7 Not to sell or offer for sale where the marks had been tampered with, not to sell or offer for sale to a private individual or co-operative society below list price, not to supply black-listed individuals and not to exhibit or export the goods without permission. This totals nine obligations undertaken in relation to three goods (tyres, covers and tubes) producing a total of 27 undertakings.

offend the compensation principle which Macneil takes as his starting point (cf. Edlin and Schwartz, 2003, p. 44, for an efficiency-based argument that such clauses should be enforced). However, Macneil provides an elegant explanation by way of another mini-essay in a footnote for the lack of symmetry between the considerable judicial concern when a contract clause 'overliquidates' damages compared to the indifference where it 'underliquidates' them. Both under- and overliquidation of loss constitute 'an alteration of the social tool of contract', but there is 'an important difference' between them according to Macneil. When a party 'contracts, but limits liability' in a situation where he would otherwise be free to decline to contract at all, 'he is altering the nature of the social tool of contract in the direction of his right not to contract at all' (Macneil, 1962, n. 54).

2. The subsequent literature on penalty clauses

There is an extensive literature, much written from a law and economics perspective, examining the *policy* that justifies the current, or a different, approach to the enforceability of stipulated damages clauses in contracts, some of which has already been mentioned (e.g. Johnston, 1990; and Markovits, 2004, discussed above). Attempts to summarize the literature (either alone, Edlin and Schwartz, 2003; and Walt, 2009; or alongside other related scholarship, E Posner, 2003) have required articles in themselves. Therefore, in this section I will only offer a few general comments which might help to contextualize the subsequent acknowledgment, or otherwise, of Macneil's contribution to this debate.

The early, less technical, literature emphasized factors such as the use of stipulated damages provisions as an efficient means to provide insurance against otherwise uncompensable idiosyncratic losses (Goetz and Scott, 1977). Other authors emphasized the need to structure the law in a way that deters contractors from indulging in activity designed only to manoeuvre their contractual partner into a breach of contract (Clarkson et al., 1978; and Crasswell, 1988). Different analyses support different conclusions. The first study just referred to argues for the abolition of the present division between enforceable liquidated damages clauses and unenforceable penalties and the second recommends its retention. However, these earlier studies have subsequently been shown to have been premised upon assumptions about the equal availability of information to the contractors ('symmetric information models'). Later studies try to model informational asymmetries with respect to a number of variables including: the cost of contractual renegotiation, different third-party valuations of the contract goods and the parties' investment incentives (Chung, 1992; Spier and Whinston 1995; Edlin and Reichelstein 1996; Chung, 1998; all discussed in

Edlin and Schwartz, 2003, pp. 42–52; and Eric Posner, 2003, pp. 859–63); and yield results generally criticizing the current legal position.

It is difficult to draw clear conclusions from these studies. They convincingly demonstrate that, *in certain circumstances*, stipulated damages clauses set at particular levels are economically desirable, but in different circumstances they are not. As Aaron Edlin and Alan Schwartz (2003, p. 53) put it: 'Multipliers of *any size* [meaning recovery of stipulated damages which might underliquidate, perfectly liquidate or overliquidate the promisee's actual losses] thus can be efficient or inefficient, depending on the parties' circumstances.' However, the variables modelled by the writers do not correspond to any of the criteria which the courts refer to when determining the enforceability of a stipulated damages provision. Further, each contribution to the debate tends to concentrate upon a single variable and so yields predictions justified by that factor alone. Few have attempted to bring together this scholarship into a single multifactorial approach capable of judicial application (Edlin and Schwartz, 2003, is perhaps the most ambitious attempt). Posing the rhetorical question whether this literature shows that the penalty doctrine is efficient, Eric Posner (2003, p. 862) concedes that 'under certain conditions' the enforcement of stipulated damages 'can produce negative externalities'. He observes that, despite this, 'the fit is poor' and the 'penalty doctrine does not incorporate any of the variables in the literature'. It is true that these different studies generally trend to the same policy prescription, i.e. that stipulated damages clauses should be more routinely enforced than they are at present (Goetz and Scott, 1977; Ham, 1990; Schwartz, 1990; Edlin and Schwartz, 2003; Scott and Triantis, 2004; and Klass, 2007; but contra the following who support some variant of the present regime: Clarkson et al., 1978; Johnston, 1990; and Markovits, 2004). However, the different approaches taken mean that 'we are left with a sterile normative defense of freedom of contract, one that is closely tied to its premise that parties know more about their interests than courts do' (E Posner, 2003, p. 863).

3. The influence of *Power of Contract*

a. Judicial citation

This section contains a formal assessment of the influence of Macneil's *Power of Contract* upon the courts and a brief look at its incorporation into the academic literature. My researches have revealed six cases in the US[8]

---

8 *Re AJ Lane* (1990) 113 BR 821; *Schmidt v US* (1996) 912 P 2d 871; *Security Safety Corp v Kuznicki* (1966) 213 NE 2d 866; *Grand Bissell Towers v Joan Gagnon Ent* (1983) 657 SW 2d 378; *Vines v Orchard Hills* (1980) 435 A 2d 1022; *Wallace Real Estate v Groves* (1994) 881 P2d 1010; *Wassenaar v Panos* (1983) 331 NW 2d 357.

and none in England and Wales in which *Power of Contract* has been referred to. In four cases, the court relied upon arguments in the article to support important conclusions in difficult areas; in another case, Macneil's argument is discussed and, I believe wrongly, rejected; and a final case refers to the article when endorsing a principle which cannot really be derived from the article.

In *Re AJ Lane*, the Massachusetts Bankruptcy Court had to consider whether a clause in a loan agreement requiring the debtor to make a 'prepayment charge' if the loan was settled early fell within the penalty jurisdiction. The court held that it did and by application of the test discussed in, and with reference to, *Power of Contract*, held that the prepayment could not be considered as an 'alternative performance', and so avoid the penalty rule, because when the loan was made the creditor had no reason to believe that the loans would not be repaid in the normal way. In *Wallace Real Estate*, the Supreme Court of Washington referred to *Power of Contract* to support its rejection of the previous approach of the courts in Washington (*Lind v Pacific Bellevue Developments* (1989) 781 P 2d 1322), which had been to insist on a requirement of proof of actual loss before recovery of liquidated damages could be sanctioned. The court, like Macneil, emphasized the importance of judging the enforceability of the clause by reference to the time of contracting, and quoted *Power of Contract* for the view, discussed above, that the insistence of proof of actual loss in the earlier cases was probably associated with an older general attitude of hostility to any stipulated damages provisions. While declining to embark on a 'detailed review of the chequered history of liquidated damages clauses', the Supreme Court of Connecticut has relied upon *Power of Contract* to support the proposition that the burden of showing that a clause is an unenforceable penalty is borne by the party seeking to challenge its validity (*Vines v Orchard*). So-called underliquidated clauses were referred to briefly, in a case with a reference to *Power of Contract* before the Supreme Court of Oklahoma (*Schmidt v US*). In a final, briefly reported case, in Massachusetts *Power of Contract* is noted in passing (*Security Safety Corp*).

In contrast to the *Wallace Real Estate* case discussed above, the Missouri Court of Appeals rejected the analysis in *Power of Contract* and insisted that the promisee 'must show at least some actual harm or damage ... before liquidated damages can be triggered' (*Grand Bissell Towers*). For reasons developed above, it is suggested that this conclusion should not be supported. In a final case heard by the Supreme Court of Wisconsin (*Wassenaar*), *Power of Contract* is referred to (without a particular page reference) for the proposition that the reasonableness test strikes a balance between permitting private parties 'to perform the judicial function of providing the remedy in breach of contract cases' and ensuring that there is no 'unfairness in bargaining'. The statement is perhaps inoffensive at its most general level but this is something that simply was not said by Macneil.

b. Academic citation

Many academic studies of the law applicable to stipulated damages clauses make reference to Macneil's 'thoughtful' (Eddy, 1977, n. 8) analysis in *Power of Contract*. A few illustrations are all that is possible here. Some commentators have apparently adopted part of Macneil's analysis. One academic (Eddy, 1977, pp. 92–3; cf. Macneil, 1962, pp. 500–1) proposes that a more contextual approach be taken when applying certain sections of the UCC. The development of this analysis builds on a purposive approach similar to that which lies at the heart of Macneil's conception of power of contract. In another article, a new argument is made for the more extensive enforcement of stipulated damages provisions for breach of the contractual duty to co-operate (Klass, 2007).[9] The duty to co-operate is said to derive from 'second subsidiary promises' which are enforceable on a theory similar (Klass, 2007, pp. 32–6) to that applicable to 'alternative contracts' in *Power of Contract* (n. 19).

Other articles take issue with *Power of Contract* in different ways. Some depart from Macneil's policy prescriptions with regard to stipulated damages clauses. Analyses, such as that of Charles Goetz and Scott (1977, n. 30) have tangentially, or others more directly (Kaplan, 1977, nn. 1, 13, 24, 25, 28, 29, 35 and 41), suggested that some of Macneil's reasoning is open to question, asserting that Macneil is '[r]elying upon logic which is not wholly free from circularity' when he notes that clauses found to be penalties are against public policy and that this knowledge will mean that parties do not rely upon then. For this reason Macneil believes that by declining enforcement the courts are not, within the Fuller and Perdue model, depriving the parties of their reliance interest. Other commentators such as Kaplan have also sought to challenge Macneil's analysis in a more fundamental way, at the same time making extensive reference to his arguments (Kaplan, 1977, nn. 1, 13, 24, 25, 28, 29, 35 and 41). However, these critiques often simply reflect a different set of premises and so support their conclusions by reference to a normative model of contracting which is different to the one (derived from Fuller and Perdue, 1936) that underlies *Power of Contract*.

---

9 Klass (2007) argues that such damages are necessary to avoid a 'Catch 22' situation where a claimant can only recover damages for breach of duty to co-operate if she can prove loss but the breach is effectively the breach of a duty to produce evidence of harm.

Other writers support the policy prescription of Macneil's analysis by reference to their own theory of contract, for example, Markovits (2004, p. 1450 and n. 68) who presents an account of contract as collaboration which for distinct reasons also supports the law's current hostility towards penalty clauses. Of course, other critics (e.g. Barnett, 1992) focus upon the model of relational contracting which Macneil developed many years after *Power of Contract* was published.

Perhaps inevitably, some commentators, like some judges, appear to proceed on the basis of a misunderstanding or unjustified generalization they derive from *Power of Contract*. An example would seem to be the oft repeated and seductively simplistic observation that: 'The courts' refusal to enforce such penalties ... is somewhat at odds with the deep-rooted principle of freedom of contract.' (Wachtel, 1999, n. 119) This statement seems inconsistent with Macneil's careful definition of power of contract developed in the eponymous article.[10]

4. *Power of Contract* and Macneil's relational theory

In my brief survey of the academic literature examining the penalty rules, I noted that the majority of authors express dissatisfaction with the current regime. The ban on penalty clauses is interpreted as an attempt to limit 'obdurate adherence to contractual freedom' (Mattei, 1995, p. 432). As we have seen, Eric Posner remarked that the direction of travel of the economic analyses of penalty clauses is mainly in the direction of freedom of contract and he further predicted that it will be difficult to resist this current trend (E Posner, 2003, p. 862). Yet resist is exactly what Macneil does in *Power of Contract* and this is effected by the careful definition of the concept of power to contract described in detail above.

The concept of power of contract which Macneil outlined in his 1962 article has subsequently been consistently reasserted in the course of Macneil's development of his relational theory of contract. This is recorded in key articles from 1978 and 1983 which followed shortly after what many would consider the first complete account of his relational theory of contract in his 'Many Futures' article (Macneil, 1974). In Macneil (1978, n. 55), he said succinctly that:

---

10 See also Anderson (1987, n. 249), who says: 'The rule against penalties, therefore, ultimately is an external restraint on the power of contract.' Cf. Macneil's argument that the power of contract is effectuated through the penalty rule, even if individual contractors might have their power infringed. 'Such decisions are an infringement of the plaintiff's power of contract ... the theory upon which the cases proceed is not.' (Macneil, *Power of Contract*, p. 508)

> Freedom of contract here means, of course, power of contract, eg the power to bind oneself, by agreement, to further action or consequences to which one otherwise would not have been bound.

In Macneil (1983, p. 370; and to similar effect see Macneil, 1984, n. 40), he cautioned that '[b]ecause of the confusing nature of the term "freedom of contract"':

> It is important to note that the value of sovereign non-intervention is not the same as the value of freedom of contract. Freedom of contract is almost always used to mean freedom to bind yourself by contract – that is to cause the sovereign to confer power on the other contractor to enforce the contract against one's self. This is sovereign intervention, not sovereign non-intervention.

The centrality of the concept of power of contract in the development of Macneil's relational theory of contract means that it has been scrutinized and attacked by proponents of rival theories. An example is Randy Barnett, who is associated with a theory of contract that emphasizes the role of consent in justifying initial contractual obligation and in informing the selection of appropriate default rules where the initial consent leaves lacunae (see especially Barnett, 1986). The 'consent theory' shares some features with Macneil's relational theory of contract but also has many differences, which are examined in Barnett (1992). In the course of exploring these points of overlap and distinction, Barnett criticizes Macneil's description of power of contract as 'a bit murky' (Barnett, p. 1992, n. 94). The exact cause of Barnett's objection would appear to focus upon the negative side of the definition of freedom of contract, i.e. freedom from restraint, rather than on the positive side constituted by 'a power to contract, a power to secure legal sanctions when another breaks his promise' (Macneil, 1962, p. 495).

In essence, Barnett's critique asserts that Macneil's relational theory of contract is 'surprisingly' (Barnett, 1992, p. 1194) underinclusive. This, of course, is the diametric opposite of Williamson's appeal (discussed above), which Macneil rejects, for a simplified classificatory schema. Barnett believes that Macneil's conception of freedom should rather be broadened to 'immunity from having one's entitlements transferred to another without one's consent' (Barnett, 1992, n. 94). He believes that such a reference to property rights is necessary, but that a major weakness of Macneil's relational theory is that it is not associated with a developed theory of property rights (Barnett, 1992, p. 1197). Irrespective of the merits of this criticism, it is clear on close analysis that it leaves the *positive* power to contract untouched.

5. The value of Macneil's *Power of Contract* today

In this section examining the value of Macneil's 1962 article today, I will look at examples of how the analysis or concepts developed in *Power of Contract* might assist with resolving problems currently facing the courts in this area.

a. Unconscionability and oppression

A number of commentators have recently suggested that the proper basis of the rule against penalties is unconscionability or oppression and that the jurisdiction should more explicitly reflect this (Chen-Wishart, 1996, p. 299; Downes, 1996, p. 267; and Waddhams, 2004, para. 8.130). Such an approach has found favour in the Canadian Supreme Court, where Dickson J said 'the power to strike down a penalty clause ... is designed for the sole purpose of providing relief against oppression (*Elsey v JG Collins Insurance Agencies* [1978] 83 DLR 1, p. 15). Referring to the comments of Dickson J, Tomlinson J, in *Indian Airlines Ltd v GIA International Ltd* [2002] EWHC 2361 at [71]), expressed the view that there has been 'something of a sea change in the approach of the courts to penalty clauses'. Although this case was not expressly considered by the Court of Appeal in *Murray v Leisureplay plc* [2005] EWCA Civ 963, in that case, at [49], Arden LJ expressed her clear view that she did 'not consider that oppression ... is of itself a criterion in determining whether a contractual sum is a penalty' (see also *Jeancharm Ltd T/A Beaver International v Barnet Football Club Ltd*, per Jacob J at [10]). It is suggested that the approach of Arden LJ is to be preferred on the basis of the increased certainty that is achieved by eschewing reliance upon such an ill-defined standard. This is in accord with the view Macneil expresses: 'The oft repeated reference to oppression in penalty cases somehow sounds curiously flat, as it does in the whole history of relief against forfeitures and penalties ...' (Macneil, 1962, pp. 502–3 and n. 26).

b. The false opposition[11]

In *Murray v Leisureplay plc* [2005] EWCA Civ 963, the Court of Appeal stated the orthodox view that the jurisdiction to set aside a stipulated damages clause is anomalous. The general suspicion with which common law but also civilian law jurisdictions (Mattei, 1995, p. 431) view stipulated damages clauses may be difficult to justify in economic terms but is consistent with a shared but often underemphasized judicial hostility to attempts to curb a court's remedial discretion. In *Murray*, Arden LJ (at [29]) described the penalty jurisdiction as a disapplication of the usual laissez-faire

---

11 See textual discussion at pp. 95–7 above.

approach which permits parties the maximum degree of contractual self-determination. Indeed, according to Beatson J in *General Trading Co (Holdings) Ltd v Richmond Corp Ltd* [2008] EWHC 1479 (Comm) at [123], it is this anomalous character that justifies the imposition upon the party challenging such a clause of the burden of proving that it is a penalty. The Court of Appeal repeated the view taken in *Murray* the following year: 'The rule against penalties is an exception to the general principle of English law that a contract should be enforced in accordance with its terms.' (*Euro London Appointments Ltd v Claessens International Ltd* [2006] EWCA 385, [2006] 2 Lloyd's Rep 436 *per* Chadwick LJ at [17], delivering the judgment of the court) In *McAlpine v Tilebox* [2005] EWHC 281 (TCC) at [38], Colman J described the jurisdiction as a principle whose origins lay in an earlier chapter of contractual history but which atypically survived the rise of freedom of contract.

These recent judicial statements all repeat what I have termed the 'false opposition' which Macneil sought to displace with his more nuanced concept of power of contract. Whether or not the judges subscribe to the Fuller and Perdue analysis, close attention to Macneil's article should have convinced them to adopt a different vocabulary and apply it in the light of whatever normative principle they wish to endorse. It is suggested that only then can the boundary disputes (i.e. between enforceable and unenforceable contract clauses), to which the false opposition directs us, be resolved.

c. Alternative contracts

The *Abbey* litigation above illustrated how parties can avoid the application of the penalty jurisdiction by structuring their dealings to provide for two alternative modes of performance rather than, on the one hand, performance and, on the other, breach. Given that this is an evasion technique, it might be expected that the party seeking to rely upon it must express itself with some clarity. In *General Trading Co (Holdings) Ltd v Richmond Corp Ltd* [2008] EWHC 1479 (Comm), the Commercial Court had to consider a sale and purchase agreement for a business, the price to be paid as £60k cash and £540k as loan notes. The agreement further provided that, if the seller, following the buyer's notice to do so, failed to provide a guarantee within a specified period the loan notes would be cancelled. Beatson J dismissed the purchaser's argument that the sale and purchase agreement should be construed as a contract for the sale of a business at two alternative prices; £600k where the guarantee was obtained and £60k where it was not. In his view, the structure and language of the other parts of the transaction supported this conclusion. This close attention to contextual indicators of what exactly had been the subject matter of the bargain closely follows, but unfortunately does not refer to, the analysis in *Power of Contract* (pp. 499–500).

Conclusion

In *Power of Contract*, Macneil did not set out a theory of contract; instead he borrowed one from Fuller and Perdue. The act of borrowing is simultaneously limiting and farsighted. It is limiting because the premises upon which he relies are not his own. Of course, by way of atonement he spent most of the rest of his distinguished academic career formulating and then refining his own relational theory of contract. Nevertheless, *Power of Contract* is farsighted in its recognition that a resolution of many of the important issues in the law governing the enforcement of stipulated damages clauses depends upon a prior commitment to a normative theory of contract. The assessment of Macneil's success in his larger endeavour has been the subject of other chapters in this book. I now want to conclude with an evaluation of a paper written before he embarked upon that task, but will try to relate it to those later writings at different levels.

It is certainly true that stylistically *Power of Contract* shares many features with Macneil's later, better known, general works. It is very well written, the prose is dense but always attractive, clear and precise. A particular feature is that there are often two distinct discussions, one in the full text and the other contained in mini-essays in the footnotes. These are not divided by any hierarchy of importance. We have seen on several occasions that insightful analysis is contained in the footnotes.

The precise classification of a subject is of more than stylistic or expository importance; it also informs and directs our understanding of the substance of the subject classified. Macneil has always favoured a maximal approach to presentation and defended the use of rich classificatory indices. He always resisted attempts to condense these orderings to something others consider more manageable. At several points, *Power of Contract* contains categories of description that go beyond what has been presented by others and which, in some cases, still await recognition. An example that I have reserved for this conclusion is Macneil's isolation (p. 502) of five different types of uncertainty that might impede the assessment of damages. The latest edition of perhaps the leading text on the law of contract in the US reproduces this five-fold classification and then immediately notes that despite 'the wealth of potential that this analysis suggests [it] has been little explored' (Perillo, 2009, p. 532).

The major substantive link between *Power of Contract* and Macneil's subsequent work is the construction of its eponymous concept. It has been shown that this distinctive formulation is built upon in several important articles by Macneil and also helps to distinguish the relational theory they describe from rivals such as Barnett's consent theory of contract. In addition to the concepts of power of contract and uncertainty, Macneil's article contains several valuable expositions on subtopics, such as: the relevance of the contractors' intention, the timing of any applicable test, varying and hypothetical breaches, and underliquidation clauses. Courts and academics have made occasional use of some parts of *Power of Contract* to support their conclusions or help with new analyses. I must admit that I was surprised not to find more judicial citation of *Power of Contract*. However, this is positively flattering compared to the citation of articles written from an economic perspective. Eric Posner (2003, p. 870) records that between 1980 and 2003 there were only 36 judicial references to articles applying economic analysis to any aspect of contract.

On this point, there is an interesting comparison to be made with much subsequent scholarship in this area. Much of the more recent economic analysis of remedies in contract law is technical and so inaccessible to those without an economic training. In one paper (Edlin and Schwartz, 2003, p. 36), ostensibly written for 'readers without mathematical sophistication', I suspect that the first sentence many readers would comprehend fully would be the final one recommending the repeal of the sections of the UCC and the US Restatement (Second) Contracts dealing with stipulated damages clauses! This inaccessibility and lack of influence is readily admitted by those writing in that tradition: 'modern scholarship has not had a large impact on how judges or legislators decide law' (Ayres, 2003, p. 881; see also E Posner, 2003, p. 870; and Klass, 2007, p. 35).

I hope that by the only detailed review undertaken of Macneil's *Power of Contract* I have achieved two original purposes: first, to demonstrate how the concepts and vocabulary introduced in that article can be, but have not yet been, applied to address pressing problems of understanding and application in the law relating to stipulated damages, and, second, how this neglected piece of scholarship contains the nascent themes of one of the most distinctive contributions to modern contract scholarship. In sum, it seems that contrary to everything the world's most influential wine critic has said, 1962 was a great year – for law review articles at least!

References

Anderson (1987) 'Good Faith in the Enforcement of Contracts' 73 *Iowa Law Review* 299

Ayres, I (2003) 'Valuing Modern Contract Scholarship' 112 *Yale Law Journal* 881

Barnett, R E (1986) 'A Consent Theory of Contract' 86 *Columbia Law Review* 269.

Barnett, R E (1992) 'Conflicting Visions: A Critique of Ian Macneil's Relational Theory of Contract' 78 *Virginia Law Review* 1175

Beale, H and T Dugdale (1975) 'Contracts Between Businessmen: Planning and the Use of Contractual Remedies' (1975) 2 *British Journal of Law and Society* 45

Brooke, A F (1992) 'Great Expectations' 70 *Texas Law Review* 1469

Campbell, D (ed.) (2001) *The Relational Theory of Contract: Selected Works of Ian Macneil* (London: Sweet &Maxwell)

Chen-Wishart, M (1996) 'Controlling the Power to Agree Damages' in P Birks (ed.), *Wrongs and Remedies in the Twenty-First Century* (Oxford: Clarendon Press)

Chirac, J (French President) Speech on the occasion of award of Officier de la Legion d'Honneur

Chung, T Y (1992) 'On the Social Optimality of Liquidated Damage Clause: An Economic Analysis' 8 *Journal of Law, Economics and Organisation* 280

Chung, T Y (1998) 'Commitment through Specific Investment in Contractual Relationships' 31 *Canadian Journal of Economics* 1057

Clarkson, K W, R L Miller and T J Muris 'Liquidated Damages v Penalties: Sense or Nonsense' (1978) *Wisconsin Law Review* 351.

Coopersmith, J B (1990) 'Refocusing Liquidated Damages Law for Real Estate Contracts: Returning to the Historical Roots of the Penalty Doctrine' (1990) 39 *Emory Law Journal* 267

Crasswell, R (1988) 'Contract Remedies, Renegotiation and the Theory of Efficient Breach' 61 *Southern California Law Review* 629

Downes, T (1996) 'Rethinking Penalty Clauses' in P Birks (ed.), *Wrongs and Remedies in the Twenty-First Century* (Oxford: Clarendon Press)

Eddy, J A (1977) 'On the "Essential" Purposes of Limited Remedies: The Metaphysics of UCC Section 2-719(2)' 65 *California Law Review* 28

Edlin, A and S Reichelstein (1996) 'Holdups, Standard Breach Remedies, and Optimal Investment' 86 *America Economic Review* 478

Edlin, A and A Schwartz (2003) 'Optimal Penalties in Contracts' 78 *Chicago-Kent Law Review* 33

Fritz, W F (1954) '"Underliquidated" Damages as Limitation of Liability' 33 *Texas Law Review* 196

Fuller, L L and W R Perdue (1936) 'The Reliance Interest in Contract Damages' (1936–1937) 46 *Yale Law Journal* 52 and 373

Goetz, C J and R E Scott (1977) 'Liquidated Damages, Penalties and the Just Compensation Principle: Some Notes on an Enforcement Model and a Theory of Efficient Breach' (1977) 77 *Columbia Law Review* 554

Halson, R (2005) 'The Law of Contract and the Textbook Tradition' *Canterbury Law Review* 163

Halson, R (2010) 'Remedies' in M Furmston (ed.), *The Law of Contract* (London: Butterworths LexisNexis) (4th edn)

Ham, A (1990) 'The Rule against Penalties in Contract: An Economic Perspective' 17 *Melbourne University Law Review* 648

Hillman, R A (1997) *The Richness of Contract Law* (Dordrecht: Kluwer)

Hillman, R A (2000) 'The Limits of Behavioural Decision Theory in Legal Analysis: The Case of Liquidated Damages' (2000) 85 *Cornell Law Review* 717

Johnston, J S (1990) 'Strategic Bargaining and the Economic Theory of Contract Default Rules' 100 *Yale Law Journal* 615

Kaplan, P R (1977) 'A Critique of the Penalty Limitation on Liquidated Damages' 50 *Southern California Law Review* 1055

Klass, G 'Contracting for Co-operation in Recovery' (2007) 117 *Yale Law Journal* 2

Law Commission (1975) *Penalty Clauses and Forfeiture of Monies Paid* Working Paper No 61 (London: Law Commission)

Leib, E J (2010) 'Contracts and Friendships' 59 *Emory Law Journal* 649

Leff, A (1967)'Unconscionability and the Code: The Emperor's New Clause' (1967) 115 *University of Pennsylvania Law Review* 116

McGregor, H (2009) *McGregor on Damages* (London: Sweet & Maxwell)

Macaulay, S (1963) 'Non-contractual Relations in Business' (1963) 28 *American Sociological Review* 55

Macneil, I R (1962) 'The Power of Contract and Agreed Remedies' (1962) 47 *Cornell Law Quarterly* 495

Macneil, I R (1969) 'Whither Contracts' (1969) 21 *Journal of Legal Education* 403

Macneil, I R (1974) 'The Many Futures of Contract' 47 *Southern California Law Review* 691

Macneil, I R (1978) 'Contracts: Adjustment of Long-Term Economic Relations Under Classical, Neoclassical, and Relational Contract Law'(1978) 72 *Northwestern University Law Review* 854

Macneil, I R (1981) 'Economic Analysis of Contractual Relations: Its Shortfalls and the Need for a "Rich Classificatory Apparatus"' 75 *Northwestern University Law Review* 1018

Macneil, I R (1983) 'Values in Contract: Internal and External' (1983) 78 *Northwestern University Law Review* 340

Macneil, I R (1984) 'Bureaucracy and Contracts of Adhesion' (1984) 22 *Osgoode Hall Law Journal* 5

Markovits, D (2004) 'Contract and Collaboration' 113 *Yale Law Journal* 1417

Mattei, U (1995) 'The Comparative Law and Economics of Penalty Clauses in Contracts' 43 *American Journal of Comparative Law* 427

Olazabal, A M (2004) 'Formal and Operative Rules in Overliquidation Per Se Cases' 41 *American Business Law Journal* 503

Parker, R M (2003) *Bordeaux: A Consumer's Guide to the World's Finest Wines* (New York: Simon & Schuster) (4th edn)

Peel, E (2010) *Treitel: The Law of Contract* (London: Sweet & Maxwell) (13th edn)

Perillo, J (2009) *Calamari and Perillo on Contracts* (Berkeley CA: West Group) (6th edn)

Posner, E (2003) 'Economic Analysis of Contract Law after Three Decades: Success or Failure?' (2003) 112 *Yale Law Journal* 829

Posner, R (1979)'Some Uses and Abuses of Economics in Law' (1979) 46 *University of Chicago Law Review* 281

Schwartz, A (1990) 'The Myth that Promisees Prefer Supracompensatory Remedies: An Analysis of Contracting for Damage Measures' 229 *Yale Law Journal* 369

Scott, R E and G G Triantis (2004) 'Embedded Options and the Case against Compensation in Contract Law' 104 *Columbia Law Review* 1428

Speidel, R (1982) 'The New Spirit of Contract' 2 *Journal of Law and Commerce* 193

Spier, K E and M D Whinston (1995) 'On the Efficiency of Privately Stipulated Damages for Breach of Contract: Entry Barriers, Reliance and Renegotiation' 26 *Rand Journal of Economics* 180

Wachtel, J T (1999) 'Breaking up is Hard to Do' (1999) 65 *Brooklyn Law Review* 585

Waddams, S (2004) *The Law of Damages* (Toronto: Canada Law Book)

Walt, S (2009) 'Penalty Clauses and Liquidated Damages' Law and Economics Working Paper 57 (Charlottesville VA: University of Virginia), s. 2

Wightman, J (1996) *Contract: A Critical Commentary* (London: Pluto Press)

Williamson, O (1979) 'Transaction-Cost Economics: The Governance of Contractual Relations' 22 *Journal of Law and Economics* 22

6
Relational Values in English Contract Law
Hugh Beale

The theory of 'relational contract' seems to have had little impact on the law of England and Wales. It has been widely discussed by academics but a common reaction seems to be: very interesting, but what do we do with the theory? (Feinman, 2001, p.63) We can observe relational contracting taking place, and we can find examples of contracts that are designed to take into account the ongoing relationship between the parties. But it is hard to see that the theory has had any impact on general contract law as such. This chapter is in part an attempt to explain why Ian Macneil's theory seems to have fallen on stony ground. However, I will also argue that our general law of contract, as expounded by the House of Lords under the influence of Lord Hoffmann and now by the Supreme Court, now has significant relational elements, at least in terms of a greater sensitivity to the context in which the agreement was made.

I will not discuss longer-term relationships in which the parties have to leave issues open and in which their expectations for the future may be derived from their conduct during the relationship. How English contract law and contract practice allow for adjustment in longer-term relationships was very well described by Ewan McKendrick (1995) and I have nothing useful to add. Instead, I will concentrate on another aspect of Macneil's theory and consider the extent to which English contract law and practice is relational in the sense of reflecting the expectations created by the context in which the agreement was made (Macneil, 1980, pp. 68–70).

Relational contracting, discrete contracts and abstraction

Contracts or contract law?

We must start by drawing a distinction between contracts and contract law. There is probably no such thing as an entirely discrete contract, at least in modern society (Feinman, 2001, p. 61). The amount of relevant background will vary with factors such as the length or depth of the parties' relationship, but even a contract made when there has been no previous contact and will be no further contact between the parties is made against a background of facts which will give rise to some expectations. Motorists who stop to buy fruit from a farmer's roadside stand that they have never passed before and will clearly never pass again will expect at least that the farmer will not have injected poison into the apples. Moreover, contracts take place within a legal framework – the law of property and of torts, the criminal law and consumer regulation – which often bite as heavily on relatively discrete contracts as on any other. As Scott (2000, p. 852) points out, the question is not whether contracts are relational but whether contract law is relational. How much of the context does the law take into account when fixing the rights and obligations of the parties? A contract may be relational, firmly embedded in a particular context, but the law may still treat it as discrete by ignoring the context.

'Abstraction' in English contract law

Macneil's vocabulary is not always easy to grasp (Feinman, 2001, p. 63) and it may be helpful to use different terminology. For the purposes of this chapter, it may be easier to think in terms of the degree of 'abstraction'. We are used to the phrase 'abstract payment obligations' (Goode, 1991; 2009). An abstract payment obligation is one that is enforceable irrespective of whether the counter-performance has been properly made or not. (Goode, 1991, pp. 223 and 233, refers to this aspect as the autonomy of the obligation; for him an obligation is truly abstract if, in addition, it comes into being by virtue solely of its communication to the beneficiary. It is not the second aspect which concerns us here.) If an irrevocable credit has been opened in favour of the seller and the seller has presented the correct documents, the bank must pay the seller even if the goods shipped are defective. If an 'on demand' guarantee has been given, the guarantor must pay without the creditor having to show that the debtor is in default. The obligation is abstract in that it exists irrespective of the underlying facts that prompted its creation. Likewise, the law may treat a contract in an abstract way, taking little account of the context in which it was made. This abstraction may be imposed by the courts or by legislation, or it may be agreed by the parties. As Macneil put it (1980, pp. 60–2), the parties may agree that their contract should be treated as discrete (this point is helpfully discussed in Campbell, 2001, pp. 21–2).

My first argument is simply that, traditionally, English contract law and English contract practice involve a fairly high degree of abstraction. The courts have developed rules that enable them to ignore the background.

Relational theory suggests that contract law should take the context into account unless the parties have agreed that the contract should be treated discretely. English law often seems to start at the other end: the context should be ignored unless the parties have provided for it to be taken into account. Even if the courts' attitude has changed over time, it is still very common for the parties to agree to exclude contextual matter being taken into account.

Caveats

I have to make a number of caveats to my argument. The first is that I am talking primarily about the 'general' law of contract. In effect, we now have several different laws of contracts, at least if we refer to 'contract law' in the sense of the law that governs the various relationships that in normal legal parlance we refer to as contractual. This law is a mixture: it includes not only contractual liability in the narrow, supposedly consent-based, sense but also tort, restitution, and, for some types of contract, a variety of kinds of 'regulation', such as consumer protection measures. A distinction may of course be made between regulation and contract law, but that is usually for a different purpose, for example, to explain how each kind of law may be justified (Brownsword, 2011). In particular, though the law governing consumer contracts is based on the same general principles as apply to other contracts, it is subject to so much special regulation that it has been transformed and, for purposes of analysis, is better treated as separate. I suspect the same is true for employment contracts. Even with contracts between businesses, distinctions need to be drawn. Thus the Unfair Contract Terms Act 1977 imposes controls over exclusion and limitation of liability clauses, but as a recent case reminds us, the Act does not apply to international supply contracts (s. 26; see *Trident Turboprop (Dublin) Ltd v First Flight Couriers Ltd* [2009] EWCA Civ 290). Nor does it apply to contracts which are subject to English law only because the parties have chosen it as the applicable law (s. 27). Construction contracts now also have to be treated separately for some purposes, since there is now extensive regulation of at least the processes for resolving disputes (Housing Grants, Construction and Regeneration Act 1996; see *Chitty*, 2012, ch. 37). However, the general law still applies in fairly unadulterated form to most contracts between businesses, and it is on these that I will concentrate.

The second caveat is that the law is far from static. In the second part of this chapter I will discuss the recent developments which seem to point to a less abstract, or more relational, approach in English contract law.

The reasons for abstraction

There seem to be a number of reasons behind the preference for abstraction.

One concern may be accurate fact-finding. When juries were still used for contract cases, it may be that rules like the parol evidence rule were designed to prevent them hearing evidence to which they might give what the judges considered to be undue weight. It has been argued that this was the rationale for the parol evidence rule, at least in the United States (McCormick, 1932; see also Holdsworth, 1944, p. 176; in England suspicions that oral evidence was unreliable may have been more influential, see Law Commission, 1986, paras 2.1–5). Even in a trial by judge alone, if the parties' rights and obligations can be determined from a document and are not affected by the context, the law will be easier to apply. There will be less need to investigate the background or to take evidence from the parties or witnesses as to what each side's expectations really were. There will be less scope for dispute and therefore fewer disputes (see Collins, 1999, p. 206).

Much of the abstraction of English law is so embedded that we barely notice it. A prime example is the signature rule, that if you sign a contractual document you are bound by its terms, whether or not you have read the document or know what it contains, unless there was misrepresentation or an operative mistake (*L'Estrange v Graucob Ltd* [1934] 2 KB 394). The objective principle used to decide whether a party intended to contract (see *Paal Wilson & Co A/S v Partenreederi Hannah Blumenthal, The Hannah Blumenthal* [1983] 1 AC 854) tends to abstraction, as (at least on one version of the rule) the court need only decide how the normal person would have understood the other party's words or behaviour (for qualifications of both rules, see below, p. 131). The 'mirror image' rule, used to decide whether the parties have reached agreement when they have been exchanging standard forms (e.g. *Butler Machine Tool Co Ltd v Ex-Cell-O Corp (England) Ltd* [1979] 1 WLR 401), avoids the need to examine what each one understood – or might reasonably have understood – that the other was in fact prepared to agree. English law's 'bright line' approach to agreement, with only very limited liability for losses caused when negotiations unexpectedly break down, is another example. (Athough it is sometimes forgotten that there may be liability for negligently misleading a party into incurring expense on the assumption that the contract would definitely be accepted by the other: *Box v Midland Bank Ltd* [1981] 1 Lloyd's Rep 434, CA. There is not space here to explore how different this is to the celebrated US case of *Hoffmann v Red Owl Stores* 133 NW2d 267 (Wis, 1965). See further below, pp. 124–5.) The flat refusal of English law to give any remedy for a self-induced mistake as to the facts even when the mistake is known to the other party (*Smith v Hughes* (1871) LR 6 QB 597 and *Statoil ASA v Louis Dreyfus Energy Services LP (The Harriette N)* [2008] EWHC 2257 (Comm), [2008] 2 Lloyd's Rep 685), or to impose a general duty of disclosure (on the differences between English law and other laws, including that of the United States (see Beale, 2012a) enables the court to simply ignore what the parties knew or should have known in the particular context.

Abstraction is particularly evident in the rules on the content and meaning of the contract. It would clearly save a lot of time and effort if all written contracts met the Chancery lawyer's ideal that the judge could answer every conceivable question about the terms of the contract without taking his or her eyes from the document. I have referred already to the parol evidence rule. Some English courts seem to have applied this rule during the early nineteenth century (see Law Commission, 1986, paras 2.3–5). By the end of the century there was no more than strong presumption that the document contained all the terms of the bargain. In the twentieth century, if the court was convinced that a promise not contained in writing had been made and was intended still to be binding, it would either hold that the extrinsic promise formed a collateral contract (e.g. *De Lassalle v Guildford* [1901] 2 KB 215 or the majority decision in *Jacobs v Batavia and General Plantations Trust Ltd* [1924] 2 Ch 329) or simply that the contract was not intended to be wholly in writing, so that the parol evidence rule did not apply (e.g. *J Evans & Son (Portsmouth) Ltd v Andrea Merzario Ltd* [1976] 1 WLR 1078, CA). The Law Commission was called upon to consider whether the rule should be abolished; it concluded that there was nothing to abolish (Law Commission, 1986). At most, there seems to be a presumption (Treitel, 2011, para. 6-014) that if the parties have signed what looks like a complete contractual document, any promise or term not in the document was not intended to be part of the final deal. The Law Commission even suggested that a clause stating that the document was a complete record of the agreement, a 'merger' clause, would not be treated as conclusive (Law Commission, 1986, para. 2.15). But recently the courts have partly resurrected the rule as one of party autonomy: it seems that when the parties have agreed on a merger clause the court will normally treat it as conclusive: see *Inntrepreneur Pub Co Ltd v East Crown Ltd* [2002] 2 Lloyds Rep 611 and, in relation to a similar kind of clause that states there has been no reliance on any misrepresentation, *Watford Electronics Ltd v Sanderson L Ltd* [2001] EWCA Civ 317; *Peekay Intermark Ltd v Australia and New Zealand Banking Group Ltd* [2006] EWCA Civ 386, [2006] 2 Lloyd's Rep 511 at [54]–[60] and *Springwell Navigation Corp v JP Morgan Chase Bank* [2010] EWCA Civ 1221, [2010] 2 CLC 705 at [169]. (The tendency to treat the merger clause as conclusive is criticized by McLauchlan (2012).)

Abstraction was also evident in the so-called 'literal meaning' rule of contract interpretation. A good example is *Lovell & Christmas Ltd v Ward* (1911) 104 LT 85. Cozens-Hardy MR said:

> It is irrelevant and improper to ask what the parties, prior to the execution of the instrument, intended or understood. What is the meaning of the language that they have used therein? That is the problem, and the only problem. [Unless one of a list of exceptions (such as a customary meaning in the trade) applied,] it is the duty of the court, which is presumed to understand the English language, to construe the document according to the ordinary grammatical meaning of the words used therein. (p. 88)

Again the court needed only to consider the document unless it was shown to be ambiguous or obviously absurd or it contained technical terms (for the list of exceptions in which traditionally parol evidence could be given to explain the meaning of the words used, see Treitel, 2011, para. 6-021). The literal meaning rule has now been abandoned (see further below, pp. 130–1) but two firm restrictions remain: what was said in prior negotiations about the meaning of the words used may not be admitted (*Chartbrook Ltd v Persimmon Homes Ltd* [2009] UKHL 38, [2009] AC 1101), nor evidence of the parties' subsequent conduct (*James Miller & Partners v Whitworth Street Estates (Manchester) Ltd* [1970] AC 583, HL). These rules are clear examples of the courts limiting the amount of contextual material that needs to be taken into account. Lord Hoffmann's prime rationale for excluding evidence of prior negotiations was that:

> the admission of pre-contractual negotiations would create greater uncertainty of outcome in disputes over interpretation and add to the cost of advice, litigation or arbitration. Everyone engaged in the exercise would have to read the correspondence and statements would have to be taken from those who took part in oral negotiations. Not only would this be time-consuming and expensive but the scope for disagreement over whether the material affected the construction of the agreement ... would be considerably increased. (*Chartbrook v Persimmon Homes,* at [35])

Lastly, the traditional reluctance of the English courts to imply terms into a contract, especially when the term is one that would not be generally applicable to the type of contract involved, sometimes referred to as a term 'implied in fact' as opposed to a term 'implied in law', which are the standard default rules for the particular type of contract. To be 'implied in fact' the term must be one so obvious that it goes without saying (*Shirlaw v Southern Foundries (1926) Ltd* [1939] 2 KB 227 (aff'd [1940] AC 701), source of the 'officious bystander' test), also seems to have the effect of abstracting the contract from its particular context. (We will see that again there seems to be a recent change of approach here; below, p. 134.)

There are examples from other areas of contract law which are arguably examples of 'abstraction', rules which seem calculated to restrict the quantity of contextual material that is relevant. Thus in English law the doctrine of unconscionability seems to be limited to claimants who, at the time they entered the contract, were suffering from an identifiable 'bargaining disability': in *Boustany v Piggott* (1995) 69 P&CR 298, PC Lord Templeman said the stronger party must have taken unconscientious advantage of the weaker party's 'disabling condition or circumstances' (p. 303) (cf. *Commercial Bank of Australia v Amadio* (1983) 151 CLR 447, p. 474). The doctrine of frustration is narrowly confined to cases of supervening illegality and more-or-less permanent impossibility; neither commercial impracticability (Uniform Commercial Code §2–615) nor *force majeure* is a defence unless the contract so provides (as in *J Lauritzen AS v Wijsmuller BV, The Super Servant II* [1990] 1 Lloyd's Rep 1). Compared to many major continental laws (for example, Dutch and German law, which both have controls over terms of all kinds in general conditions of contract: see respectively Arts 6:231–43 BW and §§ 305–07 BGB), there are very few controls over unfair terms even when they are in standard form contracts: the Unfair Contract Terms Act 1977 is limited to clauses that exclude or restrict a party's liability (see s. 13) or which reduce the party's obligations in a way the other party does not reasonably expect (s. 3(2)(b)). The courts frequently prefer a 'perfect tender' rule to one permitting termination only when there has been a 'material' (or serious) breach (see below). All these devices reduce the relevance of the contextual background to the contract.

Reduction of litigation

The preference of English law for abstraction is not only about reducing the time and cost involved in deciding cases; it is also about reducing the incidence of litigation. The fewer facts are relevant to the legal position, the less the scope for disputes. Certainly, the courts' frequent preference for the perfect tender rule is based on a perceived need for certainty and the avoidance of litigation. The courts had been moving away from labelling many terms of contracts as conditions, breach of which would always give rise to a right to terminate (see Sale of Goods Act 1979, s. 11(3)), towards a rule that would permit the victim of a breach of contract to terminate only when the breach would have deprived it of the substance of what it was contracting for (*Hong Kong Fir Shipping Co Ltd v Kawasaki Kisen Kaisha Ltd* [1962] 2 QB 26, CA). Diplock LJ advocated a very restrictive approach: a term should be treated as a condition only if the contract or statute so provided, or if every breach of it would necessarily deprive the innocent party of the substance of what he was contracting for (*Hong Kong Fir Shipping Co*, p. 69). Subsequently, the House of Lords shied away from this flexible standard, holding that a delay in serving a notice telling the other party which ship was to carry the goods was a breach of condition (in other words, time was of the essence), even though there was no evidence that the fairly short delay caused the seller any difficulties. It was argued that a rigid, bright line rule will enable the parties to know exactly what their legal rights are: *Bunge Corp v Tradax Export SA* [1981] 1 WLR 711, HL. Whether this is really the case is questionable: the Law Commission (1987) has pointed out that when a rigid rule seems to produce a very unjust result, the courts have a tendency to fudge the issue, for example, by finding that there was no breach in the first place (para. 4.1). (See e.g. *Cehave NV v Bremer Handelsgesellschaft mbH* [1976] QB 44, the effect of which had to be corrected by amendments to the Sale of Goods Act 1979: see Law Commission, 1987, para. 4.1 and ss. 14(2) and 15A of the Act.) Be that as it may, the approach taken by the House of Lords fits with economic theory; economists have pointed out that parties who are each convinced that the court will side with them may even end up investing more in litigation than the dispute is worth (Priest, 1978).

Differing notions of fairness

It may not be wholly a question of reducing cost and the incidence of litigation. Systems of contract law based on precedents (and probably even Code-based systems, unless the Code is very detailed and prescriptive) contain the possibility of markedly different outcomes on the spectrum between individualism and communitarianism (or contractual solidarity, as Macneil seems to call it), and the balance will be struck at different places by different judges and at different times. Equally, legislation affecting contracts may not take a consistent approach, particularly if the political climate changes from one period to another. Nevertheless, in any one system there may be a tendency in a particular direction. Working with lawyers from continental Europe has made me realize that in contract cases other than consumer or employment cases the English courts have been pretty consistent in making decisions at the individualistic end of the spectrum.

An example of the approach that seems to typify English contract law is that a party will not be compensated for pre-contractual expenditure wasted when the defendant breaks off negotiations or makes unexpected demands, even if the defendant had given the claimant every reason to be confident that there would be a contract and the defendants' conduct was commercially quite unjustifiable. In *Cobbe v Yeoman's Row Management Ltd*

[2008] UKHL 55, [2008] 1 WLR 1752, a property owner and a developer had made an oral agreement for the redevelopment of a block of flats and the developer had incurred considerable expense in obtaining planning permission when the owner refused to go ahead unless given a much larger share of the profits. The Court of Appeal held that the developer was entitled to a remedy on the basis of proprietary estoppel. Even though it was accepted that the defendant had taken unconscionable advantage of the claimant (see *Cobbe v Yeoman's Row* at [28]), the House of Lords reversed the decision. This was partly on the ground that the terms of the proposed agreement had not been settled fully, but also on the basis that the claimant knew or must have known the risk. Lord Walker said:

> Mr Cobbe's case seems to me to fail on the simple but fundamental point that, as persons experienced in the property world, both parties knew that there was no legally binding contract, and that either was therefore free to discontinue the negotiations without legal liability ... Mr Cobbe ... ran a commercial risk, with his eyes open, and the outcome has proved unfortunate for him. (*Cobbe v Yeoman's Row* at [91]).

In the Australian case of *Walton Stores (Interstate) Ltd v Maher* (1988) 164 CLR 387, the defendant had indicated that it wished to take a lease of a property from the plaintiffs, which would require the plaintiffs to demolish the existing building and build afresh. The plaintiffs signed and sent their part of the contract to the defendant's solicitors who replied that 'we believe that approval will be forthcoming. We shall let you know tomorrow if any amendments are not agreed to.' The defendant changed its mind about taking the lease but did not inform the plaintiffs even though it knew that the plaintiffs were working on the premises to make them suitable for the defendants. The High Court granted a remedy based on promissory estoppel. I very much doubt that our Supreme Court would give a remedy on the same facts. This is not simply because the court does not have the technical means to do so, though on the decisions to date a party can rely on promissory estoppel when the other party has promised (without consideration) not to enforce or to give up an existing right, as in the case which first introduced the doctrine of promissory estoppel in English law, *Central London Property Trust Ltd v High Trees House Ltd* [1947] KB 130, and in *Collier v P & MJ Wright (Holdings) Ltd* [2007] EWCA Civ 1329, [2008] 1 WLR 643, but not if the promise was to create a new right: *Combe v Combe* [1951] 2 KB 215, CA. (Proprietary estoppel is not limited in this way but it would not apply here as Walton Stores was not representing that it would grant an interest in property to the plaintiffs; it was to take an interest from the plaintiffs.) Rather, I strongly suspect, it is because the English court would say that any loss was the claimant's own fault. It is true that the facts in the *Walton Stores* case were more extreme than those of *Cobbe's* case; Brennan J said that relief should not be given unless the defendant had induced a belief by the plaintiff that a legal relationship would exist between them. If the agreement were complete save that it was 'subject to contract' and the defendant had indicated that it would definitely go ahead, an English court would probably treat the defendant as 'waiving' the 'subject to contract' clause and hold that the contract was binding (*RTS Flexible Systems Ltd v Molkerei Alois Müller GmbH & Co KG (UK Production)* [2010] UKSC 14, [2010] 1 WLR 753 at [86]). But I doubt whether anything less than a deliberate statement that the requirement was being waived would suffice for an English court; a statement like that made by the defendant's solicitors in *Walton Stores* would not be enough. I am fairly sure that the court would still take the view that the claimants, or at least the claimants' solicitors, should have realized that there was no contract and that they would take any action in reliance at their own risk (cf. *Secretary of State for Transport v Christos* [2003] EWCA Civ 1073, [2004] 1 P & CR 17 at [36]–[37]), and so fairness does not require a remedy, at least from the defendant – the court might take the view that the plaintiffs' solicitors should have warned them not to start work until the contract had been signed. The claimants (or their advisors) should look after their own interests better.

There are many other examples of a similar approach. Thus there is no relief for a unilateral, self-induced mistake of fact or law, even when the mistake was known to the other party (*Smith v Hughes*: in contrast, a mistake in the terms of the offer is relevant: the offeree cannot accept an offer which he knows does not represent what the offeror intends, *Hartog v Colin and Shields* [1939] 3 All ER 566). English law has not followed the US or Canadian courts in giving relief for 'calculation' mistakes. In those jurisdictions, relief is given where the offeror's bid is too low because it has made a mistake in calculating how much work is required or what its offer should be, as opposed to making a mistake in stating the offer itself (see Farnsworth, 2004, p. 615, referring to cases such as *Boise Junior College District v Mattefs Construction Co*, 450 P 2d 604 and to Restatement 2d §153, Illustration 4; in Canada, after a complicated history starting from the English approach (see *McMaster University v Wilchar Construction Ltd* 22 DLR (3d) 9 (Ont SC), and *Imperial Glass Ltd v Consolidated Supplies Ltd* (1960), 22 DLR (2d) 759 (BC Court of Appeal), it now seems that relief will be given in equity: see McCamus (2008)). Duties of disclosure, whether direct or indirect by imposing liability for defects that were not made known to the other party, are limited to specific situations (see the list of exceptions in Chitty, 2012, paras 6-150–72; the issues are discussed at length in Beale, 2012a).

Parties should make their own enquiries. Similarly, we have already seen that the courts are reluctant to imply terms into a contract (above, p. 121). The absence of a doctrine of good faith from English law is notorious. I am not convinced that the lack of a general doctrine makes so much difference. In German law, for example, the good faith clause in §242 BGB is generally not used to control contracts or contractual behaviour directly, but is the basis on which the courts developed new doctrines to deal with omissions from the Civil Code (e.g. so-called 'positive breach of contract', such as failing to take care to avoid causing damage while performing the contract, which was incorporated into the BGB in 2001, see §241(2)) or with new phenomena such as standard form contracts (see e.g. BGH 4 June 1970, BGHZ 54, 106, NJW 1970, 1596 (translated in Beale et al., 2010, no 16.4); the controls that were later put into statutory form in the AGBG 1976 and since 2002 have been incorporated into §§305–10 BGB). English judges can reach many of the same results but they do so by developing specific rules rather than by relying on general doctrines (see the oft-quoted statement of Bingham LJ in *Interfoto Picture Library Ltd v Stilletto Visual Programmes Ltd* [1989] 1 QB 433, 439). The real question is: what rules do the courts in each country choose to develop? Sometimes they reach very similar results. Thus in each country a tenderer who has not been awarded a contract because the other party has failed to follow the published rules of the tendering procedure has been awarded loss of bargain damages (*Blackpool and Fylde Aero Club Ltd v Blackpool BC* [1990] 1 WLR 25; BGH, 25 November 1992 NJW 1993.520). At other times the results are complete opposites. German courts hold that a right to terminate a contract because of a delay, even when the contract provides that the creditor may cancel if there is any delay (a *fixgeschäft*), is qualified by the doctrine of good faith (Markesinis et al., 2006, 124–25, citing RG 12 February 1918, RGZ 92, 208 and RG 29 June 1927, RGZ 117, 354). English courts have refused to hold that the creditor must exercise its remedies in a reasonable way and have allowed termination for what appeared to be a trivial breach, such as paying an instalment of hire a few hours late, even when the creditor's motive seems to have been to escape the contract which had become unprofitable in changed market conditions (*Mardorf Peach & Co Ltd v Attica Sea Carriers Corp of Liberia (The Laconia)* [1977] AC 850, HL; see also *Union Eagle Ltd v Golden Achievement Ltd* [1997] AC 514). Instead, the English courts' reaction was that if the charterer wanted to prevent the owners from terminating in such a situation, it should put a clause to that effect in the contract (*The Laconia*, p. 833). Many charters do now include an 'anti-technicality' clause (see the recent decision in *Petroleo Brasileiro SA (Respondent) v ENE Kos 1 Ltd* [2012] UKSC 17). In other words, the parties should specify their own remedies and limits on them rather than look to the court for a solution. This may be partly a question of 'comparative advantage' that it is more efficient for the parties to prescribe the precise terms they wish to see observed than for the court to do so after the event (see Schwartz and Scott, 2003, p. 549), but it also seems to be the point that to take advantage of a technical breach is not seen as unfair; it is all part of the game. If you did not appreciate the risks or did not look after your own interests – well, that's tough: you will know for next time.

Conversely, when the parties have agreed on a term, the English courts and indeed English law show great reluctance to override it. This is evidenced by the limited nature of the statutory controls over the terms of business-to-business contracts – in effect, only over exclusion and limitation of liability clauses, with no controls at all for 'international contracts'; and by judicial statements. The following statement by Chadwick LJ, dealing with a clause by which one party acknowledged that it had not relied on any pre-contractual representation by the other, reflects what seems to be the typical judicial attitude:

> There are, as it seems to me, at least two good reasons why the courts should not refuse to give effect to an acknowledgement of non-reliance in a commercial contract between experienced parties of equal bargaining power— *a fortiori*, where those parties have the benefit of professional advice. First, it is reasonable to assume that the parties desire commercial certainty. They want to order their affairs on the basis that the bargain between them can be found within the document which they have signed. They want to avoid the uncertainty of litigation based on allegations as to the content of oral discussions at pre-contractual meetings. Second, it is reasonable to assume that the price to be paid reflects the commercial risk which each party—or, more usually, the purchaser—is willing to accept. The risk is determined, in part at least, by the warranties which the vendor is prepared to give. The tighter the warranties, the less the risk and (in principle, at least) the greater the price the vendor will require and which the purchaser will be prepared to pay. It is legitimate, and commercially desirable, that both parties should be able to measure the risk, and agree the price, on the basis of the warranties which have been given and accepted. (Chadwick LJ in *Watford Electronics* at [39], quoting his own judgment in the earlier, unreported case of *EA Grimstead & Son Ltd v McGarrigan* (27 October 1999); see also the remarks in the House of Lords in *Photo Production Ltd Respondents v Securicor Transport Ltd* [1980] AC 827, pp. 851, 852)

Chadwick LJ limits his remarks to cases of equal bargaining power, and in the relevant case the trial judge had found that there was no equality of either bargaining power or bargaining skill (see *Watford Electronics* at [23]). However, it is common to find the court treating the parties as equal in bargaining power or skill without, apparently, detailed investigation.

Abstraction by the parties

We also find examples of deliberate abstraction by the parties. The obvious examples are the merger and 'no reliance' clauses already mentioned: the background, in particular the context of what was promised or represented in the negotiating process, is not to affect the contract. Obviously, such a clause may not represent a genuine agreement; it may be a term in the party's standard conditions and the other may have been unaware of it or have had insufficient bargaining power to get it taken out. But when the parties do seem to have been skilled bargainers and are more-or-less equal in bargaining power, it seems more likely that they had a genuine desire to exclude promises and representations that were not included in the writing. There may be many reasons, including a desire for certainty, concerns about the position if rights under the contract are later assigned and simply making it easier for those who had not been involved in the negotiations to administer the contract later.

We find other examples of abstraction. Contracts frequently provide for more extensive termination rights than would exist at common law; sometimes these are very severe, allowing termination for very slight breaches (e.g. *Lombard North Central plc v Butterworth*[1987] QB 527). These are not always, I think, abuses of bargaining power by one party. Sometimes, I suspect, the parties agree to the right though they do not expect it to be exercised unless events have led to the failure of the commercial relationship. But they do not attempt, deliberately, to spell out their expectations of when the right will or will not be used. This is partly because it would be very difficult to draft suitable safeguards; but possibly also because they both recognize that giving one party a kind of 'nuclear deterrent' may be an effective way of ensuring that the contract is performed properly by the other. Think about the distributorship agreement for large panel presses in *Schuler AG v Wickman Machine Tools Sales Ltd* [1974] AC 235. This provided that 'it shall be condition' that the distributor visit each of the (then) six large motor manufacturers each week. Why was this clause inserted? Very probably because visits were crucial to sales – the way in which most large machine tools were sold was by the sales reps 'being around' when existing machines were being operated, seeing any difficulties or inefficiencies and suggesting how newer machines could overcome the problems. How could the manufacturer ensure that the distributor did visit regularly? Specific performance was out of the question. Damages would be of little use because it would be almost impossible to prove that missing a particular visit had caused a sale to be lost (a point made by Moccatta J at first instance). An agreed damages clause might have worked but the parties could not be confident that the clause would be upheld when the loss from missing some visits would be nil (see the criteria stated in *Dunlop Pneumatic Tyre Co Ltd v New Garage and Motor Co Ltd* [1915] AC 79, p. 88; they are not easy to apply). A severe right to terminate may have seemed the obvious answer, and one that the distributor might well have agreed to. The majority in the House of Lords held that the result that the contract could be terminated because of missing a single visit was so unreasonable that the term could not have been meant to be a condition. My sympathies are with the dissenting speech of Lord Wilberforce, who remarked:

> to call the clause arbitrary, capricious or fantastic, or to introduce as a test of its validity the ubiquitous reasonable man (I do not know whether he is English or German) is to assume, contrary to the evidence, that both parties to this contract adopted a standard of easygoing tolerance rather than one of aggressive, insistent punctuality and efficiency (*Schuler AG v Wickman*, p. 263).

An example of abstraction which seems regularly to be agreed between parties of equal bargaining power is the demand (or 'autonomous') guarantee. This gives one party the right to call on a guarantor, normally a bank, for the agreed sum without having to show that the party whose performance is guaranteed is even in breach of contract (for a detailed account, see Benjamin, 2010, ch. 24).

Reasons for the abstract approach

The abstract and individualist nature of English contract law is, I think, primarily to be explained by the nature of the cases which are brought before the courts – or at least in the superior courts whose decisions 'count' as precedents and are reported (see Beale, 2012b). The overwhelming bulk of the reported cases are 'commercial' cases, usually involving high-value contracts between parties who are sophisticated or at least well advised. Between such parties, the old notions of freedom and sanctity of contract, and of self-reliance – *'qui dit contractuel dit juste'* (Fouillée, 1885, p. 410; see Rolland, 2006, p. 771) – are quite plausible. It is also plausible to expect the parties to such contracts to have planned them in some detail.

An additional factor is that often the relevant market is volatile. This is an old story but one that is worth recalling. Just think how many of the leading contract and sale of goods cases seem to have been fought because the market has changed dramatically and the party who stands to lose as a result is desperately seeking a way to get out of the contract and thus shift the market risk back to the other party (as in the *Hong Kong Fir* case). This is a zero-sum game. Parties have an incentive to litigate rather than to reach a mutually beneficial arrangement (Priest, 1978).

Counter-tendencies

However, even in the relatively stable legal world of England and Wales, contract law is both dynamic and contested. Partly this is because judicial attitudes, like everyone else's, seem to be influenced by changes in the political climate. I think this is true even of judges whose analysis appears to be in purely doctrinal terms. A striking example is the decision in *Clough Mill Ltd v Martin* [1985] 1 WLR 111, decided in 1985 by the Court of Appeal under Lord Donaldson MR. The case involved a retention of title clause; the question was whether yarn which had been supplied and which was still in the buyer's possession, unused, remained the seller's property or whether the seller's interest in the yarn amounted to a charge. Earlier courts (such as *Re Bond Worth Ltd* [1980] Ch 228; *Borden (UK) Ltd v Scottish Timber Products Ltd* [1981] Ch 25) had been doubtful that the yarn could simply remain the seller's property when, unlike in the usual bailment case, the buyer had the right to use up the yarn. These doubts were swept away; Robert Goff LJ remarked that 'concepts such as bailment and fiduciary duty must not be allowed to be our masters, but must rather be regarded as the tools of our trade' (*Clough Mill v Martin*, p. 116). He went on to demonstrate how the clause could, by the implication of appropriate restrictions and by employing restitutionary remedies, be made to work fairly (pp. 117–18). But different judges also take different approaches to contract law and have different ideas of how the law can best serve the needs of the parties or society. Recent cases, and in particular a number of decisions in the House of Lords in which the leading speech was delivered by Lord Hoffmann, provide examples of this. I will refer to the cases on interpretation, on 'assumption of responsibility' and on implied terms.

I have said that at one time English law seemed to adopt the literal meaning rule of contract interpretation, under which a document would be given its literal meaning – the meaning of the words in proper parlance – unless it was shown to be ambiguous or obviously absurd or it contained terms which have a technical or customary meaning (for the list of exceptions in which traditionally parol evidence could be given to explain the meaning of the words used, see Treitel, 2011). In *Investors Compensation Scheme Ltd v West Bromwich Building Society* [1998] 1 WLR 896, Lord Hoffmann rejected the literal approach completely (the principles set out by Lord Hoffmann in this case have subsequently been adopted in numerous cases: see Chitty (2012), para. 12-050). Although his speech has been quoted many times, some of it bears quoting again:

> (1) Interpretation is the ascertainment of the meaning which the document would convey to a reasonable person having all the background knowledge which would reasonably have been available to the parties in the situation in which they were at the time of the contract.
> (2) The background includes absolutely anything which would have affected the way in which the language of the document would have been understood by a reasonable man [except what was said during negotiations] ...
> (4) The meaning which a document (or any other utterance) would convey to a reasonable man is not the same thing as the meaning of its words. The meaning of words is a matter of dictionaries and grammars; the meaning of the document is what the parties using those words against the relevant background would reasonably have been understood to mean ... (pp. 912–13)

This approach caused consternation among some judges (e.g. Saville LJ in *National Bank of Sharjah v Dellborg*, 9 July 1997, referred to by Staughton LJ in *Scottish Power plc v Britoil, Times*, 2 December 1997), and I think the reason is not hard to see. If everything in the background that the parties might have had in mind needs to be taken into account, the difficulty and cost of making a correct interpretation will be increased very significantly. Staughton LJ said:

> ... it is often difficult for a judge to restrain the enthusiasm of counsel for producing a great deal of evidence under the heading of matrix, which on examination is found to contribute little or nothing to the true understanding of the parties' contract. All, or almost all, judges are now concerned about the huge cost of litigation. I have to say that such a wide definition of surrounding circumstances, background or matrix seems likely to increase the cost, to no very obvious advantage.

It is perhaps not surprising that, in a more recent case, *Rainy Sky SA v Kookmin Bank*, the majority of the Court of Appeal ([2010] EWCA Civ 582,

[2011] 1 Lloyd's Rep 233) took a somewhat different line. In simplified form, the question was what was covered by a refund guarantee provided by the bank to the buyer of a ship that was being built. Clause 2 recited the buyer's entitlement to repayment on termination, rescission or total loss. Clause 3 stated: 'In consideration of you making pre-delivery instalments ... we undertake to pay such sums due to you under the contract.' The question was whether the guarantee applied only to refunds due on the events stated in cl. 2, or also refunds due when the builders were insolvent. Sir Simon Tuckey, dissenting, held that cl. 3 must refer to refunds of payments due for any reason, or the buyer would be left unprotected in the one case in which the guarantee was really needed, namely when the builders were insolvent. The majority refuse to depart from what appeared to them to be the reasonable meaning of the words of cl. 3, namely that the guarantee covered only refunds due in the events listed in the preceding clause. Patten LJ accepted that 'the words used may, if given a particular meaning, lead to consequences which are so extreme as to make it unlikely that the parties intended them to have that effect' (para. 39); but concluded that this was not a case:

> in which the construction contended for would produce an absurd or irrational result in the sense described in the cases I have referred to and merely to say that no credible commercial reason has been advanced for the limited scope of the bond does, in my view, put us in real danger of substituting our own judgment of the commerciality of the transaction for that of those who were actually party to it.

The decision was overturned by the Supreme Court ([2011] UKSC 50, [2011] 1 WLR 2900), which followed Lord Hoffmann's approach. Lord Clarke JSC said that:

> It is not in my judgment necessary to conclude that, unless the most natural meaning of the words produces a result so extreme as to suggest that it was unintended, the court must give effect to that meaning.
> The language used by the parties will often have more than one potential meaning. I would accept the submission made on behalf of the appellants that the exercise of construction is essentially one unitary exercise in which the court must consider the language used and ascertain what a reasonable person, that is a person who has all the background knowledge which would reasonably have been available to the parties in the situation in which they were at the time of the contract,

would have understood the parties to have meant. In doing so, the court must have regard to all the relevant surrounding circumstances. If there are two possible constructions, the court is entitled to prefer the construction which is consistent with business common sense and to reject the other. (at [20]–[21])

So the court cannot avoid considering the background unless the relevant term in the contractual document has only one possible meaning.

The result is that in matters of interpretation at least, English contract law is to be sensitive to the background in which the contract was made. This seems to me to be a deliberate move towards what Roger Brownsword (1996) has called 'dynamic' market-individualism but also towards a more relational approach.

It is arguable that this is not a deliberate shift so much as an inevitable logical development. Lord Hoffmann's approach follows logically (*Investors Compensation Scheme*, pp. 912–13) from the earlier decisions of the House of Lords in *Prenn v Simmonds* [1971] 1 WLR 1381 and *Reardon Smith Line Ltd v Yngvar Hansen-Tangen* [1976] 1 WLR 989. It is widely acknowledged that the meaning of words depends on the context in which they are used (the most frequently cited authority appears to be Wittgenstein, 2001). However, I am not sure that the other two developments I mentioned are merely inevitable logical developments.

Take first the new element of 'assumption of responsibility', which now seems to form part of the remoteness test for damages for breach of contract. Before the decision in *Transfield Shipping Inc v Mercator Shipping Inc (The Achilleas)* [2008] UKHL 48, [2008] 3 WLR 345, the general understanding had been that a party which breaks a contract is liable for losses that would appear to be the natural and probable result of the breach under the 'first limb' of *Hadley v Baxendale* 1854) 9 Ex 341. The exact likelihood of the loss has been the subject of debate (see, in particular, *Koufos v C Czarnikow Ltd, The Heron II* [1969] 1 AC 350; and Chitty, 2012, paras 26-115–118) but it seems generally agreed that losses fall within this test if they are 'not unusual'. The party in breach may also be liable for 'unusual' losses if they were reasonably contemplated by the parties at the time the contract was made. 'Contemplation' may have required more than mere knowledge on the part of the party who is to be held liable; arguably, the possibility of the losses had to be bought home to the party in such a way that it was reasonable to think the party was accepting responsibility for them (see Robert Goff J in *Satef-Huttenes Albertus SpA v Paloma Tercera Shipping Co SA* [1981] 1 Lloyd's Rep 175, p. 183; Chitty, 2012, para. 26–122). But in *The Achilleas*, the majority, led it seems by Lord Hoffmann, held that the victim of a breach of contract cannot recover a loss just because it was 'not unlikely' to occur if the contract was broken. Even a 'not unlikely' loss is not recoverable if, in the circumstances in which the contract was made, it was not reasonable to think that the party who had broken the contract was assuming responsibility for a loss of the relevant kind. To me, this marks a change of approach. I had understood the earlier House of Lords case of *Koufos v C Czarnikow* to adopt exactly the opposite policy: if loss is a likely one, but a party does not wish to be liable for it should he break the contract, it is up to him to get an exclusion clause in the contract. Indeed, precisely this was the approach taken recently by Rix LJ, delivering the only full judgment, in *Rubenstein v HSBC Bank plc* [2012] EWCA Civ 1184. The old policy seemed to be that it is more appropriate that the parties should fix the limits of liability in advance, rather than the court do so after the event using a necessarily vague test such as 'assumption of responsibility' (see at [123]). True, the old remoteness test is not straightforward to apply: in particular it is unclear to what extent the test applies only to the kind of loss, the seriousness or amount of it being a matter of quantification; it sometimes seems to operate more as a financial limit on liability, which seems to be the practical effect in cases like *Victoria Laundry (Windsor) Ltd v Newman Industries Ltd* [1949] 2 KB 528 where the court treats various losses of profit as being different kinds of loss. But whether the loss was or was not unusual, even if it is a test imposed by a rule of law rather than flowing from the consent of the parties (see Lord Hoffmann's speech in *The Achilleas* at [9]) is a relatively bright line test, one that can sensibly be applied as the default rule, i.e. unless the parties have expressly agreed that one should not be liable for an identified or identifiable loss. The decision that there must also be an assumption of responsibility again seems to make the law more responsive to the context of the individual contract, but at a cost – dispute settlement will involve deeper investigation of the factual circumstances, and the application of broad standards will lead to greater uncertainty. It is perhaps not surprising that subsequent cases have indicated that the new test will make a difference only in exceptional cases: e.g. *Sylvia Shipping Co Ltd v Progress Bulk Carriers Ltd* [2010] EWHC 542 (Comm), [2010] 2 Lloyd's Rep 81.

I think a similar point can be made about Lord Hoffmann's approach to implied terms in *Att-Gen of Belize v Belize Telecom Ltd* [2009] UKPC 10, [2009] 1 WLR 1988, in which he argued that the implication of terms is essentially the same as interpretation, a question of what the reasonable man would understand the document to mean. Does the decision herald a greater readiness to rewrite the document to bring it into line with commercial expectations? I suspect it does. I agree that interpretation and the implication of terms are different points on a single spectrum – indeed, I understand that German law refers to 'supplementary' (Beale et al., 2010,

p. 749) or 'completive' interpretation' (Markesinis et al., 2006, p. 139). But I agree with Davies (2010, p. 144) that there is a difference between interpreting what is there and implying words that are not, and it seems to me to be perfectly possible to interpret the express words according to the context in which they were used but to refuse to supply additional terms on a stricter basis, say that the contract is unworkable without them. That would keep the onus on the parties to plan for themselves. Lord Hoffmann's approach is more responsive, more relational, but whether it will actually result in any change in practice I wait to see. I suspect other judges may be reluctant to follow it (see *Mediterranean Salvage & Towage Ltd v Seamar Trading & Commerce Inc (The Reborn)* [2009] EWCA Civ 531, where Lord Clarke at [17]–[18] was at pains to stress that the test remains one of necessity; *Fitzhugh v Fitzhugh* [2012] EWCA Civ 694, [2012] P & CR 14 at [17]; and Chitty, 2012, para. 13–005), because they may suspect it to be a Trojan Horse. Just how far does it go? The reasonable lawyer always reads the document and probably expects a rather literal interpretation. The reasonable businessperson may well take a different line (compare what Sir Thomas Bingham said about the interpretation of Unfair Contract Terms Act 1977, s. 3(2)(b) in *Timeload Ltd v British Telecommunications plc* [1995] EMLR 459, p. 468). Ask the businessperson, 'Does this clause saying that the ship may be withdrawn from the charter if the hire is not paid by 1 April mean that it may be withdrawn if the hire is paid a couple of hours late because of a delay at the bank?' (*The Laconia*), and I suspect the answer would be no. So do we imply an anti-technicality clause? If so, it seems to me that we would not be so far away from good faith and fair dealing. (And see now *Yam Seng Pte Ltd v International Trade Corp Ltd* [2013] EWHC 111 (QB), [2013] 1 Lloyds Rep 526.)

Conclusions

My conclusions can be stated very simply. The traditional approach of English law to business-to-business contracts has tended towards abstraction, deliberately ignoring the context in which the agreement was made, so as to reduce the amount of factual investigation required to decide cases and to reduce uncertainty. Recent developments have made the law more responsive to the contractual context, but at a cost – the cost of more investigation, of greater uncertainty and possibly a reduction in the incentives given to parties to plan for themselves. Some of these developments – particularly the recognition that the meaning of the words used always depends on the context in which they were used – seem inevitable and are probably here to stay. But I wonder whether the courts will embrace either the 'assumption of responsibility' test for contract damages or greater flexibility to imply terms when, in each case, there seems to be a more bright line rule that might be applied in the 'commercial contract' cases on which the courts seem to focus. Just possibly, English judges will turn out to be closet relationalists. But it seems more likely to me that they will conclude that greater responsiveness comes at too great a cost.

References

Beale, H (2012a) *Mistake and Non-disclosure of Facts: Models for English Contract Law* (Oxford: Oxford University Press)

Beale, H (2012b) 'Characteristics of Contract Laws and the European Optional Instrument'

Beale, H, B Fauvarque-Cosson, J Rutgers, D Tallon and S Vogenauer (eds) (2010) *Ius Commune Casebooks for the Common Law of Europe: Cases, Materials and Text on Contract Law* (Oxford: Hart Publishing) (2nd edn)

Benjamin (2010) M Bridge (ed.), *Benjamin's Sale of Goods* (London: Sweet & Maxwell) (8th edn)

Brownsword, R (1996) 'Static and Dynamic Market Individualism' in R Halson (ed.), *Exploring the Boundaries of Contract* (Aldershot: Dartmouth), p. 48

Brownsword, R (2011) 'The Theoretical Foundations of European Private Law: A Time to Stand and Stare' in R Brownsword, H-W Micklitz, L Niglia and S Weatherill (eds), *The Foundations of European Private Law* (Oxford: Hart Publishing)

Campbell, D (ed.) (2001) *The Relational Theory of Contract: Selected Works of Ian Macneil* (London: Sweet & Maxwell)

Chitty (2012) H Beale (gen. ed.), *Chitty on Contracts* (London: Sweet & Maxwell) (31st edn)

Collins, H (1999) *Regulating Contracts* (Oxford: Clarendon Press.)

Davies, P (2010) 'Recent Developments in the Law of Implied Terms' [2012] *Lloyd's Maritime and Commercial Law Quarterly* 140

Farnsworth, A (2004) *Contracts* (New York: Aspen) (4th edn)

Feinman, J (2001) 'The Reception of Ian Macneil's Work on Contract in the USA' in Campbell (2001), p. 59

Fouillée, A (1885) *La science sociale contemporaine* (Paris: Hachette) (2nd edn)

Goode (2009) C Proctor (ed.), *Goode on Payment Obligations in Commercial and Financial Transactions* (London: Sweet & Maxwell) (2nd edn)

Goode, R (1991) 'Abstract Payment Undertakings' in P Cane and J Stapleton (eds), *Essays for Patrick Atiyah* (Oxford: Clarendon Press), p. 209

Holdsworth, W S (1944) *A History of English Law* vol. IX (London: Sweet & Maxwell)

Law Commission (1986) *Law of Contract. The Parol Evidence Rule* Report No 154 Cmnd 9700 (London: HMSO)

Law Commission (1987) *Sale and Supply of Goods* Report No 160 Cmnd 137 (London: HMSO)

Macneil, I (1980) *The New Social Contract: An Enquiry into Modern Contractual Relations* (New Haven: Yale University Press)

Markesinis, B, H Unberath and A Johnston (eds) (2006) *The German Law of Contract* (Oxford: Hart Publishing) (2nd edn)

McCamus, J (2008) 'Mistaken Bids and Unilateral Mistake: A New Solution for an Old Problem' 87 *Canadian Bar Review* 1

McCormick, C (1932) 'The Parol Evidence Rule as a Procedural Device for Control of the Jury' 41 *Yale Law Journal* 365

McKendrick, E (1995) 'The Regulation of Long-term Contracts in English Law' in J Beatson and D Friedmann (eds), *Good Faith and Fault in Contract Law* (Oxford: Clarendon Press), p. 305

McLauchlan, D (2012) 'The Entire Agreement Clause: Conclusive or a Question of Weight' 128(4) *Law Quarterly Review* 521

Priest, G (1978) 'Breach and Remedy for the Tender of Non-conforming Goods' 91 *Harvard Law Review* 960

Rolland, L (2006) '"Qui dit contractual, dit juste" en trois petit bonds, a reculons' 51 *McGill Law Journal* 765

Schwartz, A and R Scott (2003) 'Contract Theory and the Limits of Contract Law' 113 *Yale Law Journal* 541

Scott, R (2000) 'The Case for Formalism in Relational Contract' 94 *Northwestern University Law Review* 847

Treitel, G H (2011) E Peel (ed.), *The Law of Contract* (London: Sweet & Maxwell) (13th edn)

Wittgenstein, L (2001) *Philosophical Investigations*, G Anscombe (trans.) (Oxford: Blackwell) (3rd edn)

7
Arcos v Ronaasen as a Relational Contract[1]
David Campbell

Introduction

I have long been of the opinion that the main reason that the relational theory of contract set out by the late Ian Macneil has encountered such resistance from mainstream understandings of the law is that it has been interpreted as a very paternalistic theory opposed to freedom of contract, one which has no or very little place for competition. I have argued at great length elsewhere that this certainly was not Macneil's intention (Campbell, 2001), and, drawing on his work, that the relational theory can readily be restated in such a way as to give competition a central place in, say, the doctrines of agreement (Campbell, 2003) and remedy (Campbell, 2005). Contracts can usefully be placed along a spectrum ranging from the simplest to the most complex, and, as I have myself argued (Campbell and Harris, 1993; Campbell, 2013), it is true that the latter more clearly evidence the self-consciously co-operative action by the parties that Stewart Macaulay called 'non-contractual relations' and Macneil, in the earlier stages of his work, called relational contracting. Nevertheless, the correct view of the relational theory is, I believe, not that there is a class of relational contracts which should be distinguished from discrete contracts, but that all contracts, including the simplest (Campbell, 1996), are relational. The reason the relational theory is so superior to the classical law of contract (and its corollary neoclassical economic understanding of exchange) is that all contracts can be fully understood only when their relational dimension is made explicit (Campbell, 1997). In this chapter, I hope to provide evidence for this claim by examining what I think it will be

---

1 I am grateful to Warren Swain, to those attending the Macneil conference and the members of the North East Regional Obligations Group for comments on this chapter.

allowed is, on the face of it, *a* if not *the* case which is most unpromising for this purpose: *Arcos Ltd v EA Ronaasen and Son*.[2]

Though commonly coupled in this respect with *In re Moore and Co Ltd and Landauer and Co* [1921] 2 KB 519, *Arcos* is perhaps the most criticized case in the entire law of the sale of goods, and, when it features in discussion of the general principles of the law of contract, it challenges the likes of *Bell v Lever Bros* [1932] AC 161 and *Junior Books v Veitchi Co* [1983] 1 AC 520 for this unwelcome distinction. It is widely regarded as the paradigm case of a rigidly formal interpretation of contract terms absurdly and unfairly trumping a sensible and fair contextual interpretation of those terms; just the sort of thing, in fact, that recent authority such as *Rainy Sky SA v Kookmin Bank* [2011] UKSC 50, [2011] 1 WLR 2900 tells us should no longer be possible after *Investors Compensation Scheme Ltd v West Bromwich Building Society* [1998] 1 WLR 896. Generalizing from its shortcomings as an approach to interpretation, *Arcos* has persuasively been argued to be evidence of the unwelcome consequences of the excessive individualism of the classical law of contract.

However, disentangling *Arcos* from the central principles of the sale of goods has not proven at all easy. It has never been overruled, and it still has a significant, unhappy influence on the interpretation of key sections of the Sale of Goods Act 1979, namely description under s. 13(1), satisfactory quality under s. 14(2), fitness for purpose under s. 14(3), and delivery of a wrong quantity under s. 30. It has had a similar influence on the definition of key terms in the law of the sale of goods, such as delivery under s. 29, acceptance under s. 35 and, most importantly, the distinction between conditions and warranties under s. 11.

After setting out the facts and issues raised by *Arcos*, I will examine the criticisms which have been made of it, focusing on those of the late Professor John Adams (sometimes writing with Professor Hector MacQueen in their edition of *Atiyah* (Adams and MacQueen, 2010)) and Professor

---

2 *Ronaasen and Son v Arcos Ltd* came before the King's Bench Division on the issue of correspondence with description on 15 December 1931, by way of a special case stated by the umpire of the arbitral tribunal which first heard the matter. It was referred back for further evidence and was given a full hearing by the King's Bench on 19 February 1932. It was heard in the Court of Appeal on 12 and 13 April 1932 and in the House of Lords on 29 November, 30 November and 1 December 1933. The King's Bench, Court of Appeal and House of Lords judgments are all reported in the *Lloyd's List Law Reports* and the Lords judgment is also reported in the *Appeal Cases*. In this chapter, the Kings Bench judgment will be referred to as *Arcos* (KBD), the Court of Appeal judgment as *Arcos* (CA), and the *Appeal Cases* report of the Lords judgment as *Arcos* (HL(E)).

There had been a previous reference by the umpire on another issue which is unreported but which will be discussed in this chapter. *Arcos* was, of course, decided under the Sale of Goods Act 1893, but, save when the argument requires it, I shall discuss the case as if the Sale of Goods Act 1979, as amended, had applied.

Roger Brownsword. My fundamental purpose is to demonstrate the superiority of the relational theory of contract over all rival theories, and Adams' and Brownsword's criticism of *Arcos* allows us to compare the relational theory, not only to the classical law of contract, but also to the welfarist law which has been the classical law's most successful rival so far, for they have been two of the leading proponents of welfarism (Brownsword, 1994; Adams and Brownsword, 2004). In regard of our concerns here, the central thrust of the welfarist law is the replacement of the excessive individualism of the classical law with an appreciation of the necessity of co-operation between the parties articulated in a doctrine of good faith.

Though I am in substantial agreement with Adams and Brownsword, I believe the welfarist conception of contract is inadequate. Despite various restatements of their early opposition between the classical 'market-individualist' and the co-operative 'consumer-welfarist' laws, their conception of the criticism of the classical law remains one of a choice between two opposed sets of values. Not only does this mean that their criticism remains exogenous to the classical law and so can be, and has been, simply put to one side by those committed to that law, but, to be frank, if this choice was the issue, I do not think the welfarist law is the one which should be chosen, for I believe that the market competition articulated by the classical law is the best economic system of which it is possible to conceive, or, rather, it would be if its values were, as Hegel would have put it, made actual. The lack of attractiveness of a welfarist law which is ultimately inimical to market competition is, in my opinion, the reason that welfarist reform of the law of sale has not been able to eliminate *Arcos* from the sale of goods, for welfarism cannot adequately fill the gaps that the removal of *Arcos* would leave.

This is because, although *Arcos* is in the end badly wrong, it makes far more sense than it is normally given credit for, both at the level of the doctrine it expounds and at the level of the individualism that is the background to that doctrine. This is not to say that *Arcos* is acceptable as law. It isn't. But, in my opinion, only a criticism of *Arcos* as failing adequately to give effect to the values of the classical law will show why this is the case. This would be not a criticism from an exogenous standpoint, but an endogenous criticism starting with the values of the classical law; an immanent criticism, as, again, Hegel would have put it. It is my belief that the relational theory is essential for this form of criticism of *Arcos*. This may appear a surprising thing to say, for *Arcos* concerned a standard commodity sold on the usual terms for unascertained goods. It therefore appears to be a paradigmatic discrete contract which could hardly be more different from the complex performance involving bespoke understandings between the parties to what Macneil used to call a relational contract. But, as I have said, the best understanding of the relational theory of contract is that it points to the relational dimensions of all contracts, including those Macneil called discrete. In my terminology, though there is a spectrum of contracts running from the simple to the complex, all contracts are relational. Identifying the relational dimensions in *Arcos* allows us both to understand its shortcomings more clearly and to posit a more adequate, non-classical law, the virtue of which is that it makes actual the values of the classical law. In *Arcos*, the particular value at issue was reciprocity, the necessity of paying for the benefit one obtains from a contract, which the doctrine of consideration purports to institutionalize. But consideration, as with all the central doctrines of the classical law, is unable to give adequate expression to the core market value which underlies it. An adequate expression requires recognition that *Arcos* is a relational contract.

The facts of *Arcos v Ronaasen*

By two contracts dated 13 November 1929, the seller, Arcos Ltd, a commercial agency of the USSR government with responsibility for UK sales, agreed to sell a large consignment of timber staves to the buyer, EA Ronaasen and Son, the staves to be shipped during the summer of 1930 from Archangel (*Arcos* (HL(E)), p. 471). Though it does not seem that the written contracts made reference to this, the buyers made it known to the sellers that the staves were to be used for the manufacture of cement barrels, and it was never challenged that the sellers had an obligation under what is now the Sale of Goods Act 1979 s. 14(3) to ensure the staves were fit for this purpose, nor that the seller satisfied that obligation (*Arcos* (KBD), p. 167 col. 2, p. 168 cols 1–2; (HL(E), p. 480). This s. 14(3) aspect of *Arcos* is dealt with in passing in the judgments, but I shall discuss it at length as it is the key to understanding the case. The written contracts did expressly specify the range of the sizes of staves to be delivered, so that, for example, one part of the consignment dispatched under the second contract was to consist of '135 to 180 standards [of staves] $\frac{1}{2}$ in [thick] by 28 in [long] by 2 in [wide]' (*Arcos* (KBD), p. 166 col. 2).[3] The written contracts provided that disputes were to be referred to arbitration, and, when it eventuated that the arbitrators appointed by the parties could not agree, the arbitrators appointed an umpire (*Arcos* (HL(E)), pp. 471–2). The Arbitration Act 1889 s. 7 provided that an arbitrator might state a special case for adjudication by the High Court, and it transpired that the umpire referred the two disputes which occurred in *Arcos* to the King's Bench Division in this way.

---

3 A standard was the 'St Petersburg standard' common to the timber trade, a 165 cubic foot bundle of lengths of timber.

The goods were shipped from Archangel on or about 9 October 1930 and landed later that month (*Arcos* (HL(E)), pp. 471–2). Delivery could be made by tender of the shipping documents, but the buyers, prior (I surmise) to the goods being landed, rejected those documents on a ground to which we will return. This rejection was referred to arbitration, the first dispute in *Arcos*, and, as was confirmed on a reference to the High Court, found to be unjustified. The buyers then, after inspection of the landed goods, rejected actual delivery on the ground that the sizes of a substantial proportion of the staves did not conform to the sizes described in the written contracts. This was the second dispute in *Arcos* and is the subject matter of the reported decisions. There were considerable difficulties in accurately measuring the staves for the purposes of obtaining evidence, but we shall ignore these and accept that there were many relevant deviations from description. For example, in regard of the staves 28 inches long which I have mentioned, which were to be half an inch thick, it was found that '[n]one are less than $\frac{1}{2}$ in. 4.3% are $\frac{1}{2}$ in. 85.3% are more than $\frac{1}{2}$ in but not more than $\frac{9}{16}$ths in. 9.4% are more than $\frac{9}{16}$ths in and not more than $\frac{5}{8}$ths in. 1% are more than $\frac{5}{8}$th in and not more than $\frac{3}{4}$ in. None are over $\frac{3}{4}$ in' (*Arcos* (KBD), p. 166 col. 2, p. 167 col. 2).

What makes *Arcos* important is that the High Court found the existence of these deviations to be a breach of the seller's obligation under what is now s. 13(1) to deliver goods which correspond to their description. This is, now under s. 13(1A), breach of an implied condition which justifies rejection of the goods and therefore a release of the buyer from its obligation to pay the price. Though the facts about the value of the goods as reported are difficult to understand, it seems that this caused the seller to entirely lose a contract price of over £200,000 adjusted to 2011 values (*Arcos* (KBD), p. 165 col. 1), and placed on it the burden of retaking possession of timber which had lain upon a London quayside since rejection (p. 167 col. 1), where it will have been to some extent damaged by exposure to the weather (p. 171 col. 1). All this was affirmed by an extremely distinguished Court of Appeal, the leading judgment being handed down by Scrutton LJ, and a House of Lords in which one of the leading speeches was given by Lord Atkin. As the judge at first instance was Wright J, soon to become Lord Wright,[4] it is really rather hard to imagine a commercial case of the period receiving a more authoritative hearing. It is truly a puzzle that the result of so distinguished a hearing has been almost universally[5] regarded as a disaster for the law of the sale of goods.

---

4 See n. 10 below.
5 I have found the divergent views of Sealy and Hooley (2009, pp. 400–1) very instructive. I have not been able to reconcile these views with those recently expressed by Professor Hooley (2013, pp. 87–8)

Arcos v Ronaasen and the problems of correspondence with description

When one assesses the impact of *Arcos* on the Sale of Goods Act, the obvious first casualty is the interpretation of the implied term of fitness for purpose under s. 14(3). I have noted that it was not challenged that the seller had satisfied its s. 14(3) obligation. The deviations in the sizes of the staves had no effect on their fitness to be made into cement barrels. *Arcos* obviously makes it difficult to understand the relationship between having and satisfying a s. 14(3) obligation and discharging the contract by performance.

The same problem arises in regard of what is now the implied term of satisfactory quality under s. 14(2). For the umpire also found the deviations in the sizes of the staves were not of a magnitude to prevent 'the staves when shipped [being] merchantable under the contract specification' (*Arcos* (KBD), p. 168 col. 2), ample evidence for which was that 'the goods as tendered were worth as much in money as they would have been if they had been precisely of the contract specification' (p. 170 col. 1).

The buyer was able to reject goods which were fit for purpose and of satisfactory quality because, as I have noted, it was found that the deviations in size amounted to a breach of the implied condition that the goods correspond with their description under s. 13(1). Two points of great difficulty immediately arise from this finding: first, the relationship of s. 13 to s. 14, and, secondly, the operation of s. 13(1) in such a way that minor deviations of the type that arose in *Arcos* generate a right of complete rejection.

Wright J's reasoning on the first point was that the umpire's findings as to fitness for purpose and satisfactory quality only dealt with s. 14 issues:

> and that leaves the more important question which has to be decided as a question of law on the award, whether the implied condition under s 13 ... has also been satisfied, because these ... conditions are cumulative, and the satisfaction of [either of the first two] does not dispense the sellers from the obligation of satisfying the other (*Arcos* (KBD), p. 167 col. 2).

This treatment of the implied terms as 'cumulative' was confirmed in the House of Lords by Lord Atkin, who used the word 'additional' in order to make it clear that, on the view taken in *Arcos*, the existence of a s. 14 obligation does not mean that such a sale is not also a sale by description:

> It may be desirable to add that the result in this case is in no way affected by the umpire's finding that the goods were fit for the particular purpose for which they were required. The implied

condition under s 14[(3)], unless of course the contract provides otherwise, is additional to the condition under s 13[(1)]. A man may require goods for a particular purpose and make it known to the seller so as to secure the implied condition of fitness for that purpose; but there is no reason why he should not abandon that purpose if he pleases, and apply the goods to any purpose for which the description makes them suitable. If they do not correspond with the description there seems no business or legal reason why he should not reject them if he finds it convenient to do so. (*Arcos* (HL(E)), p. 480)

I shall, towards the end of this chapter, argue that the claim that these obligations are cumulative or additional are what is fundamentally unacceptable about *Arcos*. But even at a first blush, it is clear that the problems with this claim are very serious, for they expose the shortcomings of what seems to be drafting which was questionable at the time, certainly is now obsolete, and as such prone to cause much mischief. Leaving aside the distinction between sale by description and sale by sample (Sale of Goods Act 1979 ss. 13(2), 15), it would seem (Stoljar, 1952, pp. 432–6) that in sale by description Chalmers had in mind a distinction derived from nineteenth-century commercial practice between unascertained and specific goods, when the latter were existing, ascertained goods which were available for inspection, and the buyer had to rely on its inspection (or its choice not to inspect) rather than on any statement about the goods (other than a fraudulent statement). This was always a minority of sales, and with the growth of consumer contracting, it is now a very small minority indeed, represented by, say, some diamond sales or some car auctions. The demarcation of this true sphere of *caveat emptor* as an exception to what, for want of a better term having emerged from the law of sale of goods, I will call normal sales, which logically embraces all sales of unascertained goods and which are anything but *caveat emptor*, is but poorly accomplished by the Sale of Goods Act. This can, however, be put to one side.

In respect of normal sales, s. 13 is unnecessary. The description is given in the express statements about the goods by the seller, that is to say, leaving aside the problems of distinguishing between representations and terms (Sale of Goods Act 1979, s. 62(2)), the description is part of the statement of the seller's primary obligations which essentially constitutes the contract. By making satisfactory quality and fitness for purpose implied terms, s. 14 adds to the content of the contract. But s. 13, effectively saying the seller must deliver what it has undertaken to deliver, adds nothing, but merely duplicates, in the form of an implied term, the obligation the seller has expressly undertaken by describing the goods in a way on which the buyer relies, which, in terms of the 1979 Act, could readily be based upon s. 27. Or, one should rather say, s. 13(1) adds nothing positive. The duplication is imperfect and this has caused many problems.

The error in duplication that concerns us is the mandatory treatment of a breach of s. 13(1) as a breach of condition. As Adams and MacQueen (2010, p. 87) tell us, 'the position was the same with respect to ... the seller's duties, whether they were implied conditions under the Act or ... conditions laid down by the contract'. But, of course, if the description was regarded as a matter determined by the statement of the terms of the contract, the consequences of breach would depend on the seriousness of the breach regulated by the distinction between conditions and warranties under s. 11. This distinction must now be understood in light of *Hong Kong Fir Shipping Co Ltd v Kawasaki Kisen Kaisha* [1962] 2 QB 26 and subsequent cases. If, performing the contortions necessary to allow that there was a breach in *Arcos*, this law were applied, that breach would have been regarded as a breach of warranty and damages would have been low or even nominal, for, as we have seen, the goods were of satisfactory quality and their market value was equivalent to the contract price (though it does appear a small proportion of the goods were actually defective in quality and a small allowance might have been made in respect of them (*Arcos* (KBD), p. 166 col. 1)). This is, of course, entirely different than the very large loss rejection caused to the seller because s. 13(1) mandated the classification of the breach as a breach of condition and the buyer chose to reject.

It would be difficult to overstate the malign influence of this aspect of *Arcos* on the development of the law of sale of goods. The *ratio* of *Arcos* has been taken to be what came to be called the 'perfect tender rule', requiring, as Adams and MacQueen put it (2010, p. 86), that s. 13(1) 'duties must be strictly complied with and that any breach of these conditions, however trivial, *prima facie* justifies the buyer in refusing to accept the goods'. Adams and MacQueen are merely giving authoritative statement to the modern view when they say that they are in 'no doubt that [this] law permitted rejection on capricious and technical grounds' (2010, p. 499) 'for many breaches of no serious import at all' (2010, p. 87).

That the perfect tender rule is on its face preposterous was recognized in *Arcos* itself. *Benjamin* (Guest et al., 2006, para. 8.050) tells us that '[s]ome slight elasticity in carrying out a commercial contract for the supply of goods in bulk is unavoidable'. With sufficiently accurate mensuration, almost all goods, and certainly all commercial commodities such as the timber in *Arcos*, could always be shown not to correspond with description. The vanishingly small set of goods that could not (unless they actually did not correspond) are the very goods that are used in work that explores the limits of mensuration, such as some components of an electron microscope. To deal with this undeniable problem in *Arcos* itself, Wright J allowed that 'some microscopic variation ... might be permissible' under the doctrine of *de minimis non curat lex*, but that 'no further degree of elasticity would be permissible than is involved in the application of that doctrine' (*Arcos* (KBD), pp. 169 col. 2–170 col. 1). This was also allowed, and the word microscopic used, by Scrutton LJ in the Court of Appeal (*Arcos* (CA), p. 5 col. 1) and Lord Atkin in the House of Lords (*Arcos* (HL(E)), p. 479).

One can avoid utter unworkability of the perfect tender rule by invoking *de minimis* in this way, but it has been repeatedly urged that this simply gives rise to the problem of deciding what is *de minimis*. *Arcos* is commonly criticized for not being very helpful about this, but, in my opinion, this is not so. *Arcos* sets out a clear position about *de minimis* in connection with s. 13(1); it is just that, as we shall find, it is not, in the end, a position which addresses the real issue in the case. The law of *de minimis* is dominated by, and the use of microscopic is derived from, *Shipton, Anderson and Co v Weil Bros and Co* [1912] 1 KB 574, where a delivery of 4950 tons and 55 lbs was held not to be a s. 13(1) breach of a sale of 4500 tons of wheat ± 10 per cent, which is to say that a deviation of 0.000496 per cent could be ignored. Scrutton LJ thought this case 'an excellent illustration of the sort of thing that the court is thinking about when it says microscopic' (*Arcos* (CA), p. 5 col. 1).

In respect of the staves 28 inches long which I have mentioned, none were less than the stipulated thickness of $^1/_2$ inch, but 85.3 per cent were $^1/_{16}$ inch thicker, a 12.5 per cent deviation; 9.4 per cent were $^1/_8$ inch thicker, a 25 per cent deviation; and 1 per cent were $^1/_4$ inch thicker, a 50 per cent deviation. If one assesses these deviations as it were quantitatively, just on the basis of s. 13(1) correspondence, then it must be acknowledged that these deviations are not microscopic, that *Arcos* can be distinguished from *Shipton, Anderson*, and that Wright J, after referring to *Shipton, Anderson*, was not taking up an absurd position when he concluded that those deviations went 'far beyond any elasticity which would be permissible on the most benevolent application of the maxim *de minimis*' (*Arcos* (KBD), p. 170 col. 1). But, on the ground that he did 'not wish to dogmatise as to what degree of elasticity might be permissible in the measurements under a contract like this' (p. 170 col. 1), Wright J did not tell us where the line could be drawn, and it is not possible for a judge to do this in an, as it were, arithmetic fashion. What if the deviation had been, not 50 per cent or 0.000496 per cent, but 10 per cent, or 1 per cent or 0.1 per cent? Nothing said by any of the courts that heard *Arcos* provides real guidance about any arithmetic limits of *de minimis*. I myself am little troubled by this as I do not see what is especially problematic about the application of *de minimis* to particular sales, once we understand that the issue is not arithmetical but is one of reasonable commercial judgment, and that *de minimis* means microscopic, not, the word I used earlier, minor; but mine certainly is a minority view. Nevertheless, the law as left by *Shipton, Anderson* and *Arcos* can be said to be that almost any normal sale is made on the basis of a s. 13(1) implied condition of correspondence that is absolute, save for microscopic deviations.

The solutions to the problems of correspondence with description which are possible within the law of sale of goods

What Adams and MacQueen (2010, pp. 89, 142) have called the 'legal revolution' in the interpretation of the distinction between conditions and warranties brought about by the line of cases following *Hong Kong Fir Shipping* has, of course, posed a challenge to *Arcos's* absolute interpretation of s. 13(1): 'in light of [these] cases ... it may be wondered whether this famous decision, though of the highest authority, is not now somewhat suspect' (Adams and MacQueen, 2010, p. 137). These cases were not, in the main, sale of goods cases, and *Arcos* is not prominently discussed in them. In the case which is of most direct relevance, *Reardon Smith Lines Ltd v Yngvar Hansen Tangen* [1976] 1 WLR 989, *Arcos* is not cited. But Lord Wilberforce did, speaking for the majority of the House of Lords in *Reardon Smith*, find *Moore and Landauer* to be 'excessively technical and due for fresh consideration' (*Reardon Smith*, p. 998D), and, after *Reardon Smith*, it would be most unwise to rely on *Arcos* in any general consideration of whether or not a term was a condition.

Especially as I will argue that this is not as entirely happy a position as it is now generally taken to be, I am anxious to be precise about what I mean by this, and, in this connection, the remarkable facts of *Moore and Landauer* and *Reardon Smith* are worth recapping. In the former (heard inter alia by Scrutton LJ and Atkin LJ as he then was), 3000 tins of peaches were to be delivered packed 30 tins to a case. Because delivery was of 24 tins to the case, the goods were able to be rejected, despite the arbitrator finding that 24 tins to the case are as 'valuable commercially' as 30 tins to the case (*Moore and Landauer*, p. 524). In *Reardon Smith*, an oil tanker under construction by a Japanese company was, in accordance with Japanese shipbuilding practice, described in way which was based on identifying the yard in which the tanker was to be built. It was, in fact, built at another yard, and so had a different identification. This was not a sale, for the ship was not being sold but rather chartered to the defendant under a novel and controversial financing arrangement. The defendant nevertheless purported to refuse to take delivery of the tanker on the basis that the different identification constituted a lack of correspondence with description, although that lack was found to be of no material significance whatsoever. Lord Wilberforce did not even consider the possibility of regarding the lack of correspondence as *de minimis*, but found the rejection to be unlawful on the basis of what has become the doctrine of substantial performance, which he was anxious to advance. The point I wish to make about this is that it is in complete contradiction of the position taken by Lord Atkin in *Arcos*, in which he categorically rejected the seller's contention:

> that in all commercial contracts the question was whether there was a 'substantial' compliance with the contract; there always must be some margin, and it is for the tribunal of fact to determine whether the margin is exceeded or not (*Arcos* (HL(E)), p. 479).

As Adams and MacQueen (2010, p. 89, n. 31) tell us, in light of the changed attitude to substantial breach, changes have been made to the 1979 Act itself, and it is their opinion that these changes 'should obviate many of the difficulties caused by this old case law'. The Sale and Supply of Goods Act 1994 s. 4(1) inserted s. 15A into the 1979 Act, which provides that a commercial buyer may not avail itself of its right to reject goods for a breach of ss. 13 or 14 (or 15) implied terms when, as s. 15A(1) has it, 'the breach is so slight that it would be unreasonable for him to reject them', and therefore 'the breach is not to be treated as a breach of condition but may be treated as a breach of warranty'. This drafting is open to serious criticism. Even to understand what is intended one has to realize that 'so slight' is an oblique way of bringing in the doctrine of substantial performance; that 'may' has to be interpreted as doing the work of 'must' if one is to counter the mischief of the mandatory classification of breach as breach of condition; and that the basic drafting strategy, which is to leave ss. 13(1), 14(2) and 14(3) as mandatory conditions, and then purport to take this away when 'the breach is so slight that it would be unreasonable' not to do so, leaves the seller's duty to a commercial buyer a curious and inconsistent, indeed, in my opinion, ultimately incomprehensible, mixture of the absolute and the flexible.[6]

---

[6] Even such distinguished commentators as Professor Goode and Professor McKendrick get into a terrible tangle when trying to state the current law. Building on Goode's previous work, McKendrick tells us that *Arcos* is authority for the propositions 'that any disconformity, however minor, infringes [s.] 13' and that '[t]he right to reject does not have to be exercised reasonably', all of which evidences the want of a doctrine of good faith that is 'the most reprehensible feature of English contract law'. But he then goes on to tell us that 's 15A ... places a limit on the entitlement of the non-consumer buyer to reject' so that it cannot reject when 'it would be unreasonable' to do so (McKendrick, 2010, pp. 317, 368, 125, 368 n. 9, 125 n. 358). Well, which is it?

Adams and MacQueen (2010, p. 149), following other distinguished commentators (e.g. McKendrick, 2010, p. 298), hint at what surely is the solution to the problems I have discussed insofar as they can be narrowly regarded as problems of the construction of s. 13(1), which is to abolish it. The duplication of the express statement of terms of the sale and the implied condition of sale by description, and the errors in that duplication, can be eliminated by doing away with the duplication to leave only the express statement of the terms of the sale. I need say no more about this here, not only because I am not directly interested in the sale of goods as such, but because all I could hope to say has been said by Professor Michael Bridge (2008) in an outstanding essay on *Reardon Smith*, which should be placed in the context of his wider criticisms of the condition and warranty dichotomy (Bridge, 2006). I will point out only that Bridge draws it to our attention that, for example, the Uniform Commercial Code did away with the provision as to description under the former Uniform Sales Act 1906, preserving only that Act's provision as to the seller's express undertakings as Uniform Commercial Code art. 2-313 (Bridge, 2008, pp. 344–5).

In *Arcos* itself, a subsidiary aspect of this problem was dwelt on at length. Section 30(3) of the 1893 Act provided that:

> Where the seller delivers to the buyer the goods he contracted to sell mixed with goods of a different description not included in the contract, the buyer may accept the goods which are in accordance with the contract and reject the rest, or he may reject the whole.

The timber delivered in *Arcos* was a 'mixed' delivery in that some of the staves corresponded with description and some did not. In respect of the 28-inch staves, we have seen that 4.3 per cent were $^1/_2$ in thick and so in correspondence, but this, of course, meant that 95.7 per cent were not. It was argued before Wright J (*Arcos* (KBD), p. 167 col. 2) that s. 30 allowed rejection of the entire delivery. The s. 13 finding made it unnecessary for Wright J to decide the matter, and he did not do so, but Scrutton LJ, obviously *obiter*, made it plain that he would have found for the buyer on this point (*Arcos* (CA), p. 4 col. 2). In general, s. 30(3) of the 1893 Act indisputably allowed a buyer to convert lack of correspondence of part of the goods, an issue about quality, if it may be put this way, into a breach of the rules about quantity which granted a wide power of rejection which it is highly unlikely that Chalmers intended s. 30 to convey. In the climate set by *Hong Kong Fir Shipping*, it became clear there was no justification for this, and s. 30(3), which had been re-enacted as s. 30(4) of the 1979 Act, has rightly simply been repealed by the 1994 Act s. 3(3).[7]

But whilst repeal may deal with s. 13(1) and s. 30(4) as such, it cannot, of course, deal with the underlying problems of regulating the use of rejection, and termination more widely, and the way to further consider these problems is to return to the distinction between conditions and warranties as it now is under s. 15A of the 1979 Act.

Certainty and flexibility in the distinction between conditions and warranties

Adams and MacQueen (2010, p. 87) did not deny the value in certain circumstances, 'especially perhaps in the nineteenth century', but even now, of the 'certainty' which *Arcos* and associated cases created. They accordingly allowed that the main problem to which s. 15A leads, which the Law Commissions identified in their joint Consultation Paper that eventually led to the passing of the 1994 Act (Law Commission and Scottish Law Commission, 1983, para. 4.60), is that it 'would introduce some element of uncertainty where previously the right of rejection was unqualified' (Adams and MacQueen, 2010, p. 299). But, like the Commissions in their joint *Report* (Law Commission and Scottish Law Commission, 1987, para. 4.23), after balancing this cost against the benefit of s. 15A, Adams and MacQueen (2010, p. 499) concluded that 'this may well be an acceptable price to pay for penalising totally unreasonable commercial behaviour'.

It is effectively possible to contract out of s. 15A, for s. 15A(2) provides that s. 15 'applies unless a contrary intention appears in, or is to be implied from, the contract'. This is to allow parties which agree to do so to stipulate that specific terms are conditions in pursuit of certainty. That this serves a valuable function in light of what s. 15A now generally provides seems to be unanimously agreed. Even in *Hong Kong Fir Shipping* (p. 998D), Lord Wilberforce immediately followed the famous observation on *Moore and Landauer* quoted above with the reservation that it might be right to take 'a strict and technical view ... as regards the description of unascertained future goods (eg commodities), as to which each detail of the description must be assumed to be vital'. Adams and MacQueen (2010, p. 147) insightfully suggest that, when saying this, His Lordship 'probably had *Arcos v EA Ronaasen* particularly in mind'. But this is a remarkable thing to say, for

---

7 The Sale and Supply of Goods Act 1994 s. 4(2) introduced s. 30(2A), a parallel to s. 15A, into the 1979 Act, modifying the pure quantity obligations under ss. 30(1)(2) in respect of 'slight' shortfall or excess.

surely it is a concession that, for some sales at least, *Arcos* is good law, not merely in the sense that it remains the applicable law, but that that law is good policy! In a brilliant essay on *Suisse Atlantique Société d'Armament SA v NV Rotterdamsche Kolen Centrale* [1967] 1 AC 361 to which I shall return, Brownsword (2008, p. 320) says that the *Arcos* position, which in this essay he calls 'self-reliance', 'might be the appropriate ethic in some markets'. In my opinion, this concession is made because the law under *Arcos* is, in fact, not nearly so different from the law under s. 15A as is commonly believed.

If we put to one side the extent to which a court's yielding to the temptation to do justice might in current times override even the clear intentions of the parties, s. 15A(1) in conjunction with s. 15A(2) should allow parties to contract on the basis of either substantive performance under s. 15A(1), or on any other basis they choose, including the basis of absolute correspondence with description. This is not really a dramatic change, for, although this is not generally recognized, this was the law in *Arcos*! Section 13(1) mandates that a lack of correspondence with description is a breach of condition, but, of course, the seller can alter the description.[8] The duplication of the express specification of the goods and the mandatory classification of a breach which I have so criticized does contain the possibility of solving the correspondence with description problem. This possibility was explored at length in *Arcos* itself.

In *Arcos*, counsel for the sellers sought to rely on *Vigers Bros v Sanderson Bros* [1901] 1 KB 608, in which the existence of deviations of a proportion much more like those in *Arcos* than those in *Shipton, Anderson* did not allow the buyer to reject a consignment of timber. But in *Vigers Bros* (p. 611) the express terms of the contract constituting the s. 13(1) description were that the goods were to be 'of about the specification stated below'. Wright J, having obliged the seller's counsel to agree that 'the word "about" is not to be found anywhere in' the contracts in *Arcos*, readily distinguished the cases on this basis (*Arcos* (KBD), pp. 168 col. 2–170 col. 1). The *de minimis* doctrine was not the basis of this distinction. The parties had allowed for a more than *de minimis* deviation in *Vigers Bros*, but not in *Arcos*.

This argument about *Vigers Bros* in particular and about the possibility of providing for deviation in general was accepted by Scrutton LJ and Lord Atkin, the latter summing up the point by saying that '[i]f the seller wants a margin he must ... stipulate for it' (*Arcos* (HL(E)), p. 479). And in fact this happened in the case itself. It will be recalled that between 135–80 standards of the 28-inch staves were to be delivered, and Scrutton LJ was of the

---

8 I am trying to make a different point than the possibility of negativing or varying s. 13 under s. 55 of the 1979 Act (subject to the Unfair Contract Terms Act 1977 (c. 50) ss. 3, 6(2)), the metaphysical dimensions of which I am glad to ignore.

opinion this meant that 'the seller is given liberty to deliver either 135 or 180 standards' (*Arcos* (CA), p. 5 col. 1). I do not read the term as did Scrutton LJ, and I do not think it is possible to say what the correct reading is from the reported facts, but the point is that flexibility, when provided for, was in principle accepted readily enough in *Arcos*. (I will not discuss the way that some other statements purporting to convey flexibility were, after consideration, held not to support the seller's position, for they do not affect the point of principle I am trying to make.)

The difference between *Arcos* and the law as we now have it after *Hong Kong Fir* is not that the range of possibilities open to the parties when negotiating their contracts is different; it is that the default law is different.[9] Under the current law, the default law is substantial performance, from which the parties can contract out, and we have seen that it is allowed that it may be right that it should do so, in order to take 'a strict and technical view' of correspondence in appropriate cases. The law in *Arcos* is the reverse. The default law is strict and technical. If the seller wants to be able to deviate from this, it has to make express provision, perhaps, as it was dwelt on in the case under the influence of *Vigers Bros*, by use of the word 'about'.

But although I wish to point to the fundamental similarity of the current law and the law in *Arcos*, I am strongly of the opinion that the current law is a superior default. I have noted that almost all commodities are physical things which will, when sold commercially, involve a departure from description which will not be microscopic, and the timber in *Arcos* is a good example. It appears to me that delivery of such a commodity is usually best governed by substantial performance. But contracting out of this default in order to stipulate absolute correspondence subject to *de minimis* must be possible, and if it is, and if the relationship between default rule and bespoke rule is properly understood by the parties, then the necessity of taking a view on this will diminish, for competition should determine which clauses are adopted by the parties in accordance with freedom of contract, and this is, of course, the optimum outcome.

Support of flexibility in interpretation of the contract terms when it was believed to be appropriate was possible in *Arcos* because the case does not actually display a generally excessive commitment to formalism. Adams and MacQueen (2010, p. 155) point to a number of cases in which *Arcos* has been distinguished in order that a term 'be construed as business men would construe it', particularly when, as the 'goods have acquired a trade

---

9   Constraints of space prevent me from engaging properly with Brownsword's (2008) account of the default rules, which is outstandingly penetrating, but which, to take only this point, seems to me to evidence a belief that the current 'default provisions are set on the basis of a robust individualistic ethic' (p. 320), when I believe the opposite to be the case.

description they may correspond to their description even when they are not what a literal reading of the trade description suggests they are'. But this possibility was perfectly well recognized in *Arcos*, with Lord Atkin, for example, saying that 'by recognized trade usage particular figures may be given a different meaning, as in a baker's dozen' (*Arcos* (HL(E)), p. 479), and an actual instance of it formed part of the dispute. It will be recalled that the buyer initially rejected the shipping documents prior to the landing of the goods. The ground on which it did so was that the contract provided for 'shipment during the summer', but the goods were not shipped until on or about 9 October. A previous arbitral award, confirmed in an unreported King's Bench judgment, found that, in the timber trade, October deliveries could be regarded as summer deliveries, and dismissed rejection on this basis. Wright J let this pass without any criticism (*Arcos* (KBD), p. 167 col. 1), as did Lord Atkin (*Arcos* (HL(E)), p. 478), and it was enthusiastically affirmed, again obviously *obiter*, by Scrutton LJ (*Arcos* (CA), p. 5 col. 2).

At the levels of the sales law of correspondence with description and the general stance towards the interpretation of the contracts of commercial parties, it is, I submit, wrong to regard *Arcos* as as poor a case as it is generally believed to be. There is no overall commitment to excessive formalism in *Arcos*.[10] Section 13(1) now seems to be a legislative mistake and should be repealed, but this is a problem with the 1893 Act, not specifically with *Arcos*. *Arcos* interpreted the underlying issue, which would not be resolved by repeal of s. 13(1), of determining the seriousness of lack of correspondence with description when it is treated as a breach of the seller's basic obligation to deliver, in a way which is far inferior as a default rule to the law on substantial performance we now have, but the *Arcos* position must be available as a bespoke term if the modern law is to be sound.

But, in saying all this, I do not mean to say that *Arcos* is overall a defensible decision. It is not. But in order to see why it is not, we must go behind description, indeed behind the express contract as such, and examine the normative basis of rejection by the buyer in *Arcos*.

---

10 Constraints of space prevent me from going into the background interpretive stances of the three distinguished judges on whom my discussion of *Arcos* concentrates, but the remarkable events in the career of Wright J around the time he heard this case demand some comment. In April 1932, less than two months after Wright had heard *Arcos*, Sankey LC took the remarkable step of appointing him directly to the House of Lords as Sankey felt there was a desperate need to strengthen the quality of the Lords of Appeal. Within three months of his appointment to the Lords, Wright gave a speech in *Hillas and Co Ltd v Arcos Ltd* [1932] All ER Rep 494 which is now generally regarded as an exemplary instance of taking a sensibly contextual approach to the interpretation of contracts. In sum, Wright was not a formalist (Duxbury, 2009).

Adams and Brownsword on *Arcos v Ronaasen*

The buyer in *Arcos* could, of course, have waived the condition and accepted the goods which were, after all, both of satisfactory quality and fit for purpose. Why didn't it do so? Adams and MacQueen believe that the motive behind rejection had nothing to do with breach of any part of ss. 13–14 (or s. 30). *Arcos* is believed to be one of a number of cases, including *Shipton, Anderson* and *Moore and Landauer*, in which 'the buyer's real motive in rejecting the goods was that market prices had fallen since the contract was made' (Adams and MacQueen, 2010, p. 499). There is no actual evidence about the movement of timber prices in *Arcos*, and this motive is nowhere set out in so many words. But rejection of satisfactory goods fit for purpose on the grounds of a minor, if not microscopic, lack of correspondence, especially after the even more insubstantial attempt to reject on the grounds of the time of dispatch, is inexplicable on any other basis. All commentators who express a view are in agreement with Adams and MacQueen about the real motive for rejection. I myself do not doubt it, and I will simply accept it without further argument.

Those commentators have also more or less uniformly argued that *Arcos* is compelling evidence that a want of a doctrine of good faith is a grave shortcoming of the sale of goods, and of the general principles of the English law of contract, for rejection motivated by a wish to take advantage of a falling market which purports to be a rejection for breach of s. 13(1) is breach in bad faith. Adams and MacQueen (2010, p. 92) think it regrettable that 'the innocent party ... is not required to act reasonably, or in good faith, in exercising his rights', allowing 'technical breaches of condition [to be] treated as grounds for termination where the innocent party is seeking a way out of the contract because market conditions have changed'. These views can be related to the comments on *Arcos* in Adams' work with Brownsword in which they have stated one of the most important criticisms of the market-individualist moral orientation of the classical law of contract.[11]

In the way it allowed a buyer 'to be able to escape from the contract in order to take advantage of falling prices on the timber market' (Adams and Brownsword, 1995, p. 226), *Arcos* is, Adams and Brownsword tell us, 'a blatant example of ... economic opportunism' (1995, p. 170 n. 27). It is not legitimate 'to play the market', for when 'economic self-interest prevails' 'over contractual commitment' in this way, it is an instance of 'bad faith'

---

11 Though I shall confine myself to other statements of their views on *Arcos*, the reader should also consult Brownsword (1992).

(1995, p. 226). The buyer, they complain, was 'not actually rejecting *for breach* (except in the technical legal sense); the seller's breach was merely a pretext for getting out of the bargain' (1995, pp. 171–2). Like Adams and MacQueen, they point to the reforms of the Sale of Goods Act I have discussed as a way forward (1995, p. 171, n. 31), and to the developments in the common law around *Hong Kong Fir* as representing a far superior position: 'a plausible view [of *Hong Kong Fir Shipping*] must be that the court set ... a difficult threshold for withdrawal precisely in order to block opportunistic withdrawals of the kind exercised by the buyers in *Arcos v Ronaasen*' (Adams and Brownsword, 2004, p. 167).

But the great obstacle to this line of criticism, which Adams and Brownsword are somewhat distinguished from most other commentators in clearly seeing, is that it can hardly be said that those who heard *Arcos* were unaware of, in effect, this criticism of bad faith and excessive individualism. They saw it perfectly well. But the point is that they didn't see anything wrong with what has since been so criticized. Adams and Brownsword (2004, p. 167) have rightly told us that 'the House of Lords, being perfectly well aware of what was going on, saw no problem', and Brownsword (2010, para. 1.23, n. 8) has further told us that Lord Atkin 'was party to the unanimous House of Lords' view that sellers who failed to deliver goods corresponding precisely to the contractual description had no cause for complaint if buyers then rejected the goods purely for their own economic advantage' (see also Brownsword, 2003, p. 127).

In a number of their discussions of the point, Adams and Brownsword quote the relevant part of Lord Atkin's speech and I will also do so:

> the right view is that the conditions of the contract must be strictly performed. If a condition is not performed the buyer has a right to reject ... No doubt, in business, men often find it unnecessary or inexpedient to insist on their strict legal rights. In a normal market if they get something substantially like the specified goods they may take them with or without grumbling and a claim for an allowance. But in a falling market I find that the buyers are often eager to insist on their legal rights as courts are ready to maintain them ... Buyers are not, as far as my experience goes, inclined to think that the rights defined in the [Sale of Goods Act] are in excess of business needs. (*Arcos* (HL(E)), p. 480)

Lord Atkin was of the opinion that the contract gave the buyer the right to reject, not, as Adams and Brownsword put it, 'actually ... *for breach*', but just to take advantage of a falling market. And this has what is, to most modern eyes, the objectionable effect that it would not have made any difference if the English law of sale of goods, or the general principles of contract, had then had a doctrine of good faith. As Adams and Brownsword (1995, p. 227) very acutely put it, if the House of Lords in *Arcos*:

> had employed the concept of good faith ... the question would have been whether the relevant commercial community would have regarded the buyers' rejection as a bad faith withdrawal – and, on the evidence of Lord Atkin's judgment, we can take it that the answer would have been in the negative, with the result that a good faith requirement would not have altered the outcome of the case.

What precisely, then, do Adams and Brownsword think is wrong with the view Lord Atkin took? It was that 'a market-individualist judge' (1995, p. 227) took 'the classical view ... that where one party is in breach of contract, then the innocent party may legitimately take up any of the legally available options irrespective of whether this is for self-serving economic advantage' (Brownsword, 2008, p. 307). This is an 'uncompromising view [which] is seen ... as being congruent with business practice and expectation' (p. 307). This view condones 'bad faith in the illegitimate exercise of contractual discretion', even though this is 'driven by market-playing reasons' and is not 'compatible with respect for the co-operative ideal of contract' (Adams and Brownsword, 1995, pp. 228–9). This analysis poses, as Brownsword (2008, p. 127) has put it when summing up the issue generally in his essay on *Suisse Atlantique*:

> a question that is about as fundamental as any question can be to the design of a contract law regime – namely whether it is geared for co-operation and trust or for self-reliance and defensive dealing.

We know the answer Adams and Brownsword have given to this question in a major body of hortative work on welfarism that now reaches back some 30 years.

What actually is wrong with *Arcos*?

I have myself expended considerable effort arguing that there is a fundamental co-operative dimension to all contracting and I do not wish anything I say here to detract from my essential agreement with Adams and Brownsword. I nevertheless cannot agree with their criticism of *Arcos*, and I think it will be of interest if I set out why.

In detail, the reason why Adams and Brownsword maintain that the buyer's failure to act in what they perceive to be bad faith, despite their acute perception that this would not have had much purchase with Lord Atkin, is that:

> Clearly, when contractors close on a deal, they forego certain options that would otherwise be available for playing the market. Minimally, if A has contracted to buy goods from B, but then C comes along and offers to supply A on more attractive terms, A has foregone the option to buy from C in preference from B and can do so only by breaking the contract with B ... Thus, when the parties contracted in *Arcos v Ronaasen*, they locked themselves into the contractual regime of prices, irrespective of rising or falling markets outside the contract, and the parties' interests must be interpreted in light of this. Hence, although the buyers had an undoubted economic interest in rejecting the timber, that interest should be regarded as trumped by the overriding and (protected) interests of the sellers as determined by the contract. (Adams and Brownsword, 1995, pp. 229–30)

In my opinion, the last clause gives the game away. As determined by the contract, as Adams and Brownsword have themselves said, the buyer had a perfect right (or discretion) to reject for any reason, including playing the market. Adams and Brownsword criticize this by applying an exogenous welfarist standard to it, for this is how they conceive of the relationship between market individualism and welfarism. They see the issue as the choice between two moral frameworks, but on what basis does one choose? Brownsword in particular has written extensively about the superiority of a co-operative ethic, but, as I have mentioned, Adams (and MacQueen) and he have never been able to deny that there may be some contracts to which the individualistic ethic is appropriate. Throughout their work, they acknowledge that, to quote Brownsword (2008, p. 320) again: 'self-reliance may be the appropriate ethic in some markets'. But if *Arcos* took place in one of these markets, as they concede it may have done, what is the ground on which they can criticize it because it is so individualist? They actually can see some ill-specified but nevertheless undeniable place for it as part of the current law. But it surely is a major shortcoming of the welfarist law that it seems it can be advocated only if the law it criticizes as morally defective is allowed to continue. The clash of values approach does not, in my opinion, ultimately ground a telling critique of *Arcos*.

It would, however, be a telling critique if *Arcos* was found to set out a position which is inconsistent with market individualism, or, as I shall put it, with the values of competitive contract. There are suggestions of this in Adams and Brownsword (Brownsword, 1996; 1997; 2010) from reflection on which I have greatly benefited, and I shall unfairly ignore them as I shall, in the interest of clarity, set out my position, as it were, independently. In essence, I do not think absoluteness of correspondence with description is itself a problem, if it is understood to be part of a system of default and bespoke rules, and, indeed, as I have said, I think the law now based on a substantial performance default needs to allow the possibility of stipulating absoluteness of correspondence. The fundamental problem with the law of sale of goods as it is understood in *Arcos* is the way that s. 13 and s. 14 obligations are conceived of as, as Wright J had it, cumulative, or, as Lord Atkin had it, additional. This understanding of cumulative or additional is incompatible with the values of contract even when the contract is of the most competitive sort.

The sale of what I have called normal goods, with or without s. 13(1), will always be based on a description. If the goods are normal, to the description will be added a s. 14(2) requirement that the goods will be of satisfactory quality. A s. 14(3) requirement that the goods are fit for purpose may be added in circumstances where it is reasonable to do so. If the correct interpretation of the express terms of the contract is that the parties have made absolute correspondence a bespoke stipulation, then absolute correspondence can be cumulative with, or additional to, s. 14. The seller must deliver satisfactory goods or goods fit for purpose which also must absolutely correspond. But when normal goods are sold on a competitive market, it will never be possible to interpret the contract so that, by default, absolute correspondence with express description may be cumulative or additional to s. 14 in this way, though this is exactly the mistake which is compounded if s. 13(1) is mandatorily classified as a condition under s. 13(1A). Why is this so?

Though, as I have mentioned, it was dealt with only in passing, the key to *Arcos* is that the seller was obliged to deliver staves which were fit for the buyer's purpose of making cement barrels, and it performed this obligation. At the time the agreement was made, the buyer must have decided that the seller's goods were the most attractive on offer. One element of this must have been the seller's ability credibly to offer to deliver staves fit for purpose and another will have been the offer price. But the seller will have been able to make a competitively low offer price only because it prepared the timber so that it was fit for purpose, and not that it corresponded to description, save for microscopic deviations. I have only the smallest knowledge of the timber trade and have made no inquiry into the matter, but I take it that planing thousands of cubic feet of timber to microscopic tolerances is an incredibly expensive matter, and that the buyer would not pay for it as it is conveys no more fitness for purpose than would timber planed to normal commercial tolerances. A seller who offered timber planed to microscopic tolerances therefore could not compete with a seller who offered timber planed to normal commercial tolerances. The significance of this is that the buyer obtains the considerable advantage of a, one assumes, very much lower price by contracting on the basis of fitness for purpose rather than absolute correspondence.

I have quoted above the passage in which Lord Atkin uses the word 'additional', and it will be recalled that that passage began with the claim that 'the result in this case is in no way affected by the umpire's finding that the goods were fit for the particular purpose for which they were required' (*Arcos* (HL(E)), p. 480). This, we can now see, is quite wrong. In a sale of normal goods on the basis for fitness for purpose, the default interpretation of the contract must be that the goods will be manufactured to the tolerances needed to make them fit for purpose, and no more, because competitive pressure on the offer price will ensure this is the case. When Lord Atkin observes that '[t]he implied condition under s 14[(3)], unless of course the contract provides otherwise, is additional to the condition under s 13[(1)]', he interprets the contract in exactly the wrong way. By default, it cannot be the case that these conditions are additional. But, of course, the contract could, as a theoretical possibility, provide that this was so. But in *Arcos* the claimant could not, by default, reasonably be expected to put in 'about' because the case is a paradigm instance of what it is settled law is a ground for implying a term in fact: that it is too obvious to need saying. In negotiations, a seller could be persuaded to agree that the contract was for goods that are fit for purpose and also are in absolute correspondence. But this would be a most unnatural construction which would have to expressed in very clear words, and should never be thought to apply by default.

When I previously quoted the famous passage in Lord Atkin's speech that I have just discussed, I omitted a sentence which I will now restore. After observing that 'the right view is that the conditions of the contract must be strictly performed. If a condition is not performed the buyer has a right to reject', Lord Atkin then said 'I do not myself think there is any difference between business men and lawyers on this matter.' (*Arcos* (HL(E)), p. 480) This was a response to an extensive discussion by Scrutton LJ of the relationship of the legal and commercial attitudes towards the negotiation and interpretation of contracts as they are evidenced in *Arcos*. Scrutton LJ forcefully stated his opinion that '[t]he commercial mind and the legal mind are quite at variance as to the obligations of a seller and a buyer, the seller having undertaken to supply described goods' (*Arcos* (CA), p. 4 col. 2), such that 'the commercial man says: "I have undertaken to deliver a particular size, but it is reasonable that I should be allowed to deliver a certain percentage which is not that size"' (*Arcos* (CA), p. 6 col. 1), whereas '[t]he court says ... "[y]ou must deliver what you have agreed to deliver, and if you have agreed to deliver something without giving yourself any option of variation, then the inevitable consequence follows that the buyer may reject"' (*Arcos* (CA), p. 6 col. 2). Scrutton LJ had played a prominent role in the case law prior to *Arcos*, including, as I have noted, *Moore and Landauer*, in which, as he put it, 'the courts have been occupied in telling the commercial man: "[i]f you want to get your interpretation, you must put something in the contract. If you do not put in figures, you must put in 'about' or you must put in 'a margin of 10 per cent more or less'. If you, the seller, do that, you will have something that will give you the latitude which you claim"'. (*Arcos* (CA), p. 4 col. 2)

However, though the substance of what he did is quite wrong, I do not think that Scrutton LJ should be criticized for maintaining, as it were in principle, that *Arcos* was a case in which the seller, a competent commercial party, had to live up to what the law required. What is wrong with what he says is that he is mistaken about the default law. On his view, the default law is absolute correspondence, and the seller has to contract out of this. For reasons I have already given, this is quite the opposite of the relationship of default and bespoke rule that should and now does obtain. One cannot fail to be struck by the obduracy of Scrutton LJ's unwillingness (also demonstrated by Wright J and Lord Atkin) to recognize the commercial reality so properly appreciated by the umpire, and by the foolishness of his attacks on arbitrators' general practice in respect of lack of correspondence:

> I think it is obvious from the language of the arbitrator in his finding that he thinks there should be ... a ... variation allowed, although nothing is said about it in the contract. That in my view is a misunderstanding of the law. It is the same misunderstanding that most commercial arbitrators with whose cases I have had continually to deal continually make. They must make up their minds and sellers must make up their minds that unless they give themselves the liberty of deviation in their contract, if the buyer will agree to it, they will have to deliver what in the terms of the contract they have contracted to deliver, and if there is something which is not a microscopic difference between what they deliver and what they contracted to deliver, they must make up their minds that the court will say that the buyers are entitled to reject. (*Arcos* (CA), pp. 6 col. 2–7 col. 1)

But if it is entirely correct to say that '[t]he rule of strict compliance seems to have been introduced in the teeth of the findings of commercial arbitrators, especially in the timber trade' (Guest et al., 2006, para. 11.08

n. 98),[12] it is essential to understand why this *prima facie* absurd line was taken. Imposing a default rule which is quite the opposite of what the parties naturally think it is, Scrutton LJ completely misunderstands what the seller has 'contracted to deliver' by default. The default he believes applies actually is, or rather should be, impossible to apply by default.

Lord Atkin is able to maintain that there is no 'difference between businessmen and lawyers on this matter' because he approaches that matter from a different perspective; not that of the seller who wants to provide for a deviation, but that of the buyer who wants to have the discretion to accept in 'a normal market' or reject for want of absolute correspondence for any reason, in particular to take advantage of 'a falling market'. The buyer wants the goods fit for purpose and competitively priced for that 'normal market'. It also wants, in effect, an option to reject the goods in 'a falling market'. Once one appreciates the role of competitive pricing in determining the seller's performance, it is tempting to say that the attitude of such a buyer involves a contradiction, for the very good reason that indeed it does. But, of course, a purely individualistic buyer would very much like to have its cake and eat it too. It would like to get the goods at a low price and get the option of rejection in a falling market as well. What does such a buyer care about the contradiction?[13] If one tells such a buyer that its conduct is in bad faith, it will simply deny it. In the amoral jungle of the commercial world of the fevered imagination of such a buyer, such action is in perfect good faith, the good faith of the pure individualist. Macneil (1986, p. 578) has described the attitude of such a party thus:

> An individual utility maximiser may be perfectly well aware of the fact that the deal he makes creates exchange surplus, but his *sole* concern about that utility is to grab as much of it for himself as he can. He will feel nothing but regret at whatever amount is snared by the other party and nothing but happiness that the other failed to secure more of it.

---

12 A modern account of the international timber trade shows it to rely on arbitration to the almost complete exclusion of litigation (Konradi, 2009, pp. 61–4). As I say, I have made almost no inquiry into the timber trade, but one speculates that avoiding the sentiments expressed by Scrutton LJ may have played a part in this. More generally, there is no real contemporary parallel to the reference procedure under the Arbitration Act 1889. Though appeal on a point of law remains possible, in restricted circumstances, under the Arbitration Act 1996 s. 69, this is an issue on which the English law stands in marked contrast to most other domestic and international laws, and such an appeal is very unlikely indeed (Blackaby and Partsides, 2009, paras 10.20–10.27).
13 This is not the place to pursue this into Brownsword's legal philosophical work on the role of consistency in moral judgment (Beyleveld and Brownsword, 2007), but this should be done.

This is the attitude of the contracting party of the classical law, and this is why such a party's understanding of contracting receives endorsement from Lord Atkin.

But Lord Atkin is wrong about the nature of the law of contract. The law of contract legally institutionalizes market exchange, and market exchange is not a system of pure individualism. It is a system of reciprocal exchange based on agreements to bargain. Though the parties to an exchange pursue their self-interest, they can do so only by entering into a voluntary exchange which mutually recognizes each party's autonomy. A party wishing to exchange must persuade the other party to agree to enter into a contract, and the way it has to do this is by offering goods the other party values more highly than goods it is itself willing to exchange. A purported exchange which does not do this does not satisfy the positive and normative conditions of legitimate market action and should not therefore receive endorsement by the law of contract. Within contract scholarship, this point has never been made better than it was by Macneil, who has shown that all contracts are relational in the sense that the parties to contracts must respect certain common contract norms. The norm that is of particular relevance to the analysis of the defects of *Arcos* is the norm of reciprocity, simply stated as 'the principle of getting something back for something that is given' (Macneil, 1983, p. 347), which is, of course, articulated in the doctrine of consideration.

Given the nature of the goods and the sale, Lord Atkin's interpretation of the *Arcos* contract gifts the buyer the extremely valuable option of rejecting the goods at its complete discretion, including to take advantage of a falling market. I do not have any objection to such an option, if the buyer pays for it, but the point is that in *Arcos* the buyer does not have to pay for it, and, if the default law is the law in *Arcos*, no sensible negotiation about this can ever take place. The bargaining takes place over fitness for purpose, and not at all over correspondence with description, much less about granting the buyer the option to reject. No bargaining over the vital term is therefore possible. In my opinion, that the default law has been changed in the way it has, at statute and common law, now makes such negotiation possible, but this possibility will not be fully realized whilst confusion surrounds the issues at stake in *Arcos*.

I do not think it ultimately assists the resolution of this confusion to say there is a want of good faith in *Arcos*. The confusion arises because the core values of contract, especially the reciprocity which the doctrine of consideration seeks to express, are not being applied as they should. *Arcos* is a paradigmatic expression of the classical law, but, when one says this, one should not forget that the classical law is an inadequate law. It is difficult to see why a consistent pure individualism should be criticized, but the relational theory shows that pure individualism can never be consistent in the way it grounds contracting, and it is such an individualism that *Arcos* expresses. This lack of consistency matters only if we see that even highly competitive contracting is never a matter of pure individualism but of the pursuit of self-interest within an appropriate relational framework.

Conclusion

It has been my aim in this chapter to add to my previous attempts to argue that the main point of the relational theory of contract is not that there is a class of relational contracts which should be recognized in addition to the class of discrete contracts, but that all contracts are relational. I have sought to do this by analysis of a case which may now be the most criticized case, not merely in the sale of goods, but in the law of contract generally, because it is believed to embody all the defects of the discrete contract; in essence that it is absurdly formal and endorses an excessive individualism. But against the low esteem in which *Arcos* is held, one must set the fact that it still has a very important influence on our thinking about sale and contract, and this, I believe, follows from the shortcomings of both the classical law and its welfarist critique. The buyer's rejection in *Arcos* follows from a wholly untrammelled individualism which is endorsed from the classical law's perspective by those who heard the case, for this was taken to be the legitimate self-interest pursued in market exchange. That this is unacceptable is now accepted, but the welfarist critique of this as an exercise in bad faith is persuasive only to a limited extent, for, as Adams and Brownsword acutely realize, from the classical law perspective, it is not bad faith to behave in this way. In my opinion, it has never been satisfactorily established why we should choose the welfarist over the market-individualist law, and this follows from the way that, by being set against market-individualism, welfarism undermines itself, for, despite its shortcomings, market-individualism is, after all, essential to the working of the market, and so at the core of the legitimacy of liberal-democratic society.

In my opinion, the way to criticize market-individualism is to show it cannot realize its own aspiration to institutionalize the values of freedom of contract expressed in contract's core doctrines. This can be done only by the relational theory, for those values express the objective relations which the parties to contracts must use to make their exchanges possible, and they cannot be derived from the subjective intentions of the parties conceived of as atomistic individuals. The relational theory is the strongest basis on which we can move toward a coherent general awareness that even the simplest contract is not a subjective agreement between two parties, but is the result of their relationship objectively mediated by a third party, the state, which gives effect only to socially understood and politically endorsed intentions.

This is shown, as it were by exception, in *Arcos*, the shortcoming of which is that exchange which observes the value of reciprocity, which the doctrine of consideration purports to institutionalize, is impossible on the basis of the reasoning even of the outstanding judges which heard that case. Locked in the categories of the classical law, those judges sought to endorse an individualism which simply is not an adequate positive or moral description of the action of parties who participate in welfare-enhancing market exchange legally institutionalized in contract. I hope to have shown that appreciation of this is possible only if we realize that *Arcos v Ronaasen*, like all contracts, is a relational contract.

References

Adams, J and R Brownsword (1995) *Key Issues in Contract* (London: Butterworths)
Adams, J and R Brownsword (2004) *Understanding Contract Law* (London: Sweet & Maxwell)
Adams, J and H MacQueen (2010) *Atiyah's Sale of Goods* (Harlow: Pearson Education) (12th edn)
Beyleveld, D and R Brownsword (2007) *Consent in the Law* (Oxford: Hart Publishing)
Blackaby, N and C Partasides (2009) *Redfern and Hunter on International Arbitration* (Oxford: Oxford University Press) (5th edn)
Bridge, M G (2006) 'Do We Need a Sale of Goods Act?' in J Lowry and L Mistelis (eds), *Commercial Law: Perspectives and Practice* (London: LexisNexis Butterworths)
Bridge, M G (2008) '*Reardon Smith Lines Ltd v Yngvar Hansen-Tangen, The Diana Prosperity* (1976)' in C Mitchell and P Mitchell (eds), *Landmark Cases in the Law of Contract* (Oxford: Hart Publishing)
Brownsword, R (1992) 'Retrieving Reasons, Retrieving Rationality? A New Look at the Right to Withdraw for Breach of Contract' 5 *Journal of Contract Law* 83
Brownsword, R (1994) 'The Philosophy of Welfarism and its Emergence in Modern English Contract Law' in R Brownsword et al. (eds), *Welfarism in Contract Law* (Aldershot: Dartmouth)
Brownsword, R (1996) 'Static and Dynamic Market Individualism' in R Halson (ed.), *Exploring the Boundaries of Contract* (Aldershot: Dartmouth)
Brownsword, R (1997) 'Contract, Co-operation and Good Faith: The Movement from Static to Dynamic Market Individualism' in S Deakin and J Michie (eds), *Contracts, Co-operation and Competition* (Oxford: Oxford University Press)
Brownsword, R (2003) 'After Investors: Interpretation, Expectation and the Implicit Dimension of the "New Contextualism"' in D Campbell et al. (eds), *Implicit Dimensions of Contract* (Oxford: Hart Publishing)
Brownsword, R (2008) '*Suisse Atlantique Société d'Armament SA v NV Rotterdamsche Kolen Centrale* (1967)' in C Mitchell and P Mitchell (eds), *Landmark Cases in the Law of Contract* (Oxford: Hart Publishing)

Brownsword, R (2010) 'General Considerations' in M Furmston (ed.), *The Law of Contract* (London: LexisNexis) (4th edn)
Campbell, D (1996) 'The Relational Constitution of the Discrete Contract' in D Campbell and P Vincent-Jones (eds), *Contract and Economic Organisation: Socio-legal Initiatives* (Aldershot: Dartmouth)
Campbell, D (1997) 'The Relational Constitution of Contract and the Limits of "Economics": Kenneth Arrow on the Social Background of Markets' in S Deakin and J Michie (eds), *Contracts, Co-operation and Competition: Studies in Economics, Management and Law* (Oxford: Oxford University Press)
Campbell, D (2001) 'Ian Macneil and the Relational Theory of Contract' in I R Macneil, *The Relational Theory of Contract* (London: Sweet & Maxwell)
Campbell, D (2003) 'The Relational Constitution of Contractual Agreement' in P Heugens et al. (eds), *The Social Institutions of Capitalism: Evolution and Design of Social Contracts* (Cheltenham: Edward Elgar Publishing)
Campbell, D (2005) 'The Relational Constitution of Remedy: Co-operation as the Implicit Second Principle of Remedies for Breach of Contract' 11 *Texas Wesleyan Law Review* 455
Campbell, D (2013) 'What Do We Mean by the Non-use of Contract?' in J Braucher et al. (eds), *Revisiting the Contracts Scholarship of Stewart Macaulay: On the Empirical and the Lyrical* (Oxford: Hart Publishing)
Campbell, D and D Harris (1993) 'Flexibility in Long-term Contractual Relationships: The Role of Co-operation' 20 *Journal of Law and Society* 166
Duxbury, N (2009) 'Lord Wright and Innovative Traditionalism' 59 *University of Toronto Law Journal* 265
Guest, A G et al. (2006) *Benjamin's Sale of Goods* (London: Sweet & Maxwell)
Hooley, R (2013) 'Controlling Contractual Discretion' *Cambridge Law Journal* 65
Konradi, W (2009) 'The Role of *Lex Mercatoria* in Supporting Globalised Transactions: An Empirical Insight into the Governance Structure of the Timber Industry' in V Gessner (ed.), *Contractual Certainty in International Trade* (Oxford: Hart Publishing)
Law Commission and Scottish Law Commission (1983) *Sale and Supply of Goods* Consultation Paper [1983] EWLC C85
Law Commission and Scottish Law Commission (1987) *Sale and Supply of Goods* Report [1987] EWLC 160
Macneil, I R (1983) 'Values in Contract: Internal and External' 78 *Northwestern University Law Review* 340
Macneil, I R (1986) 'Exchange Revisited: Individual Utility and Social Solidarity' 96 *Ethics* 567
Goode on Commercial Law (London: Penguin Books) (4th edn)
Sealey, L S and R J A Hooley (2009) *Commercial Law* (Oxford: Oxford University Press) (4th edn)
Stoljar, S J (1952) 'Conditions, Warranties and Descriptions of Quality in Sale of Goods I' 15 *Modern Law Review* 425

8
In Defence of *Baird Textiles*: A Sceptical View of Relational Contract Law
Jonathan Morgan

Introduction

Baird Textile Holdings Ltd v Marks and Spencer plc

For 30 years Baird Textiles was one of the four major clothing suppliers to the pre-eminent retailer of underwear to the middle classes, Marks and Spencer plc (M&S). But in October 1999, M&S informed Baird that at the end of the current production run it would place no further orders with the company. Baird claimed that 'this sudden and unexpected cessation of their business relationship with M&S ha[d] caused them considerable loss' (*Baird Textile Holdings Ltd v Marks and Spencer plc* QBD, 29 June 2000, unreported, Morison J, at [6]). Baird alleged that M&S had never before summarily terminated a relationship with any of its major suppliers (Baird's particulars of claim, 9.23). Indeed, the chief executive of M&S had written to Baird's chairman in December 1998 to affirm M&S's relationship with its suppliers as a 'fundamental asset' and 'point of competitive difference' (Baird's particulars of claim, 9.24).

Baird therefore claimed that there had been an implied 'overarching' contract between the parties in addition to the actual orders placed twice per year. Under this alleged contract, M&S had been obliged to 'acquire garments in quantities and at prices which in all the circumstances was reasonable and would deal with [Baird] in good faith and reasonably having regard to the objective of the relationship'; the contract was to 'continue long term' and terminable only 'on the giving of reasonable notice' (Baird's particulars of claim, 9). Baird also claimed that M&S was estopped from denying the belief that it had induced in Baird that any relationship between them short of contract would be terminated only on reasonable notice (three years was suggested as a reasonable period for Baird to have disentangled its affairs from M&S) (*Baird* QBD, at [17]).

In the High Court Morison J dismissed Baird's contract claim. Since, as Baird stated, M&S had deliberately refrained from entering into any express 'overarching' contract, there could be no implied common intention to enter into such a contract. Its terms were anyway 'far too imprecise to be capable of being enforced' (*Baird* QBD, [13]–[14]; Baird's particulars of claim, 9.28). But Morison J held that notwithstanding 'formidable' doctrinal obstacles in the way of using promissory estoppel to found a cause of action, that aspect of the case should go to trial because it had importance for other manufacturer–retailer relationships and the law in this area was developing (*Baird* QBD, [20]).

The Court of Appeal dismissed both grounds of Baird's claim and entered summary judgment for M&S (*Baird Textile Holdings Ltd v Marks and Spencer plc* [2001] EWCA Civ 274; [2002] 1 All ER (Comm) 737). Morritt V-C held that the ordinary rules on formation and certainty applied to 'relational contracts' – and the 'academic discussion' to which counsel had referred the court had apparently not suggested otherwise (at [16]). In his Lordship's opinion, the alleged overarching contract was insufficiently certain because there were 'no objective criteria by which the court could assess what [orders] would be reasonable either as to quantity or price'; implying the contract was, moreover, 'not necessary to give business reality to the commercial relationship between M&S and Baird' (at [30]). Mance LJ agreed that the test for implication of a contract was *necessity*, and that it was impossible to spell out the alleged contract with sufficient precision:

> The more I have heard and read about the closeness of the parties' commercial co-operation in the past, the less able I have felt to see how its effect could be expressed in terms having any contractual certainty. (at [65])

To attempt this would, in effect, be to write a contract for the parties. To counsel's suggestion that evidence of the parties' own behaviour could flesh out the obligation, Mance LJ pointed out that the court would have to rule only 'where actual co-operation had broken down' meaning it 'would be expected to undertake the exercise in the very situation where the parties' actual behaviour could no longer serve as a guide to the answer' (at [68]). His Lordship commented:

> I do not think that the law should be ready to seek to fetter business relationships, even – and perhaps especially – those as long and as close as the present, with its own view of what might represent appropriate business conduct, when the parties have not chosen, or have not been willing or able, to do so in any identifiable legal fashion or terms themselves. (at [78])

Baird's promissory estoppel claim failed too. If it was impossible to express the alleged contract with sufficient certainty, then the same obstacle would be fatal for an estoppel claim (at [38], Morritt V-C, citing *Woodhouse AC Israel Cocoa Ltd v Nigeria Produce Marketing Co Ltd* [1972] AC 741). Mance LJ doubted that Baird's claim was (as they 'ostensibly' suggested) truly limited to 'reliance' loss ([80]–[82]), and in any case this could not justify the court's imposing its own view of acceptable business conduct when the parties had been unable or unwilling to define it themselves (at [94]). They must have been well aware of the significance of not entering into an overarching contract and, accordingly, the risk of the relationship ending fell on Baird (at [96]). In any event, it was settled law that promissory estoppel is not a cause of action (at [91], Mance LJ; cf. *Combe v Combe* [1951] 2 KB 215). As the law was clear, the fact that the House of Lords might theoretically accept Baird's invitation to follow the Australian lead and allow estoppel to found a cause of action (cf. *Waltons Stores (Interstate) Ltd v Maher* (1988) 164 CLR 387; *Commonwealth of Australia v Verwayen* (1990) 170 CLR 394) was not sufficient reason to allow the action to go to trial ([2001] EWCA Civ 274, at [39], Morritt V-C).

The relational critique of *Baird Textiles*

Ian Macneil comprehensively debunked the classical, individualist paradigm of contractual behaviour. Far from displaying unbridled self-interest, contracting parties greatly value ongoing relationships. Trust and co-operation pervade commerce and are of vital importance to it. The truly 'discrete' exchange, existing in isolation from a deeper, embedded relationship of mutual trust is, according to Macneil, a striking exception rather than (as contract lawyers have tended to assume) the archetype.

This chapter does not seek to detract from Macneil's towering achievement. His realistic description of the behaviour of those doing deals and carrying on business is of the first importance. Any serious social-scientific approach to the law of contract must begin with an accurate account of contracting behaviour. We will, however, argue that attempting straightforwardly to extrapolate a relational contract *law* from Macneil's pioneering account of relational contracting *behaviour* is misguided. At their simplest, such relational theories require the law to discern, define and enforce the co-operative relationship underlying individual transactions, rather than limiting its focus to those 'discrete' contracts.

It will be readily apparent that advocates of relational contract law must view the decision in *Baird Textiles* with dismay, for the courts explicitly rejected an invitation to enforce the relational dimension of Baird's dealings with M&S. Linda Mulcahy and Cathy Andrews (2010) accordingly proffer a relational critique of *Baird Textiles*. Inverting Morritt V-C's claim

(*Baird* CA, [30], quoted above), Mulcahy and Andrews argue that enforcing the overarching contract was indeed necessary to make sense of the parties' relationship and uphold their reasonable expectations. M&S had been more intricately involved in Baird's affairs than if they had dealt at arm's length. For example, M&S had participated in Baird's investment and design decisions and required disclosure of Baird's commercially confidential information. Many features of the relationship and of Baird's decision-making were explicable only on the basis of a healthy future order book – meaning that M&S would not summarily withdraw. Indeed, this was the core of M&S's own much-vaunted 'supplier partnerships'.

Mulcahy and Andrews' critique seems very appealing. Morison J recognized that Baird's relationship with M&S was necessarily very close, so that popular clothing lines could be re-ordered rapidly and unpopular ones replaced with new designs, and that, while the relationship was short of a formal partnership, it was 'akin to it' (*Baird* QBD, at [3–4]). Was it not therefore erroneous for the courts to deny that the overarching agreement was necessary to give effect to the parties' relationship? If the doctrine of certainty was the only obstacle, had it not been applied too strictly? Lord Tomlin long ago stated that the real question is whether the obligations could be *rendered* certain (*WN Hillas & Co Ltd v Arcos Ltd* (1932) 147 LT 503); *pace* Mance LJ's objections (*Baird*, CA, [68], quoted above), there was 30 years of the parties' relationship prior to its breakdown to assist in the task of rendering the overarching contract certain. It was most unfortunate that the Court of Appeal decided that it was incapable of precise definition (and entered summary judgment for M&S) without this evidence, which could only have emerged after a trial.

As for Morritt V-C's enigmatic and vague reference to academic analysis of relational contracting not supporting relaxation of the rules on formation and certainty this seems surprising if not (with respect) plain wrong. As Mulcahy and Andrews' own paper exemplifies, relational contract law scholarship characteristically calls for such doctrinal flexibility. Relationships emerge, shift and dissolve in a gradual way rather than obeying the 'sharp in, sharp out' pattern supposed by classical contract doctrine (Macneil, 1974, pp. 750–53). Therefore, it has frequently been argued, doctrine must necessarily change to reflect this reality and so commercial expectations.

Baird Textiles might therefore appear a tragic missed opportunity. The courts recognized the importance of the commercial relationship between Baird and M&S as a matter of fact. These were certainly not parties dealing 'at arm's length'. But by adhering to rigid notions of certainty the courts refused to give legal effect to that relationship. An element of farce was introduced by Morritt V-C's claim that relational contract scholarship has not recommended any relaxation in contract doctrine. The opposite is true. In fact, such scholarship *invariably* calls for the law of contract to accommodate the greater flexibility of relationships of trust and co-operation. *Baird Textiles* ironically exemplifies how English contract law has failed to do just that.

How then does this chapter seek to criticize the critique and defend *Baird Textiles*? The failings of 'relational contract law' are, we suggest, twofold. First, such theories underestimate the difficulty of giving legal effect to the relational dimension of contracts. So, we will question whether the law *can* properly enforce relationships as opposed to discrete contracts. Secondly, and much more importantly, we question whether the law even *should* (attempt to) do so. There is evidence that this may be simply futile or, worse still, actually counter-productive. It is arguable that law cannot maintain trust between parties where mutual co-operation has ceased. Moreover, some studies suggest that formal enforcement of relational norms may 'crowd out' true trust (e.g. Frey, 1993; Malhotra and Murningham, 2002, discussed below). If correct, these two arguments would indicate that relational contract law is a well-meaning but misguided attempt to 'support' (at considerable cost) implicit dimensions of contract that work perfectly well – or arguably much better – without legal intervention. Thus, paradoxically, it may be that relational contracting is perfectly compatible with discrete, classical contract law (as still generally prevails in England) after all (see Schwartz and Scott, 2003). These general doubts about relational contract law will be discussed before we return to the defence of *Baird Textiles*.

1. Scepticism about relational contract law

Should the law enforce relational contracts?

Doubts arise over contract law's ability to discern and enforce relational contracts. But a prior and more important question is whether the law should even be trying to do this. This point has been relatively neglected in the relational contract literature (Kimel, 2007). Usually, sympathetic commentators confidently assume that contract law *must* enforce the norms that Macneil has revealed to us. However, this is far from clear. As Kimel points out, the interface between legal and social norms is intricate and difficult. Law may replicate (and enforce) or ignore social norms, or impose others, depending on both moral questions and practicalities.

There are two particular problems with the enforcement of relational norms. First, that attempting to curb trust-corroding behaviour is doomed to failure. Secondly, that attempting positive enforcement of norms of trust may be counter-productive: judicialization changes and weakens those norms. In addition to concerns about the futility and counter-productiveness of legal enforcement, it may be unnecessary: social norms may be rendered sufficiently robust by the social sanctions that back them up. We outline these points below, along with evidence that some businesses actually prefer formal, discrete (in short, non-relational) dispute-resolution norms.

Do relational norms need to be legally enforced?

It is fallacious to assume that relational norms can exist only if they are legally enforced. It is perfectly possible to have 'order without law' as Robert Ellickson's (1991) study of the norms governing relations between cattle farmers in Shasta County, California, famously puts it. Elinor Ostrom (1990) shows that the absence of formal legal regulation (e.g. private property rights) does *not* inevitably mean ungovernable and mutually destructive competition – the 'grazing out' of common resources.[1] The norms that evolve are robust without legal enforcement. This directly challenges the lawyer's typical 'Leviathan assumption' – that without law life is necessarily 'solitary, poor, nasty, brutish, and short' (Hobbes, 1651).

A number of studies have shown how informal norms also flourish in the commercial context. This might not be very surprising within tight-knit groups such as the Jewish diamond traders considered by Lisa Bernstein (1992; cf. Richman, 2009) or Chong Ju Choi's (1994) ethnically Chinese merchant networks. The small-scale manufacturers interviewed by Stewart Macaulay (1963) in Wisconsin and by Hugh Beale and Tony Dugdale (1975) around Bristol mostly did business with (and therefore knew) each other. This might be thought to explain their invariable preference for informal dispute resolution rather than litigation. Perhaps the importance of social networks for commerce explains other features of capitalist societies. F H Buckley (2005, p. 164) suggests that the longstanding tendency of Americans to be 'joiners' and club-formers (remarked upon by Alexis de Toqueville) is due to the needs of a highly commercial society, and not Americans' supposed natural gregariousness ('A naïve explanation').

But informal norms can successfully govern commercial transactions within much more impersonal market settings too. An example is John Armour and Simon Deakin's study (2001) of the 'London Approach' to the affairs of insolvent companies. This obliged creditors (usually banks) not to use their formal legal remedies, triggering insolvency proceedings, unilaterally in a manner that might damage the interests of other creditors. Instead,

---

1 Ostrom shared the Nobel Prize for Economics in 2009 for this work. Cf. Hardin (1968).

creditors were expected to work out a mutually optimal solution to the debtor's distress. The key point is that the 'approach' was entirely informal; it did not depend on legal rules, and indeed its main purpose was to restrain use of legal remedies that creditors had every right to exercise. Yet for all that, Armour and Deakin report that the London Approach was remarkably successful, ensuring co-operation rather than cut-throat competition between City creditors. The modern City of London is no longer a *Mary Poppins*-era 'Gentlemen's Club'[2] – it is globalized *par excellence*. To like effect is Alan Morrison and William Wilhelm's (2007) historical account of investment banking, and the crucial role of reputation, trust and relationships within investment banks and between such banks and their clients. Both studies contradict suggestions that social norms can only prove robust within small communities, kinship or ethnic groups.

The efficacy of social norms within such settings largely depends on extra-legal sanctions. David Charny (1990) has stressed how effective such sanctions can be even in the impersonal markets of global commerce. Reputation is the key, as seen in the history of investment banking. Obviously, firms with a reputation for untrustworthy conduct will face disadvantageous terms from potential business partners – if any will do business with them at all. Even in the depersonalized world of the multinational corporation, reputational considerations remain highly pertinent. Charny points to the considerable appetite and market for information in the financial press. He argues that stock markets are also excellent dissemination mechanisms for information about the health of companies – reputational as well as narrowly financial. Of course, in a globalized marketplace most participants will not know (or know about) each other personally, but other channels for reputational information have grown up to supply the same need.

None of this can demonstrate, of itself, that informal social sanctions and internalized norms are the optimal way of enforcing relational norms between contracting parties. What it does show is that legal enforcement is not *necessarily* required for such norms to exist and flourish. Both Macneil's and Macaulay's pioneering research shows that relational contracting has historically flourished in spite of the law of contract. For three decades, as seen, Baird Textiles worked very closely with M&S despite the absence of any explicit (or as ultimately transpired, enforceable implicit) long-term contract. The 'discrete' law has not proved an insuperable obstacle to 'relational' practice. Of course, it may be that a relational contract *law* would support relational contracting better still, as Hugh Collins (1999) and many

---

2 It is hard to imagine kite-flying, bowler-hat-wearing Edwardian paterfamilias Mr Banks manipulating Libor in the fashion of Barclays Bank plc.

others have argued. But there is reason to doubt whether this is so. It may be that there are two orders of norms: within an ongoing relationship trust and communication are the keys to success, and the contract forms are ignored; however, 'silky talk' cannot govern all risks (such as bankruptcy), and the law of contract may ultimately be needed to unwind relationships that sour (Jennings, 1995). Accordingly, it may be better to leave relational norms to an informal life backed by social sanctions, retaining contract law in its accustomed discrete form to resolve end-game litigation (see Bernstein, 1996, discussed below). That suggests that the Court of Appeal was quite right to refuse to enforce the implicit relational dimension of the Baird–M&S relationship.

Counter-productive effects of enforcing relational norms

Judicializing relational norms could prove actively harmful. The theory is that enforcing co-operative norms may 'crowd out' the true spirit of co-operation rather than promoting it. There is a growing body of evidence to support this claim, from both laboratory experiments and field studies. If true then, paradoxically, 'fairness imposed is fairness denied' (Scott, 2004).

A famous study by Uni Gneezy and Aldo Rustichini (2000) shows how replacing an informal sanction with a formalized payment can transform the underlying norm. An infant school introduced fines for parents who collected their children late at the end of the school day. But tardy collection was found to *increase* significantly when the fines were instituted. Gneezy and Rustichini conjectured that the payments exacted were being interpreted by parents as a 'babysitting price', and one worth paying. It thereby undermined the social norm of punctuality that had previously governed the parent–school relationship.

Others have experimentally studied agreements made with and without externally enforced sanctions. Deepak Malhotra and J Keith Murnighan (2002) found that such sanctions (equivalent, of course, to the law of contract) undermined trust between the parties. In the absence of sanctions, performance was credited to the trustworthiness and reliability of the promisor. With sanctions present, however, performance was attributed to the threat of their imposition instead of true commitment to the agreement. Apparently trustworthy behaviour was not now seen as heartfelt, but only as contractually induced. Bruno Frey (1993) has found a similar effect in the workplace. Close monitoring of employees paradoxically decreases their work effort. Intrinsic motivation seems to be crowded out by micro-regulation of the way people go about their tasks. Frey suggests that whereas unmonitored workers can show trustworthiness (which may be rewarded by the employer) through a high work effort, such efforts no longer signal trustworthiness when shirking has anyway been made impossible by the employer's close monitoring. Both these studies suggest a need for some 'gaps' in which trust can develop – or rather, be demonstrated to the other party.

There is certainly evidence that concentrating too much on contract drafting can send out signals of distrust. Undue concern with contract law was widely seen as suspect by businesses in the classic studies by Macaulay (1963) and Beale and Dugdale (1975). Such studies are corroborated by experiments in which more complete contracts were seen to signal lower levels of trust and to induce less co-operation (Chou et al., 2011). Seeking security by drafting more detailed contracts can apparently trigger a cycle of distrust. Such negotiation can be seen to signal that a relationship is to be more businesslike and less personal. Ironically, contracts can therefore exacerbate negative expectations and make the problems that they are intended to solve more likely to occur. Whereas incomplete contracts may generate more positive relational signals and so increase co-operation.

What to make of this evidence? It does not prove to a certainty that legal enforcement is inimical to trust (cf. for recent argument that trust and contract may be complementary not rivalrous: Mitchell, 2009). But it surely gives grounds for caution. The fear is that even if the law could perfectly enforce relational norms (or, negatively, punish opportunistic defections from relational norms), to do so would undermine the relationship. Parties could no longer tell whether apparently trustworthy behaviour was motivated by true relational commitment, or a tactical decision to simulate co-operation to avert legal liability. This may damage the relationship in the long run. Paradoxically, it may be better to have contracts (and a law of contract) limited to enforcing the main obligations on both sides. This provides a basic guarantee of performance (or its monetary equivalent) while leaving space for genuine trust to develop in the interstices. Again, this supports Baird's and M&S's decision not to enter an express long-term contract, and the court's decision not to imply one.

The capability problem: can the courts accurately define and enforce relational norms?

Even were it a good idea to enforce relational norms in principle, are the courts able to do it successfully in practice? Judicial regulatory capacity in contract cases has been debated for decades (see Danzig, 1978). The enforcement of relational norms sets especially formidable challenges. Such norms are implicit rather than explicit (by contrast with written contract terms). They evolve with the relationship rather than being fixed at the moment of 'formation': Macneil stressed the impossibility of 'presentiating' relational norms. A flavour of the difficulties of enforcing such immanent, fluctuating standards is provided by Macneil's description of the court's role. Its involvement would be both active and ongoing (compared to the reactive, one-off nature of classical adjudication), because disputes are 'not between private individuals about private rights but ... about the operation of policies of the overall contractual relation'. Remedies in relational contract law would have to be 'forward-looking [and] fashioned *ad hoc* on flexible and broadly remedial lines, often having important consequences for many persons, including absentees' (Macneil, 1978, p. 892). Clearly this would involve a considerable enhancement of the court's powers compared to traditional models of adjudication. Jay Feinman (2000) reasonably comments that Macneil totally rejected doctrinal reasoning in favour of policy analysis.

Does this matter? Certainly, many contract lawyers remain committed to a formal, doctrinal approach in the interest of providing maximum predictability for contracting parties. It is rather difficult to measure certainty, but it seems plausible enough that the judicial application of strict doctrinal rules will be easier to predict than a wide-ranging search for immanent relational norms. In contrast, Macneil (1968) maintained that contract law is an instrument of social policy and doctrinal 'certainty' an illusion. Against this, William Whitford (2003) accepts that a rule-based law of contract is more likely to be successful (i.e. stable and certain) in the professional, centralized English legal system compared to the exuberant pluralism of US law.

Collins (1999) argues extensively for the 'productive disintegration' of private law by relaxing the obsession with inward-looking doctrinal reasoning. Good judicial policy-making would, indeed, in Collins's view, require the bold, active and open stance from the courts that Macneil (1978) identifies. This should be welcomed, in Collins's view.

However, many doubt whether procedural innovations and an overt concern with policy reasoning would equip courts to perform the daunting tasks that relational contract law demands of them. John Kidwell (1985) notes that it is no good the law attempting a 'true reflection' of relational norms if it then lacks sufficient certainty to guide contracting parties' conduct. Ewan McKendrick (1995) asserts that courts lack expertise to modify long-term contracts (non-intervention will encourage the parties to agree, in McKendrick's view). In their review article of Collins's book, John Gava and Janey Greene (2004, p. 620) sum up the criticisms, complaining that he sets a regulatory task for the judiciary at which even a 'superhuman would baulk'.

Not everyone accepts such scepticism. William Woodward (2001) correctly notes that calls for formalism in law are always designed to remove power from the courts. He argues that there is no empirical evidence for claims (from Danzig, 1978, onwards) about judicial incompetence. Macaulay (2003) claims that formalist attacks on the courts' competence to develop relational contract law are based purely on anti-government ideology. But ostensibly at least, the critics' concern is a pragmatic not an ideological one: that courts are not able to meet the strenuous demands of discovering and enforcing relational norms. This argument is another reason for caution before translating Macneil's sociological findings into contract law doctrine. We will explore in further detail below the difficulties inherent in defining and enforcing the alleged relational contract in *Baird Textiles*.

Sceptical evidence: what do contracting parties want?

There is some evidence that sophisticated commercial parties do prefer a strict and formal law of contract to contextual, relational obligations. Robert Scott (2004) states that the rise of contextual standards in US contract law (the Uniform Commercial Code (UCC) and Restatement (Second) of Contracts) has coincided with an exodus from the law. Commercial contractors increasingly prefer other means of dispute resolution. Arbitration clauses are increasingly common. Scott argues that this is no coincidence. The open-textured rules in the UCC may satisfy the courts (giving them discretion to fashion 'just' results) but commercial parties have been voting with their feet to avoid them. If contract law is primarily a service for such clients, this must be a cause for concern.

What evidence exists for Scott's indictment? Lisa Bernstein has found a preference for strict rules amongst some trade associations and their members. Bernstein's (1996) study of the National Grain and Feed Association reveals a textual approach to interpretation of obligations by the association's tribunal, excluding trade custom and the course of dealings between the parties. 'Good faith' was defined as nothing more than performing the letter of the contract. Bernstein comments that this is quite different to the philosophy of the UCC – although we could note the similarity with Lord Diplock's view of 'justice' in English commercial law (*The Maratha Envoy* [1978] AC 1, pp. 13–14). Bernstein suggests that very different rules are desired (and applied) in the 'end game' compared with the 'relationship-preserving norms' that govern ongoing commercial relationships. Enforcing those relational norms would be counter-productive: potentially discouraging concessions (for fear that they would be held legally enforceable contract modifications). Moreover, parties prefer formal, clear rules for swift and predictable resolution of disputes.

Bernstein's (2001) investigation of the cotton industry provides further evidence. Again, the rules governing disputes between cotton traders were found to be distinctly formal compared to the UCC, prizing clarity over justice (e.g. excluding recovery of any losses consequent on breach of contract – making the rule much easier to apply, at the expense of 'full compensation'). Cotton industry tribunals duly apply these rules in a formalistic (rather than flexible, contextual or relational) fashion. How then can relational contracting take place against the backdrop of such decidedly un-relational rules for dispute settlement? Bernstein finds that pricing was highly sensitive to reputation: untrustworthy traders would be at a major competitive disadvantage. There is evidence here for the division of labour mentioned above – relational norms as the preserve of *extra-legal* enforcement with the legal (or rather arbitral) dispute resolution remaining limited and formal.

Bernstein's findings are a fascinating mirror image of the usual story of arbitration. Typically, it is presented as a way that commercial parties can contract out of the narrowly legal world of the courts and have their disputes resolved by other merchants, using the 'business context'. Maybe this has some plausibility in England where contract law does remain relatively formal.[3] In the US the reverse is apparently true, if Bernstein's research points to a general trend. As US contract law has declined in formality, so alternative dispute resolution (ADR) has offered the formal alternative that at least some commercial parties evidently desire. Perhaps the traditionalism of English contract law has something to commend it after all – and its practitioners have not been slow to proclaim the benefits of a clear and uncluttered approach to enforcing commercial contracts in the international 'market for law'.

Naturally, this is not to say that all commercial ADR must be so formal. The arbitrator may act as an 'amiable compositor' imposing a compromise and using flexible norms, as in the continental tradition of academic arbitrators (Dezalay and Garth, 1996). However, Sir Michael Mustill and Stewart Boyd (1989, p. 75) state that such clauses are not usually found in England. Linda Mulcahy (2013, this volume) draws attention to the soaring popularity of commercial *mediation*, an important corrective to the normal preoccupation with arbitration. Mediation aims to facilitate compromise between the disputants – standing in opposition to the austere strictness and winner-takes-all outcomes of the arbitral rules described by Bernstein.

Mediation is an emerging, important and neglected subject. Perhaps though (using Bernstein's taxonomy) it properly falls within the 'relationship-preserving' stage: mediation can succeed only if it ends with agreement between the parties. Its solutions do not have the same imposed (and likely relationship-*ending*) quality as decisions at law (or in arbitration).

---

3 But cf. the extraordinary arbitral insubordination to a House of Lords' decision (viz. *A-G v Blake* [2001] 1 AC 268) in *The 'Sine Nomine'* [2002] 1 Lloyd's Rep 805. The common law was here thought not certain enough!

However, some such rule will still be needed to resolve disputes when the parties ultimately cannot agree (even after mediation). Bernstein's division between relationship preservation and dispute resolution arguably reflects that between mediation and litigation/arbitration. Bernstein argues that it is optimal for the rules at the latter stage to be clear and formal even though the relationship-preserving norms are flexible and informal. If so then, contrary to Mulcahy's argument, the consensual norms evident in commercial mediation should not inspire a revolutionized relational contract law. Mediation represents a fundamentally different normative order from litigation, when the parties truly are in the end game of their commercial relationship. At the very least, Bernstein provides clear evidence that some commercial parties do prefer strict and formal contract norms and, if the law does not supply them, they will contract out of the law of contract. There was no positive evidence of whether the parties in *Baird Textiles* preferred *ex ante* a 'discrete' or 'relational' contract law to govern any disputes between them. The Bernstein argument does show, at least, that the relational option cannot be assumed simply because there was a long-term commercial relationship.

Relational default rules

What then do commercial parties demand from the law of contract? Accepting the importance and ubiquity of relational contracting, it does not follow that they are necessarily best served by a relational contract *law*, for the following reasons. One can reasonably doubt the courts' capacity to define and enforce the tacit, ever-changing norms which characterize commercial relations. Looking negatively at opportunistic breaches of the contractual relationship, the law is again faced with a formidable regulatory puzzle. Attempts to curb opportunism arguably cause as many problems as they solve, given its 'reflexive' nature (see Campbell, 2004). But even if courts could precisely define and faultlessly enforce relational norms (which they cannot), there are still reasons why this might be undesirable. Arguably, for true trust to develop there must be 'gaps' in which co-operative behaviour is given credit as such, and not attributed to compliance with law (coerced by the threat of legal liability). Scott (2003) argues for this reason that sometimes parties deliberately enter into unenforceable agreements – and it would be a mistake to render them enforceable (e.g. by straining the doctrine of certainty).

The real question is what the *default* approach of the law should be. We suggest that contract law's starting point should remain strict, formal and rule-based. Rules should be applied without the court seeking to inquire into 'opportunism': *Arcos v Ronaasen & Son* [1933] AC 470 should remain the default approach. The courts should not seek to imply (really, to impose) duties of trust, co-operation and good faith upon the parties: the philosophy behind *Walford v Miles* [1992] 2 AC 128 remains sound. Why, though, should the default rules remain in the classical rigid form, and not reflect the relational reality that Macneil and Macaulay have revealed? The answer lies in the nature of default rules. They are only the starting point: governing what is to happen *unless* the parties say otherwise. It is therefore desirable for default rules to be plain and modest. This facilitates contracting out of the default position. Delivery of timber $1/2$ inch thick means just that – unless the parties themselves say otherwise. And, of course, they easily could stipulate for a certain tolerance and (according to the very experienced commercial judges in *Arcos v Ronaasen*) they frequently do. The perfect tender rule is clear, and easy for the court to apply (compared with deciding whether it would be 'unreasonable' to reject non-conforming goods, let alone formulating a standard for tolerance such as +/– 5%). If the parties wish for something more nuanced then they had better say so (cf. David Campbell's discussion of *Arcos*, this volume).

Simple default rules facilitate the stipulation of more complex standards where those are desired. Because the defaults are straightforward, clear and predictable the parties know precisely out of what they must opt. The onus is on them to come up with relational standards if that is what they want the court to enforce. The parties' task is made easier by the stark clarity of the non-relational default rules. All that is required for a successful policy of judicial abstention in this fashion is that the courts enforce *express* relational clauses when the parties *do* include them in the contract. There is no good reason why the courts should not – the argument here is only that the *default* position should not be relational, and not that relational terms should *never* be judicially enforced. The *dicta* about 'margins' in *Arcos* show the court's receptiveness to *party-stipulated* softening of the perfect tender rule; the courts have given ample effect to 'anti-technicality' clauses designed to curb opportunistic withdrawal of chartered ships (e.g. *The Afovos* [1983] 1 WLR 195). Compare also the refusal to *imply* duties of good faith in *Walford v Miles* with Longmore LJ's opinion that 'it would be a strong thing to declare unenforceable a [good faith] clause into which the parties have *deliberately and expressly* entered' (*Petromec Inc v Petroleo Brasileiro SA Petrobas* [2005] EWCA Civ 891; [2006] 1 Lloyd's Rep 161, at [121] (emphasis added)).

The economic debate about default rules (whether majoritarian or penalty) gets bogged down in complexity. It ultimately seems to founder for want of the empirical data necessary to apply the economic models (Posner, 2003). We suggest a simple rule of thumb instead. The publicly supplied law of contract should be *minimalist*. Simple default rules are the easiest for the court to formulate and apply. Their clarity and predictability also makes them the easiest rules to contract away from. These twin advantages avoid the costs of a more ambitious law of contract that attempts to 'support' (i.e. enforce) relational norms. Any enterprise of elaborate judicial default-rule creation is 'seldom cost justified' according to Alan Schwartz (1998):

> This is due to high costs of state rule creation, party heterogeneity (too many contractual solutions are needed), the inability of the state to know what the benefits of good defaults are, and the state's relative lack of expertise in creating efficient contract terms. (p. 282)

Relational norms should, we suggest, be judicially enforced only when the parties have explicitly incorporated them into the terms of the contract. The failure to draw up an express long-term contract between Baird and M&S was rightly held fatal. They failed to contract out of the default discrete regime – when they could have done so quite easily.

Summary of the argument against relational contract law

To sum up the argument so far, we first reiterate that most rules in contract law are ultimately just 'defaults' – i.e. rules that apply in the absence of agreement to the contrary. Even remedies for breach of contract are such default rules.[4] A vital question for contract lawyers (one which underlies most debates about contract doctrine) is how such defaults should be formulated. The majoritarian approach suggests that the law should reproduce what most parties would like to happen in the given situation. This is the familiar territory of 'satisfying reasonable expectations'. Given Macneil's research, it might seem to follow that default rules should be 'relational'. However, we have sought to argue above that there are good reasons why commercial parties might not desire relational contract doctrine, notwithstanding the importance of trust and co-operation in their business relationships. The supporting evidence is probably not conclusive (it is hard to see that the empirical debate will ever be finally determined). But it is enough to raise legitimate doubts about a 'majoritarian relational' strategy – and yet that approach has been assumed as the natural one in the relational contracting literature.

Instead, we have sought to argue that the important thing about default rules is their *default* nature. One has to start somewhere. The law of contract must have *some* sanctions for breach (and rules on when breach has taken place, and indeed whether a contract has been formed) if it is to exist at all. The key is to emphasize that whatever these rules are, they are indeed only

---

4 With certain exceptions, e.g. the inability to stipulate for specific performance and the penalty clause doctrine. Cf. *Photo Production Ltd v Securicor Transport Ltd* [1980] AC 827, pp. 848–51, *per* Lord Diplock.

the starting point. Parties are free to contract out of them. (It is, incidentally, dubious to invest contract law doctrine with any great moral significance given this optional character.) Therefore, we defend the formalist doctrine of classical English contract law. Its clarity and relative simplicity not only promotes certainty (and thereby dispute resolution). Furthermore, parties can contract out of it easily. This is not quite the encouragement of contracting-out by 'penalty defaults' (cf. Ayres and Gertner, 1989). Our approach *facilitates* rather than actively incentivizes contracting-out.

In short, parties that want relational contract law can and should contract for it – and the courts should enforce any such agreement. But the starting point should be austere minimalism. Relational contract *law*, as the default position, may actually be harmful for the reasons canvassed above. It is also unnecessary when the parties are perfectly able to indicate that relational norms are to be used to resolve contractual disputes, if they so desire. As Campbell (2004) comments, it is difficult to justify public subsidies (in the guise of a judicial contract-renegotiation service) for businesses which can either draft their contracts properly in the first place or pay for private dispute resolution. The law of contract should be plain and simple, minimizing its complexity and cost. In this form it is likely to appeal to the maximum number of contracting parties (whose heterogeneity renders the provision of norms that are both general and relationship-specific an unachievable oxymoron). At least, all parties are confronted with the same *tabula rasa* on which they may paint a relational picture where this best suits their needs. The argument then is for non-relational contract law to remain the default position, but with full freedom to opt for relational norms for those parties that wish it.

2. In defence of *Baird Textiles*

In *Baird Textiles*, the parties could have entered into an express overarching contract, but did not. There is little doubt that if they had done so, the court would have given legal effect to the agreement (cf. Mouzas and Furmston, 2008). Consistent with the argument above, the decision to dismiss Baird's claim was therefore correct. The court should not imply a contract when the parties declined the opportunity to do so themselves – and indeed where this was a 'deliberate matter of policy' on the part of M&S ([2001] EWCA Civ 274, at [73], Mance LJ; Baird's particulars of claim, 9.28). There are numerous reasons why the parties may have decided not to conclude an express 'umbrella' agreement. Chief among these is the central argument developed above: that long-term business relationships, despite their undoubted importance (illustrated by the facts of *Baird Textiles*), may function better if governed by *extra-legal* sanctions and norms.

Thus, it cannot be assumed that reasonable expectations in a situation such as *Baird Textiles* always envisage *legal* enforcement. It is begging the question to say that there is a 'gap' here (that needs filling) in the first place. An umbrella agreement certainly does not 'go without saying' (so as to be impliedly intended). Mance LJ was correct to recognize and maintain a sharp distinction between legal obligations and the relational norms that undoubtedly underlay the parties' 'extremely good long-term commercial relationship' ([2001] EWCA Civ 274, at [69]). It is by no means obvious that even close business partners necessarily want an enforceable long-term contract. While all business depends on trust, goodwill and good intentions, economic conditions and intentions may change and businesses can be taken to know that 'without specific contractual protection, their business may suffer in consequence' ([2001] EWCA Civ 274, at [76], Mance LJ).

There are further difficulties if courts over-enthusiastically imply (really, impose) long-term contracts between parties with ongoing business relationships. As noted above, the most important thing about default rules is just that – parties can contract out of them. This is obviously possible with implied terms (subject to the courts' sporadic determination to preserve certain kinds of liability despite express contractual exclusions of it). However, it is considerably more challenging to exclude an entire implied *contract*. By definition, there is no (express) contract there at all, and no express terms by which to exclude the court-implied contract. Must the parties enter into an express contract whose sole purpose is to state that there is no contract between them? This would be contract law *Through the Looking-Glass* rather than 'reflecting reasonable expectations'. At the least, advertent parties fearing an imposed relational contract would have to make explicit, positive statements that there was no intention to create legal relations of that kind, to prevent a contract being foisted upon them. Compare the effects in the US of the significant expansion in pre-contractual liability in cases such as *Hoffman v Red Owl Stores* 133 NW 2d 267 (Wisconsin 1965). According to Eric Posner (2000, p. 163), the consequence has been express disclaimers of such liability at every step of negotiations leading up to a contract, which Posner dubs the 'new formality'. It was suggested above that a highly desirable quality of default contract terms is ease of contracting-out. It is much easier to execute an express long-term contract where that is desired than to exclude a judicially imposed contract when it is not.[5] On this ground too, the default rule of non-enforcement illustrated by *Baird Textiles* is preferable.

---

5 Compare the use of 'subject to contract' clauses in England: *Regalian Properties plc v London Docklands Development Corporation* [1995] 1 All ER 1005; cf. *RTS Flexible Systems Ltd v Molkerei Alois Müller GmbH* [2010] UKSC 14.

Complexity

How best to structure procurement is a complex economic question for manufacturers and retailers (see generally Williamson, 1985). This obliges courts to proceed cautiously before imposing ('implying') a particular solution. A steel smelter needing iron ore could buy its requirements from time to time on the open market; or enter a long-term supply contract with a mining company; or become an iron miner itself ('vertical integration' between manufacturing and abstraction). These solutions are in increasing order of 'relationism' (see Macneil, 1981, pp. 1025–6). But each has its pros and cons – and if Nobel prize-winning economists find such questions of institutional design difficult (cf. Williamson, 1985), a court which declares that the answer is so obvious that it goes without saying (so as to imply a long-term contract) is, at best, hubristic (or, more likely, unburdened by knowledge of the difficulties). Understanding the complexity of the problem undermines confidence in a simple judicial solution. It is therefore far from clear that an enforceable long-term contract was the optimal way of governing the relationship in *Baird Textiles* – this certainly did not 'go without saying' (the traditional standard for implying a contract).

Promissory estoppel

Estoppel seems full of potential for protecting relational norms – in particular by its protection of reliance. Vulnerability to opportunism in long-term contracts stems from relationship-specific investments which will be lost if the deal ends. A party with such losses at stake may be compelled to accept highly unfavourable modifications – as the other party will be well aware. If estoppel were to compensate such reliance losses, a major cause of opportunism could be addressed.

Doctrinal obstacles have prevented promissory estoppel from playing such a role in England so far. Prime among these (and the one that prevailed in *Baird Textiles*) is the rule that promissory estoppel may prevent the other party from enforcing their strict legal rights but cannot be used 'as a sword' to generate new rights (*Combe v Combe*). With respect to the learned judges involved, and commentators who have tried (Halson, 1999; Barnes, 2011), this rule is impossible rationally to defend – and has been abolished in Australia (cf. *Waltons Stores*). A second potential doctrinal hurdle, also raised in *Baird Textiles*, is the need for a clear promise by the defendant (not) to do the particular thing before he can be estopped. This has played a prominent role in some cases, notably when judges have feared that claims will be established too readily (cf. *Collier v P & MJ Wright (Holdings) Ltd* [2007] EWCA Civ 1329, at [45], *per* Longmore LJ). But the negative attitude has not been consistent. In one of the leading 'proprietary estoppel' cases, *Crabb v Arun District Council* [1976] Ch 179, the trial judge dismissed the claim because there had been no clear promise by the defendant council to grant the alleged right of way. But the Court of Appeal granted relief to the plaintiff undaunted, Scarman LJ instead emphasizing the necessity of examining the entire conduct and relationship of the parties. Paul Finn (1989) argues that the Australian doctrine illustrates increasing concern with relational factors, 'the actual conduct of the parties in the relationship, the known assumptions upon which one or both act(s), and so on'.

This relational approach sees its logical end in the arguments of Daniel Farber and John Matheson (1985). They argue for a much wider test of enforcement: any promise made for economic gain, or made within an economic relationship, should be legally enforceable. It is often difficult, they point out, to identify a definite 'exchange' or indeed reliance (it is hard to show that an employee has worked harder in reliance on some benefit promised by the employer!). 'In the context of ongoing relationships, exchange is a continuing rather than a discrete event.'

This is an accurate description of relational contracting. It explains the difficulty of applying the orthodox consideration doctrine to such relationships. Their enforceability should not be compromised by zealous insistence on a narrow *quid pro quo* – or indeed identifiable reliance. That is Farber and Matheson's argument. But it seems much too wide. Accepting that doctrinal technicalities should not obstruct proper analysis of complex problems, we cannot agree with the statement that *every* understanding within an economic relationship should be enforceable. This begs the question that has been discussed at some length above, whether relational norms should be enforced by the law. Simply observing (correctly) that such norms are vital in many economic relationships does nothing to resolve that debate.

At the heart of Farber and Matheson's argument is the protection of trust. When promises are broken it undermines the trust that is necessary for the general flourishing of the economy (which is therefore a public good). Such negative externalities ought to be deterred by law. Farber and Matheson's exemplar case is *United Steel Workers, Local 1330 v US Steel Corp* 631 F 2d 1264 (6th Cir 1980) in which US Steel had promised to keep open two steelworks marked for closure if their workers could make them profitable. US Steel concluded that this had not happened (the workers had saved enough to cover the fixed costs of the plants' operations, but not made a profit); the workers' union sought enforcement of the agreement via promissory estoppel. The court held that it was a condition precedent of the agreement that the plants become profitable, and the claim failed. US Steel was entitled to close the factory.

Farber and Matheson (1985) are highly critical of this result. The defendant company had violated the trust of its loyal workforce. It was permitted to take the benefits of their extra efforts to keep the plants open, for which the workers had seen no return. Such behaviour damages society as a whole:

> Employees will be less likely to put forth the extra effort to save a plant if employers can violate their promises by semantic quibbles. In breaching its understanding with its employees, U.S. Steel polluted the pool of trust from which it had drawn. The pool is large and individual breaches of trust may be small, but the effect of pollution is cumulative. (p. 942)

In a time of economic distress, co-operation is vital but distrust likely to be present. It is just here where, contrary to *United Steel Workers*, 'the need to reinforce trust with legal sanctions is especially strong' (Farber and Matheson, 1985, p. 939).

This sounds very appealing. But as already noted, it is far from clear that legal sanctions are necessarily the best way of fostering true co-operation. Can law really force parties to trust each other? Moreover, comparing the facts of *United Steel Workers* and *Baird Textiles*, can the law (and should it) seek to uphold uneconomic activities? Both US Steel and M&S saw their profitability undercut by cheaper foreign goods. It was rational, if regrettable, that American steelworks should close and long-standing British suppliers be replaced by cheaper factories overseas, if their businesses were to survive at all. Accepting that relational norms were broken here, it was for understandable economic reasons. Should the law really seek to deter such decisions – taking a Canute-like stand against the rising tide of globalization?

It is important not to overplay this point. English contract law is (traditionally at least) tolerant of breach. In the leading cases on specific performance, the House of Lords went out of its way *not* to condemn a quite deliberate decision to break a long-term contract that had ceased to be profitable (*Cooperative Insurance Society Ltd v Argyll Stores (Holdings) Ltd* [1998] AC 1). Their Lordships (in contrast to the Court of Appeal) declined to order specific performance, limiting the promisee to its remedy in damages (cf. [1996] Ch 286). Campbell (2001, pp. 687–91) stresses that the real 'efficiency' of breach is in limiting waste by permitting non-performance of unforeseeably expensive obligations.

But does this permissive attitude towards breach not enable the violations of trust that Farber and Matheson (1985) condemn? Seana Shiffrin (2007, p. 720) worries that if contract law allows deliberate breach to maximize profits this may weaken 'the conditions for the maintenance of moral character' in society generally. Whether or not this is very plausible, English contract law has started to move away from its tolerance of breach, notably by ordering disgorgement of profits from egregious contract-breakers (*Attorney-General v Blake* [2001] 1 AC 268). More generally, there is a growing emphasis (at least amongst academic commentators) upon the *right* to performance, and breach of contract as a violation of that right (e.g. Friedmann, 1995; Webb, 2006; Pearce and Halson, 2008; Stevens, 2009). In general, one can detect the rise in England of what Finn (1989) described as the characteristic language of the new Australian contract law – ' [t]he evocative, and morally judgemental, adjective'. Vindicating the promisee's rights, of course, encourages condemnation of the promisor's breach of them.

It is, however, questionable (for the reasons already discussed) whether *punishing* breach will really encourage trust between contracting parties. It may well encourage uneconomic decisions – outright waste – if the sanctions are sufficiently great. Campbell (2011) accordingly attacks the drift of English law towards the condemnation of breach of contract. Campbell argues again that permitting breach is essential and necessary for economic flexibility. Moreover, by requiring the disappointed promisee to take reasonable steps to minimize his or her losses, the law enlists the promisee's co-operation in limiting the damaging consequences of the deal that has turned sour. Simply, the classical doctrine on breach of contract requires co-operation between the parties – and hence remedies in their traditional permissive form enjoy a 'relational constitution' (Campbell, 2005).

What of promissory estoppel? The economically distorting incentives may be smaller here, to the extent that estoppel remedies' concern is purely with 'reversing detriment'. In the relational context that would mean protection of relationship-specific investment. However, it is questionable whether a sharp line between 'reliance' and 'expectation' measures can in the end be maintained. Despite the theoretical emphasis on protecting reliance in modern Australian estoppel (cf. *Commonwealth of Australia v Verwayen*), courts have consistently protected the plaintiff's *expectation* – i.e. awarded what was promised (this was true in all of the first 24 cases following *Verwayen*: Robertson, 1996, p. 829). Andrew Robertson (2008) explains this continuing phenomenon in the following way. Detriment is incalculable in the numerous proprietary estoppel cases involving families and homes, and even in commercial disputes it is difficult to quantify since the usual detriment in relying on a promise is *lost opportunities*. Rather than risk under-compensating such reliance, it is better simply to enforce the promise. (Of course, this is the same argument that Lon Fuller and William Purdue (1936) used for expectation damages in *contract* – a proxy for hard-to-calculate lost opportunities.) So the difference between estoppel and contract remedies may be more apparent than real.

Moreover, in England as in Australia, estoppel is an equitable doctrine with an emphasis on *unconscionability*: whether going back on the promise 'would be inequitable having regard to the dealings which have taken place between the parties' (*Hughes v Metropolitan Railway Co* (1877) 2 App Cas 439, p. 448, Lord Cairns LC; but cf. Neuberger, 2010, discussed below). By definition then, when the court upholds an estoppel claim it is condemning the defendant's conduct. From Farber and Matheson's (1985) perspective, this is a positive benefit. But it is questionable whether economically sensible decisions such as M&S's in *Baird Textiles* should be castigated with 'morally judgemental adjectives'. It is, furthermore, doubtful whether this would promote trust in business relations.

Conclusion

Fully accepting the truth of Macneil's account of relational contracting, we have nevertheless sought to argue against a relational contract *law*. The core argument is that law is unlikely to promote trust and co-operation because of its inherent limits. The identification of relational norms (or, speaking negatively, opportunism) is a difficult task for the courts. There will be a high failure rate. Even assuming (implausibly) that this can be done perfectly, or even satisfactorily, should it even be attempted? There is evidence that trying to enforce such norms is at best futile, and at worst positively harmful. The hostility engendered by litigation seems inimical to the restoration of that mutual trust upon which a relational contract depends (but the potential for relationship preservation through commercial *mediation* requires emphasis here, cf. Mulcahy, this volume).

Given these doubts, we suggest that the case for a 'relational transformation' of English contract law has not been made out. The law should instead be relatively simple and minimalistic. Plainness and clarity in the default rules supplied by law enhances the ease of contracting out of them. Therefore parties that wish for rules enforcing co-operation, or deterring opportunism, may easily stipulate for this. A limited contract law maximizes freedom of contract.

Alternatively, sophisticated commercial parties may well (we conjecture) prefer a twin-pronged strategy for the regulation of their relational contracts. During the currency of the relationship, norms of trust and co-operation are enforced by the mutual self-interest of the parties in maintaining a good relationship, backed up by reputational damage to businesses that act in opportunistic ways. Law is unnecessary here. But in situations where the parties really cannot agree, or where external shocks end the relationship (e.g. insolvency), there needs to be a set of rules to resolve the dispute between them. This corresponds to Bernstein's (1996) sequential taxonomy of relationship-preserving (extra-legal) norms and end-game (legal) norms.

It means a limited role for the law of contract. Scott (1987) suggests that long-term contractors enter into legal contracts because, even if co-operation grows naturally between them, there needs to be some external sanction to deter 'defection' when its pay-offs look particularly large. Despite his call to close the gap between 'the real and the paper deal' (Macaulay, 2003), Macaulay seems basically to agree. He expresses himself 'sceptical' about contract law's role in facilitating trust, suggesting it probably has most effect on those who know least about it – a vague sense of unpleasant threat (Macaulay, 1996). Macaulay (2004) finds that business views law as inimical to trust: it has the wrong language, that of being *right* (while the other side is wrong!) with the state's power on your side (cf. discussion of 'vindication remedies', pp. 186–7 above). But Macaulay would not abolish contract law altogether, or there would be no deterrence for 'outrageous' behaviour, which would lead to serious harm to trust and the economy (Macaulay, 2004). *Pace* Macaulay (2003), however, it is in our view sufficient for such limited purposes that the law holds parties liable for breach of the express terms of their contracts. It need not attempt to enforce all the richness of the implicit relationship between them.

Finally, is there not a streak of amorality or indeed immorality in all of this (cf. Shiffrin, 2007)? The standard relational-contract argument runs thus: the classical model of contract law is based on erroneous assumptions about how contracting parties behave. Since Macneil has uncovered the relational truth, the law's assumptions have been demonstrably falsified, and therefore its doctrines should change accordingly. For contract law to continue in its hide-bound way with doctrines premised on wholly selfish behaviour when real contractors behave co-operatively might seem little short of immoral.

However, it is mistaken to attribute too much moral significance to the doctrines of the law of contract when (public policy aside) the parties are free to contract out of them. Indeed, a major strand of our argument here is concerned with facilitating such contracting-out. Secondly, Macneil emphasized that the trust and co-operation at the heart of relational contracting is ultimately a matter of enlightened self-interest. It is dubious to equiparate it with self-sacrificial behaviour of true moral worth.

Finn (1989) praises the 'moralizing' of Australian contract law but England has remained considerably more hard-nosed. In *Banque Financiere de la Cite SA v Westgate Insurance Co,* the Court of Appeal, holding that an insurer did not owe a duty of care to the insured bank, observed that it was: 'one of those many cases where the legal obligation falls short of the moral imperatives ... The law cannot police the fairness of every commercial contract by reference to moral principles.' ([1990] 1 QB 665, p. 802, affirmed [1991] 2 AC 249) The spirit of *Smith v Hughes* is alive and well (cf. (1871) LR 6 QB 597, 607, *per* Blackburn J).

Lord Neuberger (2010), in a lecture on estoppel, deplores the reliance on the defendant's 'dishonourable behaviour' by both the Court of Appeal and Etherton J in the commercial property-development case of *Cobbe v Yeomen's Row Management Ltd* [2006] EWCA Civ 1139; [2005] EWHC 266 (Ch). The 'fundamental problem', says the Master of the Rolls, is that 'equity is not a sort of moral US fifth cavalry riding to the rescue any time a court thinks that a defendant has behaved badly'. If the House of Lords' decision in *Cobbe* [2008] UKHL 55 has led to the 'death of estoppel' in the commercial context, then in Lord Neuberger's view, it is 'probably all to the good' (Neuberger, 2010, p. 229; cf. Macfarlane and Robertson, 2008). The courts should not wield 'some Denningesque sword of justice to rescue a miscalculating, improvident or optimistic property developer from the commercially unattractive, or even ruthless, actions of a property owner, which are lawful in common law' (Neuberger, 2010, p. 230). It seems then that even the 'moral indignation' of unconscionability may be muted in English commercial law. Or rather, its applicability in commercial disputes must be tightly controlled, when 'in the business world, certainty and clarity are particularly important, and judges should be slow to encourage the introduction of uncertainties based on their views of the ethical acceptability of the behaviour of one of the parties' (p. 231).

Long may the amorality of English commercial law continue! If the arguments advanced here have any merit, this may (paradoxically enough) be the best way to support relational contracting. The traditional 'discrete' approach is certainly the right starting point (default position) for the law to adopt.

References

Armour, J and S Deakin (2001) 'Norms in Private Insolvency: The "London Approach" to the Resolution of Financial Distress' 1 *Journal of Corporate Law Studies* 21

Ayres, I and R H Gertner (1989) 'Filling Gaps in Incomplete Contracts: An Economic Theory of Default Rules' (1989) 99 *Yale Law Journal* 87

Barnes, M (2011) 'Estoppels as Swords' [2011] *LMCLQ* 372

Beale, H and T Dugdale (1975) 'Contracts between Businessmen: Planning and the Use of Contractual Remedies' (1975) 2 *British Journal of Law and Society* 45

Bernstein, L (1992) 'Opting Out of the Legal System: Extralegal Contractual Relations in the Diamond Industry' (1992) 21 *JLS* 115

Bernstein, L (1996) 'Merchant Law in a Merchant Court: Rethinking the Code's Search for Immanent Business Norms' (1996) 144 *University of Pennsylvania Law Review* 1765

Bernstein, L (2001) 'Private Commercial Law in the Cotton Industry: Creating Cooperation through Rules, Norms, and Institutions' (2001) 99 *Michigan Law Review* 1724

Buckley, F H (2005) *Just Exchange: A Theory of Contract* (London: Routledge)

Campbell, I D (2001) 'Breach and Penalty as Contractual Norm and Contractual Anomie' [2001] *Wisconsin Law Review* 681

Campbell, I D (2004) 'The Incompleteness of our Understanding of the Law and Economics of Relational Contract' [2004] *Wisconsin Law Review* 645

Campbell, I D (2005) 'The Relational Constitution of Remedy: Co-operation as the Implicit Second Principle of Remedies for Breach of Contract' (2005) 11 *Texas Wesleyan Law Review* 455

Campbell, I D (2011) 'A Relational Critique of the Third Restatement of Restitution §39' (2011) 68 *Washington and Lee Law Review* 1063

Charny, D (1990) 'Nonlegal Sanctions in Commercial Relationships' (1990) 104 *Harvard Law Review* 373

Choi, C J (1994) 'Contract Enforcement across Cultures' (1994) 15 *Organization Studies* 673

Chou, E Y, N Halevy and J K Murnighan (2011) 'The Relational Costs of Complete Contracts' IACM 24th Annual Conference Paper, via SSRN: abstract 1872569

Collins, H (1999) *Regulating Contracts* (Oxford: Oxford University Press)

Danzig, R (1978) *The Capability Problem in Contract Law* (St Paul MN: West Publishing)

Dezalay, Y and B G Garth (1996) *Dealing in Virtue: International Commercial Arbitration and the Construction of a Transnational Legal Order* (Chicago IL: University of Chicago Press)

Ellickson, R (1991) *Order Without Law: How Neighbors Settle Disputes* (Cambridge MA: Harvard University Press)

Farber, D A and J H Matheson (1985) 'Beyond Promissory Estoppel: Contract Law and the "Invisible Handshake"' (1985) 52 *University of Chicago Law Review* 903

Feinman, J (2000) 'Relational Contract Theory in Context' (2000) 94 *NWULR* 737

Finn, P (1989) 'Commerce, the Common Law and Morality' (1989) 17 *Melbourne University Law Review* 87

Frey, B S (1993) 'Does Monitoring Increase Work Effort? The Rivalry with Trust and Loyalty' (1993) 31 *Economic Inquiry* 663

Friedmann, D (1995) 'The Performance Interest in Contract Damages' (1995) 111 *LQR* 628

Fuller, L L and W R Purdue (1936) 'The Reliance Interest in Contract Damages' (1936) 46 *Yale Law Journal* 52 and 373

Gava, J and J Greene (2004) 'Do We Need a Hybrid Law of Contract? Why Hugh Collins Is Wrong and Why It Matters' [2004] *CLJ* 605

Gneezy, U and A Rustichini (2000) 'A Fine is a Price' (2000) 29 *JLS* 1

Halson, R (1999) 'The Offensive Limits of Promissory Estoppel' [1999] *LMCLQ* 256

Hardin, G (1968) 'The Tragedy of the Commons' (1968) 162 *Science* 1423

Hobbes, T (1651) *Leviathan*

Jennings, M M (1995) 'The True Meaning of Relational Contracts: We Don't Care

About the Mailbox Rule, Mirror Images, or Consideration Anymore—Are We Safe?' (1995) 73 *Denver University Law Review* 3

Kidwell, J (1985) 'A Caveat' [1985] *Wisconsin Law Review* 615

Kimel, D (2007) 'The Choice of Paradigm for Theory of Contract: Reflections on the Relational Model' (2007) 27 *OJLS* 233

Macaulay, S (1963) 'Non-Contractual Relations in Business: A Preliminary Study' (1963) 28 *American Sociological Review* 1

Macaulay, S (1996) 'Organic Transactions: Contract, Frank Lloyd Wright and the Johnson Building' [1996] *Wisconsin Law Review* 74

Macaulay, S (2003) 'The Real and the Paper Deal: Empirical Pictures of Relationships, Complexity and the Urge for Transparent Simple Rules' (2003) 66 *MLR* 44

Macaulay, S (2004) 'Freedom From Contract: Solutions in Search of a Problem?' [2004] *Wisconsin Law Review* 777

Macneil, I R (1968) *Contracts: Instruments for Social Co-operation* (Hackensack NJ: F B Rothman)

Macneil, I R (1974) 'The Many Futures of Contracts' (1974) *Southern California Law Review* 691

Macneil, I R (1978) 'Contracts: Adjustment of Long-term Economic Relations under Classical, Neoclassical, and Relational Contract Law' (1978) 72 *NWULR* 854

Macneil, I R (1981) 'Economic Analysis of Contractual Relations: Its Shortfalls and the Need for a "Rich Classificatory Apparatus"' (1981) 75 *NWULR* 1018

Malhotra, D and J K Murnighan (2002) 'The Effects of Contracts on Interpersonal Trust' (2002) 47 *Administrative Science Quarterly* 534

McFarlane, B and A Robertson (2008) 'The Death of Proprietary Estoppel' [2008] *LMCLQ* 449

McKendrick, E (1995) 'The Regulation of Long-Term Contracts in English Law' in J Beatson and D Friedmann (eds), *Good Faith and Fault in Contract Law* (Oxford: Oxford University Press)

Mitchell, C (2009) 'Contracts and Contract Law: Challenging the Distinction Between the "Real" and "Paper" Deal' (2009) 29 *OJLS* 675

Morrison, A D and W J Wilhelm Jr (2007) *Investment Banking: Institutions, Politics and Law* (Oxford: Oxford University Press)

Mouzas, S and M Furmston (2008) 'From Contract to Umbrella Agreement' [2008] *CLJ* 37

Mulcahy, L and C Andrews (2010) '*Baird Textile Holdings v Marks & Spencer plc*' in R Hunter, C McGlynn and E Rackley (eds), *Feminist Judgments: From Theory to Practice* (Oxford: Hart Publishing)

Mustill, M and S C Boyd (1989) *The Law and Practice of Commercial Arbitration in England* (London: Butterworths) (2nd edn)

Neuberger of Abbotsbury (2010) 'Thoughts on the Law of Equitable Estoppel' (2010) 84 *ALJ* 225

Ostrom, E (1990) *Governing the Commons: The Evolution of Institutions for Collective Action* (Cambridge: Cambridge University Press)

Pearce, D and R Halson (2008) 'Damages for Breach of Contract: Compensation, Restitution and Vindication' (2008) 28 *OJLS* 73

Posner, E (2000) *Law and Social Norms* (Cambridge MA: Harvard University Press)
Posner, E (2003) 'Economic Analysis of Contract Law after Three Decades: Success or Failure?' (2003) 112 *Yale Law Journal* 829
Richman, B D (2009) 'Ethnic Networks, Extra-Legal Certainty and Globalisation: Peering into the Diamond Industry' in V Gessner (ed.), *Contractual Certainty in International Trade* (Oxford: Hart Publishing)
Robertson, A (1996) 'Satisfying the Minimum Equity: Equitable Estoppel Remedies after *Verwayen*' (1996) 20 *Melbourne Law Review* 805
Robertson, A (2008) 'The Reliance Basis of Proprietary Estoppel Remedies' [2008] *Conveyancer and Property Lawyer* 295
Schwartz, A (1998) 'Incomplete Contracts' in P Newman (ed.), *The New Palgrave Dictionary of Economics and the Law*, vol. 2 (London: Macmillan)
Schwartz, A and R E Scott (2003) 'Contract Theory and the Limits of Contract Law' (2003) 113 *Yale Law Journal* 541
Scott, R E (1987) 'Conflict and Cooperation in Long-term Contracts' (1987) 75 *California Law Review* 2005
Scott, R E (2003) 'A Theory of Self-Enforcing Indefinite Agreements' (2003) 103 *Columbia Law Review* 41
Scott, R E (2004) 'The Death of Contract Law' (2004) 54 *University of Toronto Law Journal* 369
Shiffrin, S V (2007) 'The Divergence of Contract and Promise' (2007) 120 *Harvard Law Review* 708
Stevens, R (2009) 'Damages and the Right to Performance: A *Golden Victory* or Not?' in J Neyers et al. (eds), *Exploring Contract Law* (Oxford: Hart Publishing)
Webb, C (2006) 'Performance and Compensation: An Analysis of Contract Damages and Contractual Obligation' (2006) 26 *OJLS* 41
Whitford, W C (2003) 'A Comparison of British and American Attitudes towards the Exercise of Judicial Discretion in Contract Law' in D Campbell, H Collins and J Wightman (eds), *Implicit Dimensions of Contract: Discrete, Relational and Network Contracts* (Oxford: Hart Publishing)
Williamson, O E (1985) *The Economic Institutions of Capitalism: Firms, Markets, Relational Contracting* (New York: Free Press)
Woodward, W J (2001) 'Neoformalism in a Real World of Forms' [2001] *Wisconsin Law Review* 971

9
Telling Tales about Relational Contracts: How Do Judges Learn about the Lived World of Contracts?
Linda Mulcahy

Introduction

The lack of fit between relational and judicial ways of thinking about commercial relationships continues to be highly problematic to those of us who teach and study contract law. The claim made by relationalists that the neoclassical model of contract fails to adequately reflect commercial practice is suggestive of a legitimation crisis in which the jurisprudence of contract fails to recognize the needs of the community it has long sought to serve. The urgency of the problem has been made clear by a wealth of empirical studies of the lived world of contract which demonstrate that commercial actors are reluctant to bring their disputes before the courts. Significantly, this is not just as a result of the expense and delay involved but because business people perceive the law to be out of step with best business practice, injurious to commercial objectives and an inadequate mechanism for protecting their long-term financial interests (see, for instance, Beale and Dugdale, 1975; Lewis, 1982; Lyons and Mehta, 1997; Narayandas and Rangan, 2004). In endeavouring to provide access to justice and the vindication of contractual rights, it has been argued that the legal process may become an instrument for unravelling the ties of trust and confidence in commercial relations, and for preventing an accommodation which preserves the benefits expected from the transaction for both parties (Collins, 1999). What socio-legal and relational accounts of contracts have exposed is that when we teach our students through legal precedent we provide them with a skewed understanding of the role that law does, and more importantly could, play in the architecture of commercial relationships.

The great value of Macneil's contribution to scholarship in the field has been that it has allowed us to 'theorize up' from empirical studies of the lived world of contract. Relational contract theory provides us with new opportunities to reconnect the many worlds of contract as imagined by the contracting parties, the broader business community, legal practitioners, judges and academics. Not only has Macneil's work illuminated the ways in which formalist concepts of contract are out of step with the reality of commercial relationships but it has allowed us to begin to imagine 'what if' scenarios; alternative conceptual frameworks to those provided by the neoclassical paradigm which better reflect how deals are done and relationships regulated. For some scholars, relational contract theory now stands as the best rival to the classical theory of contract (Campbell, 2001). Despite this, a number of commentators have bemoaned the fact that Macneil's work has not had the impact that it deserves within the academy and courtroom (Vincent-Jones, 2001; Feinman, 2011).

This chapter looks at the interface of commercial, judicial and socio-legal visions of contract by considering where tales about relational contracts are told and to whom. It suggests that, in addition to winning intellectual arguments about the relative merits of the classical, neoclassical and relational paradigms, scholars need to consider how practitioners and judges are exposed to relational ways of thinking. Particular attention is paid to four issues. What impact has relational contract scholarship had on judicial reasoning in England to date? Are disputes with strong relational characteristics as likely to reach the attention of the judiciary as other types of contract disputes? What impact are changes to the volume of cases reaching trial likely to have on the development of contract doctrine in the future? Is the increasing use of commercial mediation facilitating different ways of talking about commercial relationships outside of the litigation system.

Judicial attitudes to relational contract theory

Neil Duxbury (2001) has quite rightly encouraged us to be circumspect about the methods commonly used to plot academic influences on the judiciary but it remains the case that evidence of scholars influencing judges through their publications has been scarce. Reflecting on the issue, Lord Neuberger (2012) has argued that:

> For a long time the relationship between judges and academics in England and Wales was that of ships passing in the night: ships that merely occasionally spoke to each other, with distant voices, before returning to silence. (p. 1)

More recently, Jack Beatson (2012) has contended that until the 1960s the English judiciary and practising lawyers generally saw the function of legal academics as parasitic on the work of judges and of no assistance in addressing new or undecided questions. As is well known, the relationship of judge and jurist in the UK stands in stark contrast to the situation in civilian traditions where the relationship between judge and jurist is generally much closer. The great distance between common law judge and jurist is reflected in the convention that academics should only be cited when dead and recognized as offering a respected view of a point of law (for a much fuller discussion of this convention than I am able to give here, see Duxbury, 2001; Beatson, 2012; and Neuberger, 2012). Scholarly works appear to have been kept at a distance by judges for a number of reasons. These include the late development of law as an academic discipline in England; lawyers' lack of prestige within the academy; the tendency for barristers and judges to have gained academic qualifications in subjects other than law in the past (Duxbury, 2001; Beatson, 2012); and the tendency of English academics to relish disagreement with each other (Neuberger, 2012). The different approaches of civilian and common law systems also reflect fundamental differences in legal methodology. While the focus of civilian systems is on principles, theory and logic, the common law judge has to fit the particular case before them into an existing schema which relies on judicial precedent. The law professor may have in mind, as did Macneil, a reformulation of a whole area of law, but the common law judge's job is to focus on the case before them and how it can be made to fit existing principles in the common law world (Beatson, 2012).

The rule that academic writing is not a source of law has been maintained, but attitudes towards the citation of living authors has changed considerably in recent years. It has been acknowledged that academics have had an increasing influence in the development of common law and statutory interpretation through their role as teachers of future generations of practising lawyers and judges (Neuberger, 2012). Beatson (2012) has also suggested that informal partnerships between bench, bar and academia have helped to breathe new life into areas of English law, such as restitution, which had for too long languished underdeveloped and constrained by mistakes of the past. Some senior judges have even claimed that judge and academic inhabit the same world and that a 'genuine dialogue now exists through the medium of judgments and academic articles between judges and scholars' (Lord Neuberger 2012, p. 17). Academic sources are increasingly cited as secondary sources and Lady Hale (2013) has provided a number of examples of ways in which the development of doctrine has been influenced by the evidence provided by socio-legal empirical scholars in the field of family law, criminal procedure and personal injury. For Beatson (2012), this suggests that senior judges are now prepared to see academics as 'players' rather than as mere observers of the evolution of law. In a similar vein, Lord Goff (1983) has spoken enthusiastically of the fusion of academic and judicial insights and has characterized academics as working alongside judges as pilgrims on the endless road to unattainable perfection (*The Spiliada* [1987] AC 460, p. 488).

Whilst there is evidence of doctrinal contract scholarship having influenced the development of the common law, the links between judicial reasoning and empirical research on the lived worlds of contract and relational contract theory are much more rare. It is noticeable that, despite the many attractions of relational contract theory, debate in the UK about whether we should radically rethink existing paradigms in favour of relational approaches has been almost exclusively confined to academic publications. Moreover, there is little evidence of prolonged discussion occurring between the business community, practitioners and academics in socio-legal publications and conferences.

The judiciary is far from immune to discussions of the many contexts in which contractual relationships are played out in the world of business or the importance of taking into account the habits of particular industries, professions or trades. The occasional English precedent in the general law of contract even appears to embrace relational ways of thinking. The recognition that not all the obligations between the parties can be accurately determined at formation and that flexible approaches to consideration in renegotiated contracts is needed was, for instance, reflected in the decision of *Williams v Roffey Brothers and Nicholls (Contractors) Ltd* [1991] 1 QB 1 (CA). Elsewhere the concepts of previous courses of dealing and custom in the implication of terms reflect a recognition of the ways in which evidence of repeat trade can provide an essential context to understanding a contractual relationship. The growing influence of the idea of relational contracts in specialist areas such as employment law has also been documented and is discussed further by Hugh Collins in this volume. Hugh Beale also argues in this collection that respect for relational elements of contracts is discernible in the laws that govern English contracts, but two points are worthy of note in relation to this argument. Firstly, these innovations have largely been achieved through legislation rather than case law, an area which Posner (2008) has argued is much more open to the influence of academic debate. An example is the focus on the concept of reciprocity in European regulations on unfair contracts. Secondly, much of the initiative for change has come from European rather than native jurisprudence. These instances of relational thinking are important, but they do not reflect a recognition of the fundamental challenges to the canon posed by the work of Macneil and his supporters. Nor do they recognize his basic contention that the ties that bind commercial parties can only be fully appreciated by reference to the broader range of behavioural norms outlined in his work.

One possible explanation for the lack of judicial engagement with relational contract theory is that judges and practitioners are neither convinced by its logic or impressed by its proponents. Supporters of Macneil have long recognized that much of his writing is highly abstract and its impact undermined by the ambiguities surrounding the links between discrete and relational components of contracts (Feinman, 2001). Macneil's choice of unfamiliar terminology can also make his work inaccessible (Andrews, 2010). In addition, commentators have drawn attention to the fact that relational contract theory has frequently either been misinterpreted or reinterpreted through a neoclassical lens which treats relational contracts as a specific sub-category of contracts. Even where Macneil's insights are accepted as reflecting commercial reality, there have been problems determining the detail of exactly how relational doctrine would work in practice (Eisenberg, 2000). Others have suggested that socio-legal and relational insights into the lived world of contract are unattractive because they reveal a messy and complex view of contracts which judges are apt to want to avoid (Mertz, 2000).

The suggestion that practitioners and judges have paid little serious attention to relational contracts is demonstrated by the fact that the senior courts have only referred to the concept in seven instances, five of which involve contracts of employment or franchise agreements considered to be special relationships which sit outside the classical paradigm.[1] The recent decision of *Yam Seng Pte Ltd v International Trade Corporation Ltd* is possibly the most important of these for relational contract theorists because it gives explicit recognition to the concept of the relational contract as a distinct type which requires a high degree of communication, co-operation and predictable performance based on mutual trust, confidence and loyalty. In this important decision, Mr Justice Leggatt made clear that there was scope to incorporate such expectations in the body of the contract. In his view, while these expectations might not have been legislated for in the express terms of the contract, they could be treated as being implicit in the parties' understanding and deemed necessary to give business efficacy to their business arrangements. The other case which has proven most ripe for a relational analysis in recent years is that of *Baird Textile Holdings Ltd v Marks &*

---

1 The search was conducted in August 2013 using Westlaw. The cases identified were: *Yam Seng Pte Ltd v International Trade Corporation Ltd* [2013] EWHC 111; *Mayer v BBC* [2004] WL 2458657; *Dymocks Franchise Systems (NSW) Pty Ltd v Todd* [2002] UKPC 50; *Morrow v Safeway Stores Plc* [2002] IRLR 9; *Johnson v Unisys Ltd* [2003] 1 AC 518; *Baird Textile Holdings Ltd v Marks & Spencer Plc* [2001] CLC 999; and *Total Gas Marketing Ltd v Arco British Ltd* [1998] CLC 1275. One of the cases involved a referral to the Privy Council from New Zealand, two were cases decided in the Employment Appeal Tribunal, two in the House of Lords and one in the Court of Appeal.

Spencer plc [2001] EWCA Civ 274, [2002] 1 All ER (Comm) 737, [2001] CLC 999, though the court was much more dismissive of the notion of the relational contract in this instance. Counsel for *Baird* argued that, in addition to the 60 or so seasonal short-term contracts which the parties had made over a 30-year relationship, there existed a relational umbrella contract, or what Stefanos Mouzas and Michael Furmston (2008) have since referred to as a constitution for the contract. However, the Court of Appeal failed to recognize the many implicit norms which could be said to have developed to govern the relationship over time and dismissed the argument that the parties had developed any enforceable obligations about how to conduct their relationship above and beyond those contained in each of the short-term seasonal contracts. As significant for present purposes was their rejection of the scholarly publications on relational contract which had been offered in support of this argument. As Sir Andrew Morritt V-C opined:

> In connection with the wide proposition counsel referred to academic discussion with regard to 'relational contracts' and the legal implications to which they may give rise. But the articles which he produced did not suggest that the normal rules as to the implication and formation of contracts or the usual requirements of certainty did not apply to 'relational contracts'. Accordingly it is to those rules that I turn. (at [16])[2]

In *Total Gas Marketing Ltd v ARCO British Ltd and Others* [1998] 2 Lloyd's Reports 209, the only other case of the seven involving a commercial contract, Lord Steyn was slightly more encouraging but retreated to a form of reasoning which considered text before context:

> The central question is whether on a correct construction of a long term contract for the sale of gas it was discharged by reason of the non-occurrence of a condition. It is a contract of a type which is sometimes called a relational contract. But there are no special rules of interpretation applicable to such contracts ... That is not to say that in an appropriate case a court may not take into account that, by reason of the changing conditions affecting such a contract, a flexible approach may best match the reasonable expectations of the parties. But, as in the case of all contracts, loyalty to the contractual text viewed against its relevant contextual background is the first principle of construction. (p. 17)

Both *Baird* and *Total Gas* are deserving of more detailed analysis than is

---

2 For an alternative vision of how this case might have been decided see Mulcahy and Andrews, 2010; see also Morgan in this volume.

possible here, but it could be argued that the reasoning in both cases reveals a fundamental lack of understanding of the challenge posed by relational contract theory. Macneil did not view relational norms as something to be taken into account when attempting to understand the context to a formal contract. The methodological turn he introduced to contractual scholarship was to argue that our understanding of relational contracts must treat the formal contract as just one source of information about the obligations assumed by the parties. Contrary to Steyn's suggestion, this means that a different interpretative approach is exactly what relationalists have called for.

Despite the claims that jurists and judges are now working more closely together than in previous decades, there continues to be evidence that they largely inhabit two distinct legal worlds and are engaged in radically different enterprises in their daily work (Duxbury, 2001; Neuberger, 2012). This suggestion has been borne out by empirical work into the everyday world of the judge. In his seminal study of the Law Lords conducted in the early 1980s, Alan Paterson (1982) claimed that the primary source of ideas for the senior judiciary remained their colleagues. More recently, Darbyshire's (2012) ethnographic study of the lives of English judges suggests that pressures of time mean that Court of Appeal judges rarely go beyond the arguments made by counsel and discussions with colleagues in deciding how a case should be determined. She remarks: 'judges often caught me laughing at the farcical contrast between the speed of setting precedents, and the leisurely, nit-picking analysis to which they would be subjected for years to come'. This apparent insularity is far from being unique to the judiciary. Modern day law professors in elite institutions are also likely to view their primary audience as being their peers (Posner, 2008; Beatson, 2012).

When scholar and judge do interact it may be that certain types of scholarship are more likely than others to be considered legitimate in the field of obligations. While citations to academic articles in judgments have undoubtedly become much more common in recent decades, it has been suggested that certain types of judges and practitioners working in particular fields such as family law or personal injury are more attuned to socio-legal academic debate (Hale, 2013). Elsewhere, Beatson (2012) has helpfully drawn our attention to a number of instances in which the work of academics has impacted on the development of the common law. However, two issues are worthy of comment in response. Firstly, it is noticeable that the journals cited as 'highly respected' by judges in this context do not include work contained in the most prestigious socio-legal journals (for instance, Neuberger, 2012, cites the *Law Quarterly Review*, *Cambridge Law Journal* and *Modern Law Review*). Secondly, the examples Beatson cites all involve doctrinal scholars and tend to focus on the sustained critique of a single rule rather than a discussion of broader principles. Lord Goff has also been keen to stress that scholarly work is at its least useful when it privileges abstract formulations which have little connection with practical experience (Beatson, 2012).

Claims to knowledge about the lived world of contract

The contention of relationists that developments in the common law are only legitimate when they reflect lived experience raises important issues about what scholars and judges can claim to know about the lived world of contract. It is easy to dismiss academics as only dealing in the abstract but socio-legal scholars have been equally critical of the failure of doctrine to reflect the everyday practices of the world of contract. Indeed, it has been suggested that the major advances in legal scholarship in recent decades have involved scholars actively distancing themselves from the study of doctrine because of this failure (Bradney, 2003). By way of contrast, relational contract theorists have drawn heavily on the insights empirical research has revealed about contractual relations across a broad range of industries. Responding to this trend, Beatson (2012) has suggested that the retreat of scholarship from doctrine is as deplorable as distancing top medical academics from the work of hospitals. In doing so, he assumes that the courts have the same exposure to a representative sample of disputes as hospitals do to a representative sample of illness and disease. In truth, it may be more accurate to suggest that the appellate courts consider a very small number of atypical disputes. As such, the courts are more akin to a specialist hospital for the treatment of rare diseases. The suggestion that the academic can have little to say about the lived world of contract may be true of some scholars but is clearly not true of them all. The law lecturer who teaches engineers or architects, the empirical researcher who spends time talking to business people, or the new breed of relationalist who has engaged with the findings of empirical research are all able to claim a legitimate role in discussions about practice. If empirical studies of the lived world of contract are correct in their assertion that the comprehensive set of contractual norms mapped out in Macneil's world reflect the 'is' rather than the 'ought' of the commercial world, then it may be that Beatson's suggestion that the socio-legal turn in legal scholarship reflects a failure to engage with practice needs to be revisited.

Judges undoubtedly have an important contributions to make to debate about the rhetoric and reality of contract doctrine but the limits of their own knowledge base also need to be recognized. If, as many socio-legal empirical accounts of contract disputes suggest, most disputants 'lump' their grievance, or negotiate a bilateral solution, then it is clear that the stories of contract that reach the lawyer's office and court may not be representative of the many problems that emerge in the commercial sphere. The fact that the vast majority of commercial disputes lodged with the courts are settled or abandoned and that 'repeat player' litigants with deep pockets and highly skilled lawyers are more likely to pursue their dispute through the litigation system than 'one-shotters' suggests that the cases that judges gain exposure to do not always reflect the realities of the commercial world (Galanter, 1974–1975).

It might also be argued that disputants are particularly likely to edit out the relational aspects of their case before they get to trial. This is because the bargaining endowment conferred by judicial precedent is likely to militate against the privileging of the real deal over the paper deal. As Macneil argued over four decades ago:

> The law has to deal largely with pathological cases. This in itself would not be so very troublesome except for the feedback of precedent: the rule of the pathological case governs the healthy contract too. To the extent that contractual behaviour is influenced by the law this feedback can have very significant effect on all contractual behaviour. (Macneil, 1969, p. 408)

If the courts are perceived to be hostile to new understandings of contracts, it is rational for disputants to filter out the relational aspects of their claims as they proceed along the litigation pathway. Indeed, lawyers would not be doing their job properly if they did not encourage their clients to frame their arguments so as to maximize the chances of winning their case. State-sanctioned adjudication is inevitably a hostile environment for those interested in making reference to extra-legal norms. The adversarial trial operates within a framework which reflects deeply held cultural norms about conflict resolution which determine what can be argued and what remedies requested. This has led Macneil to see formal law as a 'wild and dangerous animal' (1969, p. 411) and to argue that:

> [t]he legal system is ... often in the position not unlike that of a scientist who has to dry out a jellyfish before his instruments of examination can be used on it (Macneil, 1969, p. 409).

These concerns present those keen for shifts in doctrinal thinking about contracts with something of a conundrum. Relational tales about contracts need to be presented to the courts if the classical paradigm is to be exposed as an inadequate prism through which to understand the norms that bind commercial parties together. But relational tales about contract are likely to be more absent from disputing narratives the closer one gets to the trial. The result is likely to be that the fact patterns presented to the courts do not necessarily suggest a demand for shifts in the way law responds to commerce.

Diminishing opportunities for the judiciary to engage with the lived world of contract

The problems with the cases which reach the courts neither reflecting the full range of difficulties that emerge in the world of commerce nor a demand for change are exacerbated by recent reforms to the civil justice system which have led to diminishing opportunities for English judges to adjudicate commercial disputes. It is increasingly being recognized that opportunities for our judiciary to reappraise private law doctrine are becoming limited in the UK (Mulcahy, 2013). The civil trial is emerging as a major casualty in policy initiatives to promote more private ordering in the commercial sector in the aftermath of the Woolf reforms of the late 1990s. The state has long demonstrated a willingness to encourage out-of-court settlement by sanctioning the use of arbitration and promoting settlement through such procedural devices as the costs and payment-in rules. Recent years have seen a further and significant downturn in the number of cases which reach trial. The situation is such that it has prompted extensive debate about a phenomenon referred to as the 'vanishing trial' (Galanter, 2002; 2004)[3] and it is recognized that this 'development' is now a feature of several mature legal systems (Genn, 2009).

Data on UK litigation shows that while the number of trials has stabilized in the county court and Queens Bench Division (QBD) the rates of trial are flatlining at levels well below previous decades (Dingwall and Cloatre, 2006). This can be seen in Figure 9.1 which shows the number of King's Bench Division (KBD) and QBD proceedings issued from 1930 to the present. This illustrates that there was a steady rise in litigation from 1945–1990 followed by a steep reduction to rates that are much lower than those experienced during the Second World War. This downward trend in litigation is also reflected in a more recent series of statistics relating to commercial cases being conducted in the Technology and Construction Court (TCC) (see Figure 9.2).

A concern regularly alluded to in debate about the vanishing trial is that opportunities for judicial learning from disputes and the precedent-setting capacity of the superior courts will be impoverished as a result of judges having to develop doctrine from a smaller pool of litigated cases. This claim is deserving of more analysis than it has been subjected to in the literature to date. It is particularly important to recognize that, while the opportunities for learning about the lived world of contract from disputed claims undoubtedly diminishes if fewer cases get to trial, the amount of precedent

---

3 Two special issues of journals have now been devoted to this topic. See further *Journal of Empirical Legal Studies* (2004) 1 and the *Journal of Dispute Resolution* (2006) 1.

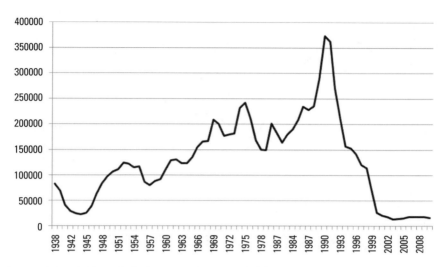

Figure 9.1 KBD and QBD proceedings issued by year 1930–2010 (Central and District) (source: compiled using *Judicial Statistics* 1938–2008)

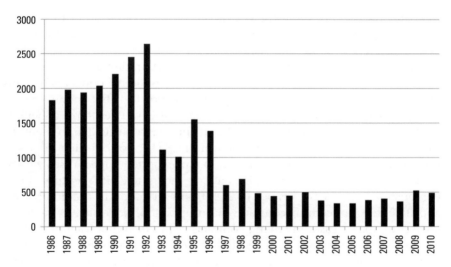

Figure 9.2 TCC total claims issued by year (source: compiled using *Judicial Statistics* 1986–2010)

generated by the senior courts is not necessarily diminished because there are fewer cases coming into the system.

The analysis of appeal cases in Figure 9.3 shows that the number of cases heard by the senior courts has been in overall decline since the 1900s but

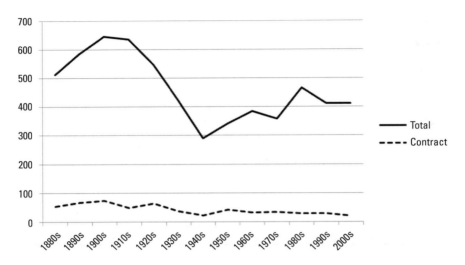

Figure 9.3 Total reported appeal cases and total that concerned contracts (source: compiled using appeal cases 1880–2010)

that they have stabilized in the last decade. For the purposes of this chapter, it is important to explore how contract cases have fared over the same period. Concerns about the dangers of the common law 'going underground' as a result of the more extensive use of arbitration are beginning to be raised (Mulcahy, 2013). Some decades ago Louis Blom-Cooper and Gavin Drewry (1972) argued that the Law Lords did not feel that they received enough appeals in some areas of law to enable them to develop a coherent body of jurisprudence and suggested that this was a particular problem in the fields of criminal law and obligations. The bottom line of data presented in Figure 9.3 charts the number of reported appeal cases which have involved contract since the end of the nineteenth century. This demonstrates that there has been a significant reduction in the number of appellate cases concerning contracts over this period. Not only has the total *number* of appeal cases involving contracts reduced from a total of 247 in the first half of the twentieth century to 169 in the second half, but the *proportion* of appeal cases involving contract has also been in decline since the high spot of 12 per cent of all appellate cases in the 1900s, 1920s and 1950s to just five per cent in the 2000s.

There has been little curiosity amongst British academics about how cases are selected as suitable for appeal but the data presented suggest that contract scholars and practitioners hoping to promote a change in thinking about doctrine may need to be more strategic in capturing the imagination of gatekeepers to the appeals process. While we can surmise from judicial statistics how many cases the Supreme Court hears per year, it remains unclear *how* decisions are made about what to include in this informal quota. The permission stage is used to ensure that cases that proceed to appeal are those with a 'real chance of success' or that there is 'some other compelling reason' why an appeal should be heard. Demonstrating a real chance of success is likely to prove difficult for an aspiring precedent-seeker to satisfy since test cases inevitably involve a certain amount of uncertainty. It will be even more difficult for proponents of relational contract theory since their expectations of how contracts should be regulated stand so squarely outside the classical paradigm. It is worthy of note in the present context that Baird Textiles failed in their leave to appeal to the House of Lords in their attempts to secure a trial of the issues.

The underground story of relational contracts

If relational tales of contract are being marginalized by the courts it may be that they are being heard in other dispute resolution forums. Macneil (1962) recognized that alternative dispute resolution (ADR) was a critical part of the disputing lexicon for relationalists in which more authentic accounts of contractual relationships could flourish. Relational contract scholars have been slow to pick up on this emphasis in his work and the tendency has been for commentators to either ignore the changing landscape of dispute resolution or to be dismissive of mediation as offering nothing more to dispute resolution than bilateral negotiations (see, for instance, Collins, 1999). To some extent this is understandable. Whilst recognizing the potential for ADR to facilitate broader discussions of what was at stake in contract disputes, Macneil's (1974) view was that, like relational contract theory more generally, the courts were highly suspicious of alternatives to court-based adjudication. In his words:

> the Western legal system especially the judiciary (real or quasi) ... is uncomfortable in the highest degree with persuasion, mediation, adjustment, compromise etc. Since, however, life cannot proceed anywhere in any legal system without such concepts in heavy everyday use, their application tends to be kept under cover and away from the eye of the 'law'. (Macneil, 1974, p. 674)

This suggests that whilst recognizing the possibility of commercial disputes being more satisfactorily resolved in these ways, Macneil considered that the tales about contract to emerge from these forums were unlikely to impact on judicial reasoning.

It may well be that the time is now ripe to question the assumption that legal systems do not look favourably upon alternative forms of dispute resolution. There is now a considerable amount of support for Macneil's contention that ADR can provide a welcoming environment for relational tales about contracts to be told. Moreover, the growing popularity of commercial mediation means that it is also an appropriate time to shift the discussion away from Macneil's focus on arbitration with its relatively limited scope to engage with the extra-legal dynamics of disputes. Of all the primary forms of dispute resolution, mediation is undoubtedly best suited to taking account of extra-legal normative frameworks which matter to the parties. Models of commercial mediation vary considerably from narrative, facilitative and evaluative approaches but certain principles underpin them all. These include a focus on brokering a sustainable deal which is commercially viable and the maintenance of relationships and respect for custom and practice.

A key principle which governs all models of mediation is that disputants' accounts of what is at stake should take precedence in the course of facilitated negotiation (Genn, 1998). Lawyers may well be present in mediation but they tend to play a much less interventionist role than is common in either the trial or arbitration. This clearly reduces opportunities for translation of the dispute into an account which fits the strictures of existing doctrine. There is evidence to suggest that mediation can serve to discipline excessive reference to legal frameworks and that mediators may deliberately minimize the input of lawyers because of their preference for legalistic approaches to resolution (Mulcahy, 2001). The importance of party control of the issues and outcome is most clearly reflected in the fact that unlike a judge or arbitrator the mediator is prohibited from imposing a solution on the disputants. The role of the mediator is to get to the root of the dispute by encouraging discussion of the context in which the dispute occurred and should be understood; to tease out realistic commercial options; test the strength of each party's case in private caucus; and identify obstacles to settlement. Moreover settlements negotiated in this way may go beyond issues pertaining to formal contractual liability and include remedies not available at trial or arbitration. These might involve undertakings about future discounts, the promise of future contracts, undertakings about publicity surrounding the case, or the advancement of cash.

Rather than being suspicious of mediation as Macneil has suggested, the UK government has been actively promoting its use. The last 15 years have seen a radical shift in the policies and ideologies which underpin the English civil justice system and commercial mediation now plays a much more prominent role within the litigation system than has ever been the case in the past. The most comprehensive dataset on the incidence of commercial mediation has been produced by the Centre for Effective Dispute Resolution (CEDR) as a

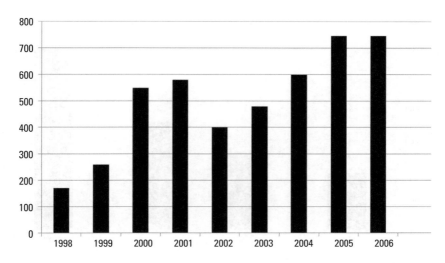

Figure 9.4   CEDR civil mediations 1997–2006 (source: compiled using CEDR annual reports 1997–2006)

result of its biannual audit of commercial mediation across the UK.[4] Drawing on these data, Figure 9.4 shows that civil mediations have increased more than sevenfold since 1997. Figure 9.5 shows that the number of commercial mediations across mediation providers surveyed has more than trebled from just under 2000 per year in 2003 to 6000 per year in 2010.

Figure 9.6 shows that if we compare the number of commercial mediations now undertaken with the level of business conducted in the QBD, it becomes clear that the incidence of mediation equates to over a third of all proceedings issued in 2010. Figure 9.6 also demonstrates that the incidence of mediation is far greater than the incidence of trials in the QBD.

Mediation is clearly becoming a very profitable option for an elite group of experienced commercial mediators. The latest CEDR audit reports that the most successful practitioners report an average earning of £7500 per case on a workload of around 80 cases a year giving an annual income of over £600,000. By collating the data from the audit with that from their own files CEDR estimates that the value of commercial cases mediated each

---

4   Some caution has to be exercised in using these statistics. The commercial mediation sector is highly competitive and it could be argued that there are incentives for CEDR competitors to inflate the number of mediations undertaken. The City UK has contended that the main ADR organizations experienced a surge in referrals between 2007 and 2009, prompted by the economic recession and financial crisis. It claims that in total the number of disputes resolved through ADR in the UK rose by 78 per cent over the two years from 19,384 in 2007 to 34,541 in 2009 (McKenzie, 2010).

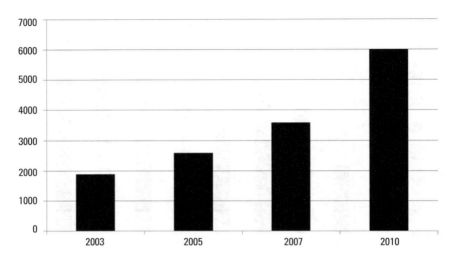

Figure 9.5   Growth in civil and commercial mediation in UK (source: CEDR audit 2010)

year is approximately £5.1 billion compared with £4.1 billion in the 2008 Audit (CEDR, 2010).[5]

This trend towards the growth of mediation is receiving the active backing of the state in a number of ways. It is possible that judges continue to be uncomfortable with persuasion, mediation and adjustment as Macneil suggested, but there is limited scope for them to express such reservations in the aftermath of the Woolf reforms. A range of policy initiatives in the UK have indicated that successive governments are keen to promote the use of mediation within the litigation system rather than it just being an alternative to it. Litigants face ever more urgent incentives to mediate at key stages of the disputing process including the period before they even issue proceedings.[6] Once litigation has commenced, the 'overriding objective' of the Civil Procedure Rules requires the parties and case management judges to consider mediation and a party filing an allocation questionnaire can now make a written request for the proceedings to be stayed, or for the court to order a stay of its own volition while the parties try to settle the case.

---

5 Significantly, the 2010 figure has been adjusted to exclude the two £1 billion pound 'outlying' corporate transactions mediated by CEDR in 2009.
6 The Practice Direction on pre-action conduct specifies that the parties have an obligation to consider whether negotiation, mediation, arbitration or early neutral evaluation might enable them to settle the matter without starting proceedings.

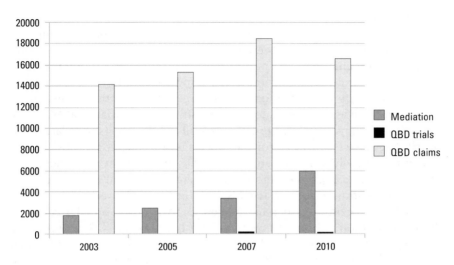

Figure 9.6 Incidence of mediation compared with QBD claims and trials (source CEDR audit 2010 and *Judicial Statistics* 2003, 2005, 2007, 2010)

These various ways of encouraging mediation have been given a boost by the Civil Procedure Rules (see CPR 44.5(3)(a)(ii)) which allows the court to take into account the settlement efforts made before and during the proceedings when determining the allocation of costs. This provision represents an exception to the long-standing rule that 'costs follow the cause' and recent case law suggests that the courts have been more than willing to use their powers to punish those who unreasonably refuse to try mediation.[7] The Ministry of Justice has embraced the rhetoric of private ordering through its Dispute Resolution Commitment of 2011 which makes clear that the government is keen to encourage businesses to take responsibility for their own disputes rather than turning to lawyers and judges to resolve contentious issues. Government ministers have also shown themselves keen to promote the UK as a centre of excellence for litigation *and* ADR[8] and the Ministry of Justice has an ongoing campaign to maximize the benefits for the UK economy of marketing the country's quality commercial courts,

---

7 The Court of Appeal first sanctioned a party for unreasonably refusing the court's invitation to mediate in *Dunnett v Railtrack* [2002] EWCA Civ 302 by denying the winner of the case its costs and, in *Hurst v Leeming* [2003] 1 Lloyd's Rep 379, Justice Lightman suggested that refusal to mediate has now become a high-risk course to take. Mediation may not yet be compulsory but these cases have clearly had an impact on the propensity to pursue an issue to trial without undertaking mediation first. CEDR has calculated that the use of mediation increased by 35 per cent in the two years following *Dunnett*. See also Hyde (2012).

8 www.justice.gov.uk/news/features/feature071211a.

lawyers and mediation services overseas (Ministry of Justice and UK Trade and Investment, 2011). The City UK's 'Unlocking Disputes' campaign provides further evidence of the ways in which the government is working with law firms, chambers and professional associations to promote London as a centre for excellence in commercial dispute resolution.[9]

In recent years there is evidence of more widespread use of mediation clauses by trade associations such as the Baltic and International Maritime Council and Lloyd's new international hull clauses in its standard form contracts. A new enthusiasm for the process is also reflected in the drafting of contracts in which agreements to mediate in the event of a dispute are becoming increasingly common. The 'tiered', 'stepped' or 'escalation' dispute resolution clauses have also become popular and commercial contracts are beginning to have references to a much broader range of dispute resolution options than was previously the norm.[10] The courts have shown themselves increasingly willing to recognize such contractual clauses. Whereas agreements to negotiate or mediate were once considered unenforceable, the decision in *Cable v Wireless plc v IBM* [2002] EWHC 2059 has altered that position as long as the clause is sufficiently certain.

Mediation practice has morphed in ways unanticipated since the time that Macneil wrote about ADR. Rather than being confined to the time period after negotiation and before arbitration or trial, recent developments have seen more pervasive use of mediation than previously anticipated. The first notable development is the growth of the concept and practice of 'transactional' mediation; that is the use of mediation in deal-making rather than just relationship-saving situations. Recognizing that making a deal can be as tense as managing it, there is burgeoning evidence of mediators working with organizations in brokering contractual agreements and even teaching mediation skills for use in everyday transactions (Peppett, 2003). Moreover, there are also indications that mediation is being used at much later stages in dispute resolution trajectories. Research on the TCC has demonstrated that mediation is the most frequently used dispute resolution process leading to settlement during or just after disclosure and that it was just as popular as negotiated settlement just before trial (Gould, 2010).

Most significantly for present purposes, it could be argued that the increasing popularity of mediation in the commercial sphere means that a

---

9 See further www.unlockingdisputes.com/.
10 The most sophisticated versions of these clauses commonly prescribe that the parties must first exchange a notice which identifies and crystallizes the issues in dispute followed by a referral for negotiation between senior managers of the organizations involved. If settlement is not reached negotiations then take place between the chief executives followed, if necessary, by mediation, arbitration or court-based litigation.

new generation of lawyers is more likely to be exposed to and presented with relational tales about contracts. Mediation is much more likely than trial or arbitration to force lawyers to familiarize themselves with the context in which commercial disputes arise and to attune themselves to the importance of the extra-legal norms which might govern it. In addition to acclimatizing to the dynamics of mediation, lawyers have shown great enthusiasm for qualifying as commercial mediators. Judges are also being encouraged to gain direct experience of mediated settlements and mediation organizations have acquired a number of high-ranking supporters amongst the senior bench. A number of prominent retired judges including Lord Woolf, Lord Irvine and Henry Brooke have now trained as mediators and there is a recently formed European Association of Judges for Mediation.[11] Somewhat controversially, we are also seeing the rise of judicial mediation. The voluntary TCC Settlement Service was launched in 2005 and allows parties to litigation to be assisted by a TCC judge in reaching a settlement. There has also been voluntary judicial mediation in Employment Tribunals since a pilot scheme was launched there in 2006 (Urwin et al., 2010).[12]

Conclusion

This volume of essays attests to the fact that doctrinal scholars and the English judiciary continue to adopt a highly cautious approach to the challenges posed by relational contract theory. It has been argued that in addition to a certain intellectual conservatism about the ways that contract law is conceived of amongst the judiciary, we also need to look to the ways in which relational tales about contracts are edited out from the disputes which reach trial. The natural tendency has been for lawyers to avoid arguments which have little backing in judicial precedent. This incentive for relational aspects of contract disputes to be marginalized has been further exacerbated by the diminishing number of trials and appeals that relate to contracts. These various factors clearly serve to limit opportunities presented to the judiciary to explore the importance of context and relational norms during trials. Viewed from this perspective, this chapter presents a bleak picture of the possibility of doctrine moving towards an understanding of contracts which better reflects the reality of commercial deals.

It has been argued that the increased use of mediation might provide new opportunities for lawyers to re-emphasize the relational aspects of

---

11 www.gemme.eu/.
12 See further www.justice.gov.uk/tribunals/employment#judicial and www.lawsociety.org.uk/advice/practice-notes/judicial-mediation/#jm8.

contract disputes. The fact that mediation is increasingly being undertaken in the course of litigation may well facilitate increased recognition of the importance of such accounts. There are undoubtedly very serious problems with this argument. On the one hand, mediation provides a forum in which relational norms can play a part in the settlement deals. On the other, it prevents change to doctrine through challenges in the courts. The result is that it is likely to lead to an even greater chasm between the tales of contract heard at trial and settlement negotiations. Indeed, in a US context, Charles Knapp (2002) has contended that such privatization of law is leading to the piece-by-piece dismantling of American contract law. Combined with existing concerns about the reduction of cases relating to obligations in the senior courts, this is clearly a cause for concern.

Discussion amongst experts in the field also indicates that there is emerging evidence of lawyers 'squaring the circle' in order to ensure that existing legal frameworks dominate mediation. The current interest in evaluative models of mediation, in which mediators undertake to formally evaluate the strength of the parties' respective cases, suggests that there will be a further 'lawyerization' of mediation procedure in the commercial sphere, a trend which some commentators have been predicting for some time (Roberts, 2009). In part this is inevitable when mediation is subsumed into the litigation system and the parties are compelled to remain alive to what could happen at trial if mediation were to fail. The gradual shift towards compulsory mediation may also serve to undermine the commitment of the parties to the principles which have underpinned the process. The proximity to the litigation system of many of the mediation schemes launched also means that the inclusion of extra-legal remedies in settlement agreements may become more rare. Anecdotal evidence certainly suggests that the spectre of a trial continues to cast a long shadow over attempts to draw out alternative discourses about contracts

The only promise that mediation is likely to deliver on is the renewed exposure of lawyers to relational tales of contract. Particularly relevant in this context is the question of whether experience of alternative stories in mediation is altering the way that lawyers and future judges think about disputes. A considerable amount of attention has been paid in the academic literature to the ways courts and lawyers have impacted on mediation practice. Much less attention has been paid to the impact that mediation might eventually have on attitudes to disputes resolved through trial. If mediation provides a forum and method of dispute resolution which is more sympathetic to the importance of the extra-legal dimensions of the dispute, it might be argued that exposure to mediation could eventually engender relational ways of thinking elsewhere in the legal system.

The purpose of this chapter has been to explore opportunities for judicial engagement with the issues raised by relational contract theory. The data presented here indicate that the judiciary has been unwilling to engage with the challenges posed by the work of scholars such as Macneil in any meaningful way. It is the case that opportunities for dominant classical paradigms to be challenged in the public forum of the courtroom are diminishing because of the vanishing trial and rise in the incidence of commercial mediation. It is contended that this should prompt serious discussion amongst relational contract theorists about how they encourage engagement outside of the academy and seek to influence debate amongst practitioners.

References

Andrews, C (2010), *Bridging the Divide: An Exploration of Ian Macneil's Relational Contract Theory and its Significance for Contract Scholarship and the Lived World of Commercial Contract* (London: University of London)

Beale, H and T Dugdale (1975) 'Contracts between Businessmen: Planning and the Use of Contractual Remedies' 2 *British Journal of Law and Society* 45–60

Beatson, J (2012) 'Legal Academics: Forgotten Players or Interlopers?' Inner Temple Reader's lecture series www.innertemple.org.uk/downloads/education/lectures/lecture_beatson.pdf

Bernstein, L (2001) 'Private Commercial Law in the Cotton Industry: Creating Co-Operation through Rules, Norms and Institutions' 99 *Michigan Law Review* 1724–90

Blom-Cooper, L and G Drewry (1972) *Final Appeal: A Study of the House of Lords in its Judicial Capacity* (Oxford: Clarendon Press)

Bradney, A (2003) *Conversations, Choices and Chances: The Liberal Law School in the Twenty-First Century* (Oxford: Hart Publishing)

Campbell, D (ed.) (2001) *The Relational Theory of Contract: Selected Works of Ian Macneil* (London: Sweet & Maxwell)

Centre for Effective Dispute Resolution (CEDR) (2010) *The Fourth Mediation Audit: A Survey of Commercial Mediator Attitudes and Experience* (London: CEDR) www.cedr.com/docslib/CEDRMediatorAudit2010.pdf

Collins, H (1999) *Regulating Contracts* (Oxford: Oxford University Press)

Darbyshire, P (2012) *Sitting in Judgment: The Working Life of Judges* (Oxford: Hart Publishing)

Dingwall, R and E Cloatre (2006) 'Vanishing Trials? An English Perspective' 1 *Journal of Dispute Resolution* 51

Duxbury, N (2001) *Jurists and Judges: An Essay on Influence* (Oxford: Hart Publishing)

Eisenberg, M A (2000) 'Why There is No Law of Relational Contracts' 94(3) *Northwestern University Law Review* 805–21

Feinman, J (2001) 'The Reception of Ian Macneil's Work on Contract in the US' in D Campbell (ed.), *The Relational Theory of Contract: Selected Works of Ian Macneil* (London: Sweet & Maxwell)

Galanter, M (1974–1975) 'Why the Haves Come out Ahead: Speculations on the Limits of Legal Change' 9 *Law and Society Review* 95

Galanter, M (2004) 'The Vanishing Trial: An Examination of Trials and Related Matters in Federal and State Courts' 1(3) *Journal of Empirical Legal Studies* 459–570

Galanter, M (2002) 'A World without Trials?' *Journal of Dispute Resolution* 1–25

Genn, H (1998) 'The Central London County Court: Pilot Mediation Scheme Evaluation Report', Lord Chancellor's Department Research Series No 5/98 (London: LCD)

Genn, H (2009) *Judging Civil Justice: The Hamlyn Lectures* (Cambridge: Cambridge University Press)

Goff, R (1983) 'In Search of Principle' 69 *Proceedings of the British Academy* 169

Gould, N (2010) *Mediating Construction Disputes: An Evaluation of Existing Practice* (London: King's College) www.kcl.ac.uk/content/1/c6/06/13/33/KCLMediating ConstructionPartsI-III.pdf

Hale, B (2013) 'Should Judges be Socio-legal Scholars', plenary lecture, Socio-legal Studies Association Annual Conference University of York www.supremecourt. gov.uk/docs/speech-130326.pdf

Hyde, J (2012) 'Court of Appeal Judge Raps Defendant for Spurning Mediation', *Law Society Gazette*, 17 May www.lawgazette.co.uk/news/coa-judge-raps-defendant-spurning-mediation

Knapp, C (2002) 'Taking Contracts Private: The Quiet Revolution in Contract Law' 71 *Fordham Law Review* 761

Lewis, R (1982) 'Contracts between Businessmen: Reform of the Law of Firm Offers and an Empirical Study of Tendering Practices in the Building Industry' 9(2) *Journal of Law and Society* 153–75

Lyons, B and J Mehta (1997) 'Private Sector Business Contracts: The Text between the Lines' in S Deakin and J Michie (eds) (1997) *Contracts, Co-operation and Competition* (Oxford: Oxford University Press)

Macneil, I (1962). 'Power of Contract and Agreed Remedies' 47(4) *Cornell Law Quarterly* 496–528

Macneil, I (1969). 'Whither Contracts' 21 *Journal of Legal Education* 403–18

Macneil, I (1974). 'The Many Futures of Contracts' 47 *Southern California Law Review* 691–816

Macneil, I (1962) 'Power of Contract and Agreed Remedies' 47(4) *Cornell Law Quarterly* 496–528

McKenzie, D (2010) *Dispute Resolution in London and the UK* (London: The City UK) www.thecityuk.com

Mertz, E (2000). 'An Afterword: Tapping the Promise of Relational Contract Theory: "Real" Legal Language and a New Legal Realism' 94(3) *Northwestern University Law Review* 909–36

Ministry of Justice and UK Trade and Investment (2011) *Plan for Growth: Promoting the UK's Legal Services Sector* (London: Ministry of Justice) www.justice.gov.uk/publications/corporate-reports/moj/2011/growth-legal-services

Mouzas, S and M Furmston (2008) 'From Contract to Umbrella Agreement' 67(1) *Cambridge Law Journal* 37–50

Mulcahy, L (2013) 'The Collective Interest in Private Dispute Resolution' 33(1) *Oxford Journal of Legal Studies* 59–80

Mulcahy, L (2001) 'Can Leopards Change their Spots? An Evaluation of the Role of Lawyers in Medical Negligence Mediation' 8(3) *International Journal of the Legal Profession* 204–24

Mulcahy, L and C Andrews (2010) *'Baird v Marks and Spencer'* in R Hunter, C McGlynn and E Rackley (eds) *Feminist Judgments: From Theory to Practice* (Oxford: Hart Publishing)

Narayandas, D and V K Rangan (2004) 'Building and Sustaining Buyer-Seller Relationships in Mature Industrial Markets' 68 *Journal of Marketing* 63–78

Neuberger, D (2012) 'Judges and Professors: Ships Passing in the Night?', speech at Max Planck Institute, Hamburg www.judiciary.gov.uk/media/speeches/2012/mr-speech-hamburg-lecture-09072012

Paterson, A (1982) *The Law Lords* (London: Macmillan)

Peppet, S (2003) 'Transactional Mediation: Using Mediators in Deals' 32(10) *The Colorado Lawyer* 81–4 http://lawweb.colorado.edu/profiles/pubpdfs/peppet/transmedcolol.pdf

Posner, R (2008) *How Judges Think* (Cambridge MA: Harvard University Press)

Roberts, S '"Listing Concentrates the Mind": The English Civil Court as an Arena for Structured Negotiation' (2009) 29 *OJLS* 457

Urwin, P, V Karuk, P Latreille, E Michielsens, L Page, B Siara and A Speckesser, with A Boon and P Chevalier (2010) *Evaluating the Use of Judicial Mediation in Employment Tribunals* Ministry of Justice Research Series 7/10 (London: Ministry of Justice)

Vincent-Jones, P (2001) 'The Reception of Ian Macneil's Work on Contract in the UK' in D Campbell (ed.), *The Relational Theory of Contract: Selected Works of Ian Macneil* (London: Sweet &Maxwell), pp. 67–85

10
Relational Contract and Social Learning in Hybrid Organization
Peter Vincent-Jones

Introduction

Ian Macneil's relational theory provides a powerful conceptual apparatus for analysing the ways in which social exchange behaviour both gives rise to and is supported by the 'common contract norms' of role integrity, reciprocity, implementation of planning, effectuation of consent, flexibility, contractual solidarity, the protection of reliance and expectation interests, the creation and restraint of power, the propriety of means, and harmonization within the social matrix (Macneil, 2000b, pp. 879–80). These norms are derived from the 'primal roots' of contract (the social conditions that need historically to have become established in order for contractual exchange to be possible): the development of society and the specialization of labour, and the capacity of human beings to exercise choice and be consciously aware of the future (Macneil, 1980, pp. 1–4). While relatively 'discrete' norms are particularly important for planning, relatively 'relational' norms are necessary to support co-operation throughout the duration of the contract. *Wherever* social interaction occurs, the quality of relationships may be assessed with reference to the configuration of such norms in the contractual environment.

This chapter considers how relational theory may be applied in the context of hybrid forms of organization, in which the state shares responsibilities for the provision of public services and the performance of public functions with a range of private and non-profit entities in sectors such as environmental management, health and social care, welfare and social security, employment and training, and policing and criminal justice.

While hybrids may take many forms,[1] the present focus is on quasi-market arrangements in which public authorities commission services on behalf of citizens on a contractual basis from competing providers (Le Grand, 1995).[2] Going beyond existing public sector studies that have drawn on Macneil (for example, in the public sector, Deakin and Walsh, 1996; Vincent-Jones and Harries, 1996; Flynn and Williams, 1997; Vincent-Jones, 1997; Walker and Davis, 1999; Rahman and Kumaraswamy, 2002; Davis, 2007; Reeves, 2008; Van der Veen, 2009; Lavoie et al., 2010; Hughes et al., 2011a; 2011b; Petsoulas et al., 2011; in the management sciences literature focusing on business-to-business (B2B) exchanges, see Kaufman and Stern, 1988; Heide and John, 1992; Gundlach and Achrol, 1993; Pilling et al., 1994; Lusch and Brown, 1996; Blois, 2002), we develop an analytical framework combining relational contract and social learning theories which may be used in the investigation of such phenomena. A theoretical connection is established between relational contract norms and behaviour on the one hand, and the capacities of the parties for social learning in exchange relationships on the other hand. The basic argument is that relational contracting is a precondition of effective social learning in all contractual relationships, including those in public service quasi-markets. However, other institutional conditions must be satisfied in order for public contracts to serve legitimately as mechanisms for problem-solving in the public interest, including the building of capacities for democratic participation on the part of citizens and stakeholders. The chapter concludes by outlining a research programme exploring the correlation between contract norms and social learning in public service networks involving collaboration between state and civil society actors.

1. Reflexive governance as social learning

The central role of social learning in decision-making and problem-solving in the public sphere is explicitly recognized in the legal–philosophical

---

1 In Britain, the development of hybrids exemplifies the 'new public contracting' – a mode of governance originating in the 1980s and subsequently adopted by governments of all political complexions, characterized by the delegation of contractual powers and responsibilities to public agencies in regulatory frameworks preserving central government controls and powers of intervention (Vincent-Jones, 2006). Public goods such as green-space management and urban regeneration are secured increasingly through contractual collaborations between local government agencies and non-governmental organizations (Peel et al., 2009; De Magalhaes, 2010; Lindholst and Bogetoft, 2011).
2 In another quasi-market variant, consumers may exercise choice directly in publicly funded vouchering schemes. Here, the role of the state, either instead of or in addition to service commissioning, is to establish the scheme and oversee the operation of contracts between citizens and service providers (Le Grand, 1995).

theory of reflexive governance as social learning (De Schutter and Lenoble, 2010; Lenoble and Maesschalck, 2010). This distinctive perspective draws elements from various strands of existing social-learning theory, most notably in the literature on organizational learning (Argyris and Schön, 1978; Schön, 1983; Easterby-Smith, 1997); deliberative democracy (Strydom, 1999; Goodin and Niemeyer, 2003); experimentalism (Sabel, 1994); and (to a lesser degree) transformative learning and policy learning (Peterson, 1997; White 2000; Mezirow, 2003). According to Jacques Lenoble and Marc Maesschalck (2010), the most intractable governance problems can ultimately be resolved in the public interest only through social-learning strategies aimed at *maximizing the fulfilment of normative expectations of participants in a collective action*. The term 'normative expectations' here refers to either what the participants believe should be done or gained, or how the interests with which they are concerned should be met. Social learning involves specific kinds of communication, deliberation and reflection by all parties with interests or stakes in the issue in question. Transcending the dualism of markets/neo-institutionalism and bureaucracies/state welfarism, the emphasis is on the need to create institutional conditions that help facilitate reflexive problem-solving on the part of key actors engaged in decision-making on matters of public interest. To simplify, these conditions are argued to take three main forms: (1) *economic–institutionalist* (concerned with increasing efficiency); (2) *pragmatist* (involving experimentation with different forms of joint enquiry such as benchmarking and learning by monitoring); and (3) *democratic–deliberative* (enhancing dialogue through increased representation).[3] Beyond the present concern with public service provision, this pragmatist problem-solving approach has been applied in other contexts where market and bureaucratic failures have occurred and where the problem of how to protect the public interest has become acute, for example, in fields such as energy (Prosser et al., 2010), biodiversity (Dedeurwaerdere, 2010) and corporate governance (Deakin and Koukiadaki, 2010).

A useful starting point for the investigation of social learning in hybrids is provided by the concept of 'organisational architecture' (Jackson, 2001), referring to a particular set of relationships between employers, employees, suppliers, customers and other organizations:

---

3 For a more detailed exposition of the theoretical perspective, including discussion of a fourth ('genetic') set of conditions of social learning in the healthcare context, see Vincent-Jones and Mullen (2010). Lenoble and Maesschalck (2010) consider that fully reflexive governance is not possible without such a genetic dimension, incorporating all the other dimensions.

> Architecture is a structure of relationships ... To understand the effectiveness of alternative architectures, one needs to concentrate on the precise nature of the relational contracts and the way in which they relate to one another within a network. Organisational architecture shapes organisational space and defines organisational context and can, therefore, empower or constrain. It is much more than simply organisation structure and transcends the transactions cost view of organisations as a 'nexus of contracts'. (p. 15)

For present purposes, the concept refers to arrangements for the provision of public services combining state and civil society actors in quasi-market organization, in which the 'horizontal' contractual relationship between the commissioning authority and service provider is nested within 'vertical' or hierarchical relationships with various tiers of government (Goldberg, 1976; Zumbansen, 2003). Economic co-ordination occurs through the devolution of contractual powers to commissioning agencies under competitive conditions in which policy-informed 'choices' have to be made, for example, concerning the form of provision, the identity of the supplier, and the trade-off between price and quality.[4] While hierarchical ordering of some kind is necessary to help generate dynamic efficiency, the overall responsiveness of quasi-markets is dependent also on the active participation of citizens and service-users which may be essential for allocative efficiency. Since in this type of quasi-market arrangement consumers cannot exercise choice directly, public participation is vital to producing services 'that individual users value and in the quantity and quality that they prefer' (Jackson, 2001, p. 18). Here the concept of 'performativity' refers ultimately to 'the capacity of a contractual system to generate added value for the stakeholders' (Davis, 2007, p. 387).

Davis suggests that an optimal organizational architecture should contribute to improved performance by enhancing the reflexive capacity of actors engaged in various forms of exchange. In his account, this reflexive capacity is associated with processes of experimentation. Similarly for Peter Jackson (2001), the framework within which such processes occur and are shaped is not fixed but rather in constant evolution:

---

[4] The relationships involved in vouchering and 'direct payment' schemes (n. 2 above) may also be analysed in terms of organizational architecture. This governance structure has the potential to lead to superior allocative efficiency than may be achieved by concentrating purchasing power in the hands of a representative public agency (Steuerle and Twombly, 2002). The capacity-building role for the local state here is to stimulate the development of competition and to encourage other market conditions that will enable citizen-consumers to make informed choices according to their needs and preference.

Architecture tends to emerge in the sense that there is a constant search for that particular constellation of relationships that results in 'excellence'. The precise set of relationships that produce high performance is 'discovered' through the testing out of hypotheses in the process of managing. In the case of private sector organizations the search is for a unique non-imitable architecture that will give a sustainable competitive advantage. This approach invites us to think in similar terms when considering the performance of public sector organizations. The search is for an efficient and effective architecture, i.e. that which adds maximum value. It is not a one-off strategic design problem. Rather it is an act of discovery, which will involve experimentation. (p. 16)

Building on this insight, organizational architectures may be considered evolving frameworks for the facilitation of social learning. Social learning in public service networks occurs through multiple, communicative relationships between professionals, purchasers, providers, service-users and other stakeholders. The exchange of information contributes a vital resource for decision-making at each 'node' in the network (Burris et al., 2005).[5] In this sense, public contracting may be seen as part of a 'collective strategy to raise the level of collective intelligence in both private and public fields of action' (Ladeur, 2007, p. 351). This mode of governance may contribute to knowledge generation by co-ordinating, and drawing on, the resources available in networks of relationships in a range of experimental projects involving collaboration between state and non-state actors. What is learned and the nature of learning are dependent on the particular kind of relationship and associated norms. For example, while some relationships entail contractual planning, others may lack this quality. Some relationships may be economic in nature and involve the transfer of money, as in purchase-of-service contracting, while others are non-monetized and based on hierarchical direction, or some other form of communicative interaction such as regulation. We return to this point in considering the possible role of different types of norm in social-learning processes in the final section.

---

5 See Burris et al. (2005): 'A node as we conceive of it is a site within an OGS (Outcome Generating System) where knowledge, capacity and resources are mobilized to manage a course of events. The node as a site governance comprises four essential characteristics: a way of thinking (mentalities); a set of methods (technologies); resources to support the node's operation; and institutions that structure the mobilization of mentalities, resources and technologies over time.' (p. 12)

2. Conditions of social learning in quasi-markets

In quasi-market organization, a basic task for institutional designers is to improve efficiency by altering incentives among economic actors. The social-learning capacities of clients and contractors are structured by economic regulation, which should help enable decision-makers to develop solutions to governance problems that maximize efficiency and minimize transaction costs, thereby satisfying at least to some extent the economic dimension of the public interest. However, well-documented problems with quasi-markets (monopoly power, bounded rationality, asymmetric information, externalities and agency) limit what may be achieved through learning based solely on economic rationality. In any case, this economic–institutionalist conception tends to ignore wider considerations, such as the need to take account of the interests of consumers and citizens who are outside the principal contractual relationship. For collective learning effectively to reflect the public interest, decision-makers must be aware of such limitations. They must avoid rational–technocratic assumptions and adopt instead a pragmatic and 'experimentalist' approach that acknowledges the need for continuous revision of basic assumptions underpinning the provisional goals and problem-solving strategies of their part of the organization (Argyris and Schön, 1978). Commissioners and providers of services may thus be seen as collectively engaged in continuous discussion of joint goals in situations of uncertainty and limited understanding. The nature of governance problems and the interests of these key players cannot be assumed to be fixed, but are rather negotiated, defined and redefined through collective engagement in various communicative, deliberative and experimental practices. Wherever social actors engage in collaborative interaction, 'they must accept the possibility that their views of themselves, or the world, and the interests arising from both – their identities, in short – will be changed unexpectedly' (Sabel, 1994, p. 145).

Decision-makers in public service networks must also be able to draw on the greatest possible pool of knowledge and experience in their efforts to address and resolve governance problems in a way that satisfies the public interest. In this democratic–deliberative conception, the active participation of citizens and service-users serves as a vital resource for collective learning (Mullen et al., 2011). In human service sectors such as health and social care, patients and consumers are also co-producers. They may help resolve problems by raising issues and posing questions that professionals have not considered (Tritter and McCallum, 2006). Effective public engagement entails constructive dialogue aimed at reshaping the relationship between professionals, managers and other stakeholders in the network (Mullen, 2008). The state has an important role to play in fostering such basic conditions of social learning. Government interventions may help build capacities for citizens and service-users to contribute in various ways, for example, by providing education and training opportunities and developing communicative skills necessary for their effective involvement (Vincent-Jones, 2007). The state can play a part also in establishing appropriate democratic fora of participation and deliberation, and in creating an institutional framework for incentivizing key decision-makers, such as commissioners and service providers, to listen and be receptive to stakeholder input. Admittedly, the experience of recent public service reforms has been disappointing measured in such terms. In the English healthcare sector, for example, successive waves of PPI (patient and public involvement) initiatives have had little success in improving the quality of democratic engagement (Vincent-Jones et al., 2009). However, rather than being seen as the inevitable consequence of state intervention (Campbell, 2007), our argument is that such policy failure is attributable at least in part to deficiencies in policy and decision-making processes associated with the absence of basic conditions of reflexive governance.

Other conditions of social learning may pose even greater difficulties. In his analysis of the part played by relational exchange in enhancing performance, Davis suggests that 'performativity' depends ultimately on reflexive changes in the capacity of the actors involved. The importance of reflexivity in this sense is apparent in the literature on organizational learning. Chris Argyris and Donald Schön (1978) focus on the need for social actors to avoid repetitive and defensive patterns of thinking associated with single-loop learning, and to engage in frame reflection involving double-loop learning: 'Double-loop learning occurs where error is detected and corrected in ways that involve the modification of an organization's underlying norms, policies and objectives.' (p. 3) Decision-makers must engage in forms of inquiry which 'resolve incompatible organizational norms by setting new priorities and weightings of norms, or by restructuring the norms themselves together with associated strategies and assumptions' (p. 18). Relationships are predicted to fail where their fundamental assumptions and routines become self-reinforcing and single-loop learning inhibits the detection and correction of error (Argyris, 1982). This particular cognitive dimension of decision-making and problem-solving is developed in greater depth in Lenoble and Maesschalck's (2010) theory of reflexive governance.[6]

---

6 According to Lenoble and Maesschalck (2010), the theoretical advance offered by the 'genetic' approach over Schönian pragmatism is the further specification of an institutional mechanism capable of facilitating the actors' engagement in the frame-reflective processes associated with double-loop learning. Rather than being taken for

Just as government may help facilitate such conditions of reflexive governance, so its policies may inhibit their development. A major problem with NHS modernization in England has been the simultaneous pursuit of voice and choice initiatives that are in mutual tension and lacking in coherent overall rationale. Policy confusion and the privileging of economic over democratic elements in the reform agenda are preventing the embedding of economic relations in social relations (Polanyi, 1957; Krippner and Alvarez, 2007), which is arguably essential in order for social learning effectively to occur in healthcare networks (Vincent-Jones, 2011). Inappropriate state interventions pose obstacles to the ability of networks to resolve governance problems to the satisfaction of those engaged in the collective action to the greatest extent possible. This conclusion is consistent with studies highlighting problems of relational contracting in other contexts, such as the procurement of public service infrastructure under the public finance initiative (PFI) (Treasury Select Committee, 2011), which are attributable to defective policies and government interference in particular projects (Reeves, 2008). The conditions of reflexive governance need to be established not only within public service networks, but also at the levels of government and in public administration. The UK government's pursuit of contradictory policy initiatives in sectors such as health and social care has nothing in common with experimentalist social learning.[7] Experimentation in policy-making can only be legitimate where it conforms to procedural and other requirements, including the clear articulation of policy purposes, and provisions for monitoring and evaluating success, and for learning from failure (Vincent-Jones, 2006; Ladeur, 2007).

This analysis points to a fundamental tension at the heart of contractualization. The state's attempted use of the essentially private governance mechanism of contract to achieve public policy objectives appears paradoxical. Certainly, the joint-welfare maximizing properties of contract (Campbell and Harris, 1993) are much more difficult to reproduce in programmes of 'positive policy-driven regulation' involving public contracting (Freedland, 1998; Vincent-Jones, 2006). A major concern is with how inappropriate central regulation may damage the norms that

---

granted, in the genetic approach the capacity for cognitive reframing and self-representation is conceived: 'as the product of an operation of "terceisation", that is, as the product of an operation that requires, as part of the process of self-construction, the invocation of a third element whose externality makes possible the actor's construction of her or his image – the image that will enable her or him to identify herself or himself (and her or his interests) in a given context for action' (p. 217).

7 It should be clear that experimentalism as presently understood cannot be reduced to a simple process of 'trial and error' (Campbell, 2007, p. 291). A key purpose of social learning theory is to help establish a sound basis for policy and decision-making that avoids this type of pragmatism (De Schutter and Lenoble, 2010).

support trust and co-operation in these contractual relations, thereby limiting the scope for social learning. However, in spite of the many difficulties in satisfying these positive and negative conditions of social learning in hybrids, there is no reason to believe that the obstacles are insurmountable. What is required in order to inform policy and decision-making in the public interest is a more robust theoretical framework for designing and evaluating experiments in hybrid organization, based – it may be suggested – on a clearer understanding of the connection between relational contracting and social learning.

3. Social learning and contract norms

Social-learning theory provides a novel lens through which the familiar theme of the relationship between contract norms and social organization may be explored. As has been seen, Ian Macneil (1980) derives the common contract norms from the social conditions that need historically to have become established in order for exchange to be possible – the so-called primal roots of contract. Assuming the existence of society and the specialization of labour, what distinguishes human 'contractual' exchange from animal behaviour is the development of *cognitive* capacities to exercise choice and plan for the future by specifying the relationship (rendering an aspect 'discrete') and bringing the future into the present ('presentation'). Where exchange relations are operating effectively, the common contract norms are likely to be in robust condition and to be supported by additional relational norms. This should enhance the capacities of the parties to learn from one another and be receptive to external sources of information, and enable them to engage in problem-solving and to deal effectively and flexibly with difficulties that inevitably arise in the course of the transaction. On the other hand, where contractual relations are in unhealthy condition, and where the contract norms are revealed in 'varying degrees of disarray' (Macneil, 1983, p. 351), social-learning capacities are likely to be reduced. Contractual relations in this condition will be characterized by disproportionate intensification of the planning and consent norms that serve to enhance discreteness and presentation: '... a sufficiently serious defect in any one of the contract norms will bring a contractual relation down over time' (Macneil, 1980, p, 168).

The suggestion here, therefore, is of a link between contract norms and behavioural qualities of relationality on the one hand, and potential for social learning in exchange relationships on the other hand. Not all the norms that govern such relationships are contractual in character – for example, the parties' expectations may be structured according to social status as well as by mutual planning (Macneil, 1974). Where the norms *are* essentially contractual, they may either be generated internally within the relationship or be imposed externally. In practice, the contract norms have overlapping internal and external dimensions, such that external norms 'become internal contractual norms, although their origins may lie outside the contractual relation' (Macneil, 1980, p. 36). The more long-term the relationship, the more the ongoing relation itself becomes a source of obligation. At this stage of Macneil's analysis there is no mention of specifically legal norms. Indeed, he laments what he calls the 'bias' given our thinking by the 'law-oriented definition of contracts': 'If we wish to understand contract, and indeed if we wish to understand contract law, we must think about exchange and such things first, and law second'. (p. 5) Again, the norms formally imposed by the state legal system are just one type of external norm: 'Custom, socially reinforced habit, morality, a host of institutional behaviour patterns, and the like typically play far more important roles, especially in everyday terms.' (p. 37) However, the point that the contract norms are not essentially legal is not, of course, to deny the importance of this dimension. Having stated that 'law is not what contracts are all about', Macneil goes on to say that law remains 'an integral part of virtually all contractual relations' (p. 5). While the debate as to how far the *law* of contract should promote relationality is of secondary importance in the present analysis, the social-learning approach must remain sensitive to the possible effects of different types of norm (both non-legal and legal) on problem-solving and decision-making in contractual relationships.

The theoretical advance made by linking the social-learning and relational contract approaches lies in helping to address the question of *why* relationality is such an important feature of contractual governance, and *how* this quality may add value in arrangements for the provision of public services. The answer, it is suggested, has to do with the potential of contracts to serve in the public interest as mechanisms for the promotion of social learning among all parties with interests or stakes in the services under consideration. In complex market exchanges, the efficiency gains associated with relational contracting are dependent at least in part on social-learning processes which enable the parties to deal effectively with difficulties and uncertainties that inevitably arise in the course of the transaction. Relational contracts may facilitate innovation, or may serve as mechanisms of innovation. Similarly, in the case of public contracting, we may posit a correlation between relational contracting and social learning. The crucial difference is that the success of governance arrangements in this setting cannot be judged solely with reference to economic exchange, but requires consideration of the public nature of the functions being performed, and the need to satisfy the interests of citizens and service-users on whose behalf contractual activities are undertaken. In both market and quasi-market settings, the majority of simple transactions may operate relationally without the need for any communicative interaction beyond what is necessary to perform the contract. However, the more complex the exchange, the greater the scope for social learning in negotiating and managing the ongoing relationship.

This social-learning approach is consistent with mainstream post-Macaulay socio-legal scholarship which focuses on the use and non-use of law in business practice, highlighting the complexity of the relationship between law and exchange processes (Campbell, 2013; Gordon, 2013). Collaborative relationships are routinely the product of a combination of formal and informal, legal and non-legal influences, and even threats of litigation need not be antithetical to relational contracting (Whitford, 2013). Gillian Hadfield and Iva Bozovic (2012) have shown how formal contract law can serve as a 'scaffolding', which 'allows transactional partners to bridge the incompleteness of inescapably informal structure of complex relationships in situations of high uncertainty'. While partners in a joint enterprise frequently structure their relationships with reference to contract law, 'they do so not in order to secure the threat of formal contract remedies – as the conventional view in the literature holds – but ... in order to coordinate the inferences each makes, and expects the other to make, about their commitment to the joint enterprise' (p. 55). Ronald Gilson et al. (2010) use the term 'braiding' to conceptualize the way in which parties respond to rising uncertainty by writing contracts that intertwine formal and informal mechanisms – 'in a way that allows each to assess the disposition and capacity of the other to respond cooperatively and effectively to unforeseen circumstances' (p. 1377). Production in capitalist economies is arguably increasingly governed through complex contractual relationships involving innovative collaborations that cannot be analysed according to traditional definitions of contract and co-operation (Jennejohn, 2006).

This literature is not particularly influenced by Macneil, if at all, and does not explore the role of contract norms in the formal and informal practices that constitute business relationships. It is suggested that research based on social-learning theory is well equipped to fill this gap. We concur with Rubin that 'empirical studies that follow a traditional social science model, although valuable, cannot penetrate these relationships ... because they do not tell us about the internal thought processes of the actor' (Rubin, 2013). Our main concern here is with social action rather than with legal structures, doctrines and regulatory frameworks. Reflexivity as a quality of governance refers ultimately to a particular kind of orientation on the part of actors in decision-making and problem-solving, both individually and in relation to other actors. While the role of norms in social learning might be studied in any contractual setting, the present focus has been on the linkages between the norms involved in different types of network relationship and learning processes within hybrid forms of organization. As has been seen, the governance problems in this context differ in kind from those found in the typical B2B exchange, reflecting the public nature of services and the need to satisfy a wider range of expectations.

A number of questions are suggested by this preliminary analysis. What sorts of social learning are made possible by, and may occur within, the various horizontal and vertical relationships within quasi-markets and other hybrid forms? How do contractual and hierarchical relationships differ in this respect? To what extent are the capacities for social learning positively related to the specifically *reciprocal* and *consensual* nature of a contractual exchange? How exactly does contractual exchange open up spaces for social learning that may not be present in other forms of co-ordination based on hierarchical direction? How do contracts that are legally binding differ from those that do not have this quality, but which may still be considered contracts on Macneil's behavioural definition? To what extent might the techniques of 'contracting for innovation' (Gilson et al., 2009) that are observable in private sector transactions be applicable in the very different context of quasi-market contracting for human services such as health and social care?

Drawing critically on the approach adopted in areas such as marketing and management studies (Blois and Ivens, 2006), these questions might be addressed by operationalizing Macneil's contract norms in empirical research. The broad aim would be to investigate how different contract norms, or constellations of norms, operate in ways that are either conducive or inimical to social learning in hybrids. The research might examine the interplay between the norms that guide behaviour, and cognitive processes such as those involving double-loop learning and frame-reflection. The importance of normative equilibrium for successful contractual relations has been emphasized at various points in this chapter, implying a productive tension between discrete and relational norms.[8] A truly welfare-enhancing relationship, it has been suggested, is not one typically in which there are no problems or difficulties, but rather in which such obstacles are recognized and overcome, and opportunities for mutual benefit identified and exploited.

---

8 Teubner's (2000) depiction of relational contract in a communitarian sense involving a 'nice and warm cooperative relation between human beings' (p. 400) owes nothing to Macneil, who has rejoined (2000a) that 'conflict is rife' both within the common contract norms (such as role integrity, reciprocity and power) and among them (for example, between flexibility and planning/consent, and between propriety of means and the other norms) (p. 433).

The research might further consider the implications for social learning of different types of norm enforcement (formal and informal procedures for sanctioning non-conformity or departure from patterns of expected behaviour), and explore the impact of litigation and the judicial process in comparison with less formal mechanisms such as arbitration and alternative dispute resolution. A related issue concerns the relationship between different 'shades' of normativity, and the behaviour which the norms reflect and to which they apply; for example, the research might examine how the same norms are applied or developed in varying private and public adjudicatory settings (mediation, arbitration, formal court processes), and investigate the different effects on business communities and networks amongst whom the results of norm enforcement are likely to be disseminated. It might investigate how the mobilization and awareness of such norms encourage the parties to reflect on their behaviour, and to learn in order to resolve problems and overcome blockages in their current understanding, based on frame reflection and identity transformation.

Conclusion

State agencies in Britain are contracting with private and non-profit providers for the provision of an expanding range of public services and functions in a variety of hybrid forms of organization. This chapter has suggested a framework for analysing such phenomena by combining Macneil's relational contract theory with insights drawn from the theoretical literature on reflexive governance. While the analysis has been national in scope, the perspective should be applicable to mixed governance regimes in developing and transitional societies as well as in Western liberal democracies. Many governance problems in capitalist systems, it may be suggested, could be addressed through experimentation with different combinations of public and private action drawing on the initiatives of state and civil society actors, informed by social-learning theory.

This conclusion as to the responsive potential of hybrids (and the interpretation of Macneil's relational theory on which it is based) is at odds with David Campbell's (2007) critique of contractualization. Campbell's argument implies that the only type of economic exchange worthy of the description 'relational' is that which occurs between private entities in appropriately constituted markets.[9] The attempt to establish relational and

---

9 Campbell's critique of hybrids is an extension of his analysis of the deficiencies of welfarism and of state intervention in the economy (1990; 1996a; 1996b; 2001). The distinctiveness of this position lies in the advocacy of the market as the mechanism by which true socialism can be achieved.

other conditions of responsiveness of hybrid organization is not only doomed to failure, but fundamentally misconceived. This argument, if correct, would render futile the project for the development of relational contract theory advocated in the present chapter. While acknowledging the continued failure of the state's attempt to use contract as a mechanism to achieve public goals in cases such as the PFI, we contest Campbell's view that this reflects fundamental problems that can only be addressed by the retreat of the state and the abandonment of contractualization.

We have argued that the state has a key role to play in economic co-ordination on matters of public interest and have defended public contracts as potentially providing part of the solution to a range of contemporary governance problems. We maintain that it is indeed possible for citizens legitimately to agree a collective purpose to be pursued by public authority, against the Hayekian notion that markets are the only means of co-ordinating diffused knowledge and capacity and of bringing order to complex systems. The social-learning approach allows for the possibility of a collective decision that particular services (for example, in fields such as social care and public security) might best be provided directly by the state due to risks and uncertainties that cannot effectively be borne by independent sector bodies. In other cases, the decision might be that services currently regarded as 'public' should lose that status and become subject to private governance regimes. However, the implication of the foregoing analysis is that many services will retain their public character, and should be provided through ongoing collaboration between the state and independent sectors as the best available means of satisfying collective expectations of citizens that cannot be spontaneously realized through the market. The development of a combined relational contract/social-learning perspective in this chapter provides a firm basis for further exploration of the factors shaping reflexive governance in the public interest in hybrid organization.

References

Argyris, C (1982) *Reasoning, Learning and Action: Individual and Organisational* (San Francisco CA: Jossey-Bass)

Argyris, C and D Schön (1978) *Organisational Learning: A Theory of Action Perspective*. (Reading MA: Addison Wesley)

Blois, K (2002) 'Business to Business Exchanges: A Rich Descriptive Apparatus Derived from Macneil's and Menger's Analyses' 39 *Journal of Management Studies* 523–52

Blois, K and B Ivens (2006) 'Measuring Relational Norms: Some Methodological Issues' 40 *European Journal of Marketing* 352–65

Burris, S, P Drahos and C Shearing (2005) 'Nodal Governance' 30 *Australian Journal of Legal Philosophy* 30

Campbell, D (1990) 'The Social Theory of Relational Contract: Macneil as the Modern Proudhon' 18 *International Journal of the Sociology of Law* 75

Campbell, D (1996a) *The Failure of Marxism* (Aldershot: Dartmouth)

Campbell, D (1996b) 'The Relational Constitution of the Discrete Contract' in D Campbell and P Vincent-Jones (eds), *Contract and Economic Organisation: Socio-Legal Initiatives* (Aldershot: Dartmouth)

Campbell, D (2001) 'Ian Macneil and the Relational Theory of Contract' in D Campbell (ed.) *Selected Papers of Ian Macneil* (London: Sweet & Maxwell)

Campbell, D (2007) 'Relational Contract and the Nature of Private Ordering: A Comment on Vincent-Jones' 14 *Indiana Journal of Global Legal Studies* 279–300

Campbell, D (2013) 'What Do We Mean by the Non-Use of Contract' in J Braucher, J Kidwell and W Whitford (eds), *Revisiting the Contracts Scholarship of Stewart Macaulay: On the Empirical and the Lyrical* (Oxford: Hart Publishing)

Campbell, D and D Harris (1993) 'Flexibility in Long-term Contractual Relationships: The Role of Cooperation' 20 *Journal of Law and Society* 166

Davis, P (2007) 'The Effectiveness of Relational Contracting in a Temporary Public Organisation: Intensive Collaboration between an English Local Authority and Private Contractors' 85 *Public Administration* 383–404

De Magalhaes, C (2010) 'Public Space and the Contracting-out of Publicness: A Framework for Analysis' 15 *Journal of Urban Design* 559–74

De Schutter, O and J Lenoble (eds) (2010) *Reflexive Governance: Re-defining the Public Interest in a Pluralistic World* (Oxford: Hart Publishing)

Deakin, N and K Walsh (1996) 'The Enabling State: The Role of Markets and Contracts' 74 *Public Administration* 33

Deakin, S and A Koukiadaki (2010) 'Reflexive Approaches to Corporate Governance' in De Schutter and Lenoble (eds) (2010)

Dedeurwaerdere, T (2010) 'The Contribution of Network Governance in Overcoming Frame Conflicts: Enabling Social Learning and Building Reflexive Abilities in Biodiversity Governance' in De Schutter and J Lenoble (eds) (2010)

Easterby-Smith, M (1997) 'Disciplines of Organisational Learning: Contributions and Critiques' 50 *Human Relations* 1085

Flynn, R and G Williams (eds) (1997) *Contracting for Health: Quasi-Markets and the National Health Service* (Oxford: Oxford University Press)

Freedland, M (1998) 'Public Law and Private Finance: Placing the Private Finance Initiative in a Public Law Frame' *Public Law* 288

Gilson, R, C Sabel and R Scott (2009) 'Contracting for Innovation: Vertical Disintegration and Interfirm Collaboration' 109 *Columbia Law Review* 431–502

Gilson, R, C Sabel and R Scott (2010) 'Braiding: The Interaction of Formal and Informal Contracting in Theory, Practice, and Doctrine' 110 *Columbia Law Review* 1377

Goldberg, V (1976) 'Regulation and Administered Contracts' 7 *The Bell Journal of Economics* 426

Goodin, R E and S J Niemeyer (2003) 'When Does Deliberation Begin? Internal

Reflection versus Public Discussion in Deliberative Democracy' 51 *Political Studies* 627

Gordon, R (2013) 'Macaulay on Law, Private Governments and Spontaneous Order' in J Braucher, J Kidwell and W Whitford (eds), *Revisiting the Contracts Scholarship of Stewart Macaulay: On the Empirical and the Lyrical* (Oxford: Hart Publishing)

Gundlach, G and R Achrol (1993) 'Governance in Exchange: Contract Law and its Alternatives' 12 *Journal of Public Policy and Marketing* 141–55

Hadfield, G and I Bozovic (2012) 'Scaffolding: Using Formal Contracts to Build Informal Relations in Support of Innovation', Law and Economics Working Paper Series No 144 (Los Angeles CA: University of Southern California Law School), p. 55

Heide, J and G John (1992) 'Do Norms Matter in Marketing Relationships?' 56 *Journal of Marketing* 32–44

Hughes, D, P Allen, S Doheny, C Petsoulas and P Vincent-Jones (2011a) 'Contracts in the English NHS: Market Levers and Social Embeddedness' 20 *Health Sociology Review* 321–37

Hughes, D, P Allen, S Doheny, C Petsoulas, J Roberts and P Vincent-Jones (2011b) 'NHS Contracting in England and Wales: Changing Contexts and Relationships', National Institute for Health Research Service Delivery and Organisation Programme, March www.sdo.nihr.ac.uk/projdetails.php?ref=08-1618-127

Jackson, P (2001) 'Public Sector Added Value: Can Bureaucracy Deliver?' 79 *Public Administration* 5–28

Jennejohn, M (2006) 'Governing Innovative Collaboration: A New Theory of Contract', Working Paper Series (New York: Columbia University School of Law), SSRN author #484873, 22 October

Kaufman, P and L Stern (1988) 'Relational Exchange Norms, Perceptions of Unfairness, and Retained Hostility in Commercial Litigation' 32 *Journal of Conflict Resolution* 534–52

Krippner, G and A Alvarez (2007) 'Embeddedness and the Intellectual Projects of Economic Sociology' 31 *Annual Review of Sociology* 219

Ladeur, K-H (2007) 'The Role of Contracts and Networks in Public Governance: The Importance of the "Social Epistemology" of Decision Making' 14 *Indiana Journal of Legal Studies* 329–51

Lavoie, J, A Boulton and J Dwyer (2010) 'Analysing Contractual Environments: Lessons from Indigenous Health in Canada, Australia and New Zealand' 88 *Public Administration* 665–79

Le Grand, J (1995) 'Knights, Knaves or Pawns? Human Behaviour and Social Policy' 26 *Journal of Social Policy* 149–61

Lenoble, J and M Maesschalck (2010) *Democracy, Law and Governance* (London: Ashgate)

Lindholst, A and P Bogetoft (2011) 'Managerial Challenges in Public Service Contracting: Lessons in Green Space Management' 89 *Public Administration* 1036–62

Lusch, R and J Brown (1996) 'Interdependency, Contracting, and Relational Behaviour in Marketing Channels' 60 *Journal of Marketing* 19–38

Macneil, I (1974) 'The Many Futures of Contracts' 47 *Southern California Law Review* 69
Macneil, I (1980) *The New Social Contract: An Inquiry into Modern Contractual Relations*. (New Haven CT and London: Yale University Press)
Macneil, I (1983) 'Values in Contract: Internal and External' 78 *Northwestern University Law Review* 340
Macneil, I (2000a) 'Contracting Worlds and Essential Contract Theory' 9 *Social and Legal Studies* 431–38
Macneil, I (2000b) 'Relational Contract Theory: Challenges and Queries' 94 *Northwestern University Law Review* 877
Mezirow, J (2003) 'Transformative Learning as Discourse' 1 *Journal of Transformative Education* 58
Mullen, C (2008) 'Representation or Reason: Consulting the Public on the Ethics of Health Policy' 16 *Health Care Analysis* 397
Mullen, C, D Hughes and P Vincent-Jones (2011) 'The Democratic Potential of Public Participation: Healthcare Governance in England' 20 *Social and Legal Studies* 1
Peel, D, G Lloyd and A Lord (2009) 'Business Improvement Districts and the Discourse of Contractualism' 17 *European Planning Studies* 401–22
Peterson, A (1997) 'The Limits of Social Learning: Translating Analysis into Action' 22 *Journal of Health Politics, Policy and Law* 1077
Petsoulas, C, P Allen, D Hughes, J Roberts and P Vincent-Jones (2011) 'The Use of Standard Contracts in the English National Health Service: A Case Study Analysis' 73 *Social Science and Medicine* 185–92
Pilling, B, L Crosby and D Jackson (1994) 'Relational Bonds in Industrial Exchange: An Experimental Test of the Transaction Cost Framework' 30 *Journal of Business Research* 237–51
Polanyi, K (1957) *The Great Transformation: The Political and Economic Origins of Our Time* (Boston MA: Beacon Press) (first published 1944)
Prosser, T, H Adlard, B Eberlein, G Britz and H Herzmann (2010) 'Neo-Institutionalist and Collaborative-Relational Approaches to Governance in Services of General Interest: The Case of Energy in the UK and Germany' in De Schutter and Lenoble (eds) (2010)
Rahman, M and M Kumaraswamy (2002) 'Joint Risk Management through Transactionally Efficient Relational Contracting' 20 *Construction Management and Economics* 45–54
Reeves, E (2008) 'The Practice of Contracting in Public Private Partnerships: Transaction Costs and Relational Contracting in the Irish Schools' 86 *Public Administration* 969–86
Rubin, E (2013) 'Law and Reality: The Evolution of Empirical Legal Scholarship', conference paper, 'Empirical and Lyrical: Revisiting the Contracts Scholarship of Stewart Macaulay', in J Braucher, J Kidwell and W Whitford (eds), *Revisiting the Contracts Scholarship of Stewart Macaulay: On the Empirical and the Lyrical* (Oxford: Hart Publishing)
Sabel, C (1994) 'Learning by Monitoring; The Institutions of Economic Development' in N Smelser and R Swedberg (eds), *The Handbook of Economic Sociology* (New York: Russell Sage Foundation)

Schön, D (1983) *The Reflective Practitioner: How Professionals Think in Action* (London: Temple Smith)
Steuerle, E and E Twombly (2002) 'Vouchers' in L M Salamon (ed.), *The Tools of Government: A Guide to the New Governance* (Oxford: Oxford University Press)
Strydom, P (1999) 'Triple Contingency: the Theoretical Problem of the Public in Communication Societies' 25 *Philosophy and Social Criticism* 1
Teubner, G (2000) 'Contracting Worlds: The Many Autonomies of Private Law' 9 *Social and Legal Studies* 399–417
Treasury Select Committee (2011) Seventeenth Report, 18 July
Tritter, J and A McCallum (2006) 'The Snakes and Ladders of User Involvement: Moving beyond Arnstein' 76 *Health Policy* 156
Van der Veen, M (2009) *Contracting for Better Places: A Relational Analysis of Development Agreements in Urban Development Projects* (Amsterdam: IOS Press)
Vincent-Jones, P (1997) 'Hybrid Organisation, Contractual Governance, and Compulsory Competitive Tendering in the Provision of Local Authority Services' in S Deakin and J Michie, *Contracts, Cooperation and Competition: Studies in Economics, Management and Law* (Oxford: Oxford University Press)
Vincent-Jones, P (2006) *The New Public Contracting: Regulation, Responsiveness, Relationality* (Oxford: Oxford University Press)
Vincent-Jones, P (2007) 'The New Public Contracting: Public Versus Private Ordering?' 14 *Indiana Journal of Global Legal Studies* 259–78
Vincent-Jones, P (2011) 'Embedding Economic Relationships through Social Learning? The Limits of Patient and Public Involvement in Healthcare Governance in England' 38 *Journal of Law and Society* 215–44
Vincent-Jones, P and A Harries (1996) 'Conflict and Cooperation in Local Authority Quasi-Markets: The Hybrid Organisation of Internal Contracting Under CCT' 22 *Local Government Studies* 187
Vincent-Jones, P, D Hughes and C Mullen (2009) 'New Labour's PPI Reforms: Patient and Public Involvement in Healthcare Governance?' 72 *Modern Law Review* 247–71
Vincent-Jones, P and C Mullen (2010) 'From Collaborative to Genetic Governance: The Example of Healthcare Services in England' in De Schutter and Lenoble (eds.) (2010)
Walker, B and H Davis (1999) 'Perspectives on Contractual Relationships and the Move to Best Value in Local Authorities' 25 *Local Government Studies* 16
White, J (2000) 'Learning from Outliers' 25 *Journal of Health Politics, Policy and Law* 743
Whitford, J (2013) 'Relational Work, Contract and Conflict in Business Organisation' in J Braucher, J Kidwell and W Whitford (eds), *Revisiting the Contracts Scholarship of Stewart Macaulay: On the Empirical and the Lyrical* (Oxford: Hart Publishing)
Zumbansen, P (2003) 'The Governance of Contracting: The Province of Administrative Law in an Era of Contractualized Government' in W Rainer Walz, H Kötz and K Schmidt, *Non Profit Law Yearbook* (Cologne: Heymanns)

Index

abstraction 2, 3, 5, 116, 117, 118, 119, 120, 122, 128, 129, 135, 183
accommodation 39, 193
alternative dispute resolution (ADR) 8, 177, 205, 206, 207, 209, 210, 228
Amazon.com 9, 14, 38, 44
arbitration 121, 141, 142, 161, 176, 177, 178, 202, 204, 206, 208, 210, 211, 228

B2B *see* exchange, business-to-business
bankruptcy 12, 105, 173
biotechnology *see* technology
bonuses 82, 83, 100
broadband
  domestic accessibility 38
  technology 41

capitalism 171, 226, 228
caveats 51, 118
  caveat emptor 144
CCTV 28
centralization 16, 17, 175
Centre for Effective Dispute Resolution (CEDR) 206, 207, 208, 209
child labour 42
Chirac, Jacques 89
coding 31
  enforced 31
  in-person moral coding 31
  intervention 32
commercial law 2, 23, 176, 189
commercial relationships 128, 167, 169, 176, 178, 182, 193, 194, 201
common law 3, 24, 65, 84, 90, 92, 93, 94, 95, 109, 128, 155, 162, 177, 189, 195, 196, 199, 200, 204, 213
communications 39, 41, 42, 45
  electronic 19
  online 18
  speed 43
  technologies 14, 17, 25, 34

competitive pricing 161
construction industry 12, 49, 73, 100, 118
contextualists 24, 25, 26
contract 1
  autonomous 80, 84
  breach of 8, 33, 34, 75, 80, 81, 82, 83, 84, 90, 91, 92, 94, 95, 97, 99, 101, 102, 103, 105, 106, 110, 112, 122, 123, 126, 127, 128, 129, 133, 142, 143, 145, 146, 148, 149, 151, 153, 154, 155, 156, 176, 178, 180, 185, 186
    hypothetical 100, 102, 112
    varying 100, 101
  computer-mediated 39
  connected 18, 23, 24, 25
  consent theory 108, 112
  consumer purchase 20, 38
  contractual behaviour 4, 68, 69, 70, 71, 72, 73, 74, 75, 76, 77, 81, 83, 86, 126, 168, 201
    multilevel theory 81
    triple framework 76, 83
  contractual relationships 4, 9, 39, 49, 51, 59, 67, 70, 72, 74, 75, 76, 77, 78, 101, 175, 178, 196, 200, 205, 217, 219, 221, 224, 225, 226, 227
  discrete 6, 10, 23, 38, 39, 40, 43, 45, 46, 47, 48, 51, 52, 58, 59, 65, 66, 68, 69, 71, 72, 73, 75, 77, 116, 117, 118, 138, 140, 141, 163, 168, 170, 171, 172, 173, 178, 180, 189, 197, 216, 224, 227
  employment 65, 66, 67, 68, 69, 71, 73, 76, 77, 78, 79, 81, 82, 83, 84, 85, 86, 87
  evasion of 94, 110
  freedom of 8, 95, 104, 107, 108, 110, 138, 152, 163, 187

235

contract (*cont.*)
  norms   4, 6, 8, 9, 39, 48, 75, 162, 178, 216, 217, 224, 225, 226, 227
  pan-European code   34
  penalty clauses   24, 103, 107, 109, 180
  power of   89, 94, 95, 96, 100, 101, 104, 106, 107, 108, 109, 110, 112
  pre-contractual representation   127
  psychological   68, 79, 80, 81, 82, 83, 84, 86, 87
  relational   1, 3, 4, 5, 6, 7, 8, 9, 10, 11, 12, 38, 39, 40, 45, 46, 47, 48, 50, 51, 52, 58, 65, 66, 67, 68, 69, 71, 72, 73, 74, 75, 76, 77, 79, 86, 87, 93, 94, 107, 108, 111, 116, 117, 118, 138, 140, 141, 162, 163, 164, 166, 167, 168, 169, 170, 171, 172, 173, 174, 175, 176, 177, 178, 179, 180, 181, 182, 183, 184, 185, 186, 187, 188, 189, 193, 194, 196, 197, 198, 199, 200, 201, 205, 211, 212, 213, 216, 217, 219, 222, 223, 224, 225, 226, 227, 228, 229
  renegotiation of   103
  social   14, 15, 16, 17, 21, 34, 40, 45
  'take or pay'   94
  umbrella   84, 85, 86, 181, 182, 198
  welfarist approach to   5, 140, 157, 163
Corbin, Arthur   2
correspondence with description   143, 147, 151, 153, 158, 162
costs   78, 180, 202
  fixed   184
  postage   56
  social   71
  transaction   47, 49, 73, 209, 221
cotton industry   176, 177
criminal justice   216
cyberspace   9, 15, 18, 19, 21

damages   96, 101, 103, 111, 126, 129, 133, 135, 145, 185, 186
  agreed clause   101, 129
  compensatory   76
  liquidated   8, 90, 91, 94, 97, 98, 99, 100, 101, 102, 105
  stipulated   94, 96, 97, 98, 99, 100, 101, 103, 104, 105, 106, 109, 111, 112
  unliquidated   96
decentralization   17
defamation   19
detriment   90, 186
diamonds
  sales   144
  traders   171
disclosure   119, 125, 169, 210
disputes   2, 6, 22, 24, 25, 69, 74, 75, 119, 121, 122, 123, 141, 142, 153, 175, 187, 193, 194, 200, 201, 207, 210, 212
  boundary   110
  commercial   186, 189, 201, 202, 205, 211
  contractual   76, 87, 181, 194, 200
  resolution of   7, 8, 9, 10, 45, 118, 171, 176, 177, 178, 181, 205, 206, 210, 212, 228
  settlement   134
  transactional   24
Dispute Resolution Commitment 2011   209
DNA profiling   28
doctrinal approach   175
  obstacles   183

eBay   9, 10, 14, 21, 28, 38, 40, 41, 43, 44, 45, 47, 52, 53, 56, 57, 58
  feedback system   41, 43, 52, 55, 56, 57, 58, 59
economic analysis   100, 112
economic distress   185
economic interest   5, 29, 70, 73, 74, 76, 79, 80, 81, 82, 83, 84, 85, 86, 157

economic rationality 6, 73, 75, 76, 78, 79, 80, 87, 221
economies
  developed 49, 50
  developing 42
  development of 41
  knowledge-based 49
  macro-level ordering 47
  monetary-based 39
  pre-barter 39
  UK 209
  world trading 49
employment
  contracts 65, 66, 67, 68, 69, 71, 73, 76, 77, 78, 79, 81, 82, 83, 84, 85, 86, 87
  tribunals 69, 177, 211
  unfair dismissal 83, 84
environmental management 216
Erewhonians 16
estoppel
  equitable 24
  promissory 124, 167, 168, 183, 184, 186, 187, 189
  proprietary 124, 186
exchange 4, 9, 10, 22, 39, 40, 45, 46, 47, 48, 51, 53, 55, 58, 65, 66, 67, 68, 70, 100, 138, 161, 162, 163, 164, 168, 184, 210, 217, 219, 220, 224, 225, 226, 227
  behaviour, social 216
  business-to-business 217, 227
  contractual 216, 224, 227
  discrete 10, 47, 59, 66
  economic 4, 225, 228
  market 162, 163, 164, 225
  reciprocal 21, 72, 162
  relational 222
  relationships, short-term 52
  voluntary 162
exclusivity 27

Facebook 14

good faith 31, 69, 76, 81, 126, 135, 140, 148, 154, 156, 161, 162, 166, 176, 179
guarantees 110, 117, 129, 132, 174

health and social care 216, 218, 221, 222, 223, 227
House of Lords 86, 87, 116, 123, 130, 134, 142, 143, 146, 155, 168, 185, 205
human rights 17, 41, 49

ICDA (interactive consumer decision aids) technology 44
intellectual property 19
International Olympic Committee 12
internet 9, 15, 18, 38, 41, 42, 43, 44, 47
  HTTP protocol 20
  online communities 20, 42, 58

joint enterprise 226
juries 119
jurisprudence 70, 71, 75, 77, 82, 193, 196, 204

Keegan, Kevin 99

Irvine, Lord 85, 86, 211

La Technique 9, 14, 15, 16, 21, 26, 31
Leff, Arthur 95
liability 23, 53, 124, 125, 174, 178, 182
  apportionment of 25
  contractual 118, 206
  exclusion of 24
  external 23, 25
  limitation of 103, 118, 119, 122, 127, 134
  negligently causing death or personal injury 24
  pre-contractual 182
litigation 6, 9, 76, 90, 121, 122, 123, 127, 161, 171, 173, 178, 187, 194, 201, 202, 206, 208, 210, 211, 212, 226, 228

litigation (*cont.*)
  cost of   131
  reduction of   122
London   142, 172, 210
  approach   171, 172
Luddites   16

Mattei, Ugo   95
mediation   8, 9, 177, 178, 187, 194, 205, 206, 207, 208, 209, 210, 211, 212, 213, 228
morality   32, 188, 189, 225

nanotechnology *see* technology
National Grain and Feed Association   176
negligence   33
neurotechnology *see* technology
networks   6, 9, 17, 21, 22, 23, 24, 25, 26, 34, 46, 57, 220, 221, 223, 228
  business   18, 22, 25, 73
  contractual   15, 21, 25, 34
  external liability   23
  global computer   18
  healthcare   223
  internal network agreements   23
    disputes   24
  loyalty   22
  merchant networks, Chinese   171
  public service   217, 220, 221, 223
  purpose   23, 25
  regulatory approach to   22
  relational   10
  self-regulation   15, 21
  social   171
  technological   48
  trading   73
non-profit providers   216, 228

Office of Fair Trading   92, 93
offline transactions   21, 57, 58
Olympic Games   12
organizational
  architecture   218, 219, 220

commitment behaviour   79
  learning   218, 222
  theory   79, 80
overdrafts, unauthorized   90, 92, 93

payments   90, 93, 132, 173
  bonus   82
PayPal   10, 45
penalty jurisdiction   90, 92, 93, 94, 97, 101, 105, 109, 110
personal injury   24, 95, 199
Post-Techniquan society   16
Post-Technique   9, 14, 15, 16, 17, 21, 25, 26, 27, 32, 33, 34, 35, 40
precedent   123, 129, 184, 193, 195, 196, 199, 201, 202, 205, 211
private law   1, 3, 11, 175, 202
public authority   229
public service networks   217, 220, 221, 223

quasi-market organization   217, 219, 221, 226, 227

radio-frequency identification (RFID)   25, 28
rail transport   32, 33, 34
refunds   132
regulation
  debate   34
  frameworks   217, 226
  guidelines   32
  interventions   25
    techno-regulatory   32
  and judicial capacity   174, 175
  purpose of   25
  regulators   15, 16, 18, 19, 26, 27, 28, 32, 33, 34
    private   26
    public   26
  regulatory control   28, 41
  regulatory environments   15, 20, 21, 25, 26, 27, 28, 29, 30, 32, 34, 35
  responses   21, 24
  restraint   15

self-regulation   15, 19, 21, 25, 26, 29, 31
  structures   41
  technologies   28
relationships
  horizontal   16, 42, 49, 219, 227
  vertical   41, 42, 43, 49, 183, 219, 227
restitution   101, 118, 130, 195
restraint   15, 95, 107, 108, 216
robotics *see* technology

sanctions   50, 95, 108, 171, 172, 173, 180, 181, 185, 186
Second Life   9, 17, 21, 42
self-assessment tax return   43
self-governance   10, 15, 16, 17, 18, 20, 21, 24, 25, 26, 34, 40
settlements   134, 177, 202, 206, 209, 210, 211, 212
social learning   9, 217, 218, 220, 221, 222, 223, 224, 225, 226, 227, 228, 229
social matrices   4, 46, 48, 216
social sanctions   171, 172, 173
state intervention   222, 223, 228
stock options   82

Technical Man   14, 15, 16, 17, 25, 26, 28, 31, 34, 40

technology   32, 33
  biotechnology   14, 32
  digital   14
  and humanity   15, 16
  nanotechnology   15
  neurotechnology   15, 43
  robotics   15
  technological control   30
  technological management   20, 21, 26, 27, 29, 30, 31, 32, 33
    in consumer products   31
    level 1   27, 29
    level 2   27, 29, 30
Thatcherism   3
tort   3, 117, 118
training   11, 78, 80, 84, 89, 112, 216, 222
trials   100, 119, 128, 167, 168, 169, 194, 201, 202, 205, 206, 207, 209, 210, 211, 212, 213
  adversarial   201
  civil   6, 202

underliquidation clauses   102, 103, 104, 106, 112

vertical integration   49, 183

Woolf reforms   202, 208
working conditions   42